ECOLOGIST

·········· guide to ··········
Fashion

ECOLOGIST

guide to

Fashion

Ruth Styles

Leaping Hare Press

First published in the UK in 2014 by

Leaping Hare Press

210 High Street, Lewes
East Sussex BN7 2NS, UK
www.leapingharepress.co.uk

British Library Cataloguing-in-Publication Data
A catalogue record for this book is available from
the British Library

ISBN: 978-1-78240-055-4
This book was conceived, designed and produced by

Leaping Hare Press

Creative Director PETER BRIDGEWATER
Publisher SUSAN KELLY
Commissioning Editor MONICA PERDONI
Art Director JAMES LAWRENCE
Senior Editors JACQUI SAYERS & JAYNE ANSELL
Designer GINNY ZEAL
Illustrator LUCY KIRK

Printed sustainably by
TJ International Ltd, Padstow, Cornwall, UK
using FSC® certified paper and vegetable based inks
Colour Origination by Ivy Press Reprographics

Distributed worldwide (except North America) by
Thames & Hudson Ltd., 181A High Holborn,
London WC1V 7QX, United Kingdom

1 3 5 7 9 10 8 6 4 2

CONTENTS

FOREWORD

The Ecologist has been setting the environmental agenda for over 40 years – bringing the critical issues of our time into the mainstream through cutting-edge reporting, as well as pioneering original thinking and inspiring action. Whether it's challenging vast corporations, exposing corruption or shining a light on unquestioned orthodoxies, *The Ecologist* remains to this day the world's leading environmental affairs title.

As the environmental debate has evolved and increasingly moved into the mainstream, *The Ecologist* has placed more emphasis on promoting ethical consumerism. This has included the publication of practical green living advice, as well as reportage around the issues concerning our day to day products and lifestyle choices.

Perhaps most well known is the critically-acclaimed Behind The Label (BTL) series, in which health commentator and ex-*Ecologist* editor Pat Thomas deconstructed the ingredients of some of our most popular and seemingly innocent products. From unearthing the chemical nasties in your body cream and revealing what's really in your bottle of tomato ketchup to examining the devastation your 'dolphin-friendly' tuna might actually be causing, this column has been scrutinizing the contents of the nation's shopping baskets for more than 8 years.

More recently, the series evolved into Behind The Brand (BTB), which took readers on a whistle-stop tour to the heart of some of the world's largest corporations. From Bernard Matthews to IKEA, the BTB columns investigated the claims made against the companies in question, and examined the 'greenwash' effect, questioning whether some companies truly were 'green'.

Elsewhere, *The Ecologist* has repeatedly exposed the 'hidden costs' of many consumerables. From palm oil to petrol, tinned tomatoes to timber, bananas to beef, its unique investigations, some of them undercover and carried out at great personal risk, have taken readers on a unique journey to some of the world's environmental front lines to bring back the often unpalatable truths about many of the consumer goods we take for granted. In recent years the intrepid Ecologist Film Unit has trod where few others have dared to go and shone a much needed spotlight on some of the world's most unreported environmental issues.

Building on all of this, *The Ecologist* is producing the much anticipated *Ecologist Guides.* Drawing from the magazine's unique archive, and containing much new material, the series will be written by leading experts in the field and will cover a range of topics on the environmental agenda, presenting the often hard truths surrounding these themes, and offering enlightening debate as they consider the changes that need to be made. The guides – sometimes surprising, sometimes controversial – will be essential reading for anyone interested in making ethical choices and living a more sustainable life.

Zac Goldsmith
*Environmental Campaigner, MP
and Editor of* The Ecologist, 1998–2007

INTRODUCTION

FIFTY SHADES OF GREEN More than any other, the fashion industry is constantly evolving, with each season bringing a host of new trends, fabrics, cuts and silhouettes to the forefront. But fashion's main strengths – innovation and creativity – are also, in environmental terms, its Achilles' heel.

Fashion is the world's fifth biggest emitter of carbon dioxide, the result of wasteful manufacturing techniques and transport. Polyester, the world's most popular fibre, accounts for 65 per cent of the textiles produced each year but, once sent to landfill, will take an estimated 500 years to biodegrade. Worse, producing it requires a staggering 70 million barrels of crude oil every year. Recycling remains an enormous challenge, with non-biodegradeable textiles making up 50 per cent of the total waste discarded by the industry every year.

Then there's the human impact of fashion. Workers in crowded Third-World factories still have few rights, trade unions are outlawed or sidelined, and conditions are poor. Pay is low, leaving many workers living below the United Nations (UN) global poverty line of a dollar a day.

But the fashion industry's environmental excesses are well documented – so do we really need another book telling us what to avoid, what's going wrong and how an industry that brings pleasure to millions is inflicting misery on millions more? No. Instead, the *Ecologist Guide to Fashion* documents the changes that have already occurred and the innovators who are bringing about a sea of change in the way we consume fashion. This is a book about the *future* of fashion.

Cast your mind back a decade and eco fashion was in the doldrums. The boom of the late 1990s and early 2000s saw eco chic pushed to the back of the conveyor belt, with Balmain's supersized shoulders and lashings of bling dominating the aesthetic. Green fashion, when brought up, was invariably dismissed as a hemp frump fest that didn't make nearly enough of a positive impact to make wearing it worthwhile.

But thanks to growing environmental awareness and a willingness on the part of green clothing brands to embrace mainstream fashion, eco fashion has never been more desirable. Initiatives such as London Fashion Week's Estethica have transformed the fashion landscape, helping emerging talents such as Beulah, Christopher Raeburn, Minna Hepburn and Ada Zanditon launch their businesses and compete with established brands. Prophetik, a US label, is producing pieces so fabulous that they regularly appear on the red carpet, while People Tree has become the eco answer to Boden. None make pieces that scream 'green' – there's no hemp or hippiness in sight – but green they are.

Even more excitingly, the rest of the fashion world is sitting up and taking notice, with an ever increasing roster of brands making over their supply chains and adding green collections to their output. Step forward Sir Philip Green, who introduced a 'Made in Britain' line to Topshop's offering. H&M's Conscious Collection improves each season, and – driven on by groups such as Greenpeace and Labour Behind the Label – the rest of the high street has made a concerted effort to clean up its act.

Slow fashion, once an abstract concept, has revived the British wool industry, while local manufacturing and traditional techniques are making a comeback, driven by the increased appetite for quality both at home and abroad. Meanwhile, the e-tail revolution has made huge strides towards a greener fashion industry, by providing a platform for small, ethical brands to promote and sell themselves as well as reducing energy consumption by getting rid of the traditional – and power hungry – boutique environment. Once an environmental pariah, the fashion industry is fast becoming a green one.

1 Textiles

INTRODUCTION

Textiles are the bricks and mortar of fashion. There are hundreds of different types, from luxuriously soft silks to plain, old-fashioned wool, and they have played an important part in human history. Whole economies were built on textiles, including that of England, which became rich from the wool trade in the Middle Ages.

The democratization of fashion in the 1950s and 60s, along with making clothes cheaper, brought environmental disaster in its wake. Pressure on natural resources, such as cotton, flax and wool increased, so manufacturers turned to fabrics based on crude oil, including polyester. Demand for wood-based textiles, among them viscose, resulted in deforestation and monocropping, while vast quantities of pesticides were – and still are – used to help cotton farmers keep up with global demand.

So what can be done? Can you justify buying cotton and polyester? Should fur, on the face of it a sustainable textile, be encouraged? Fabric might be the building block of fashion but it's also one of the most complex challenges green producers face.

KILLER COTTON

1

Cotton is a shrub so supremely useful it has been cultivated for thousands of years. The first to recognize its potential were the forebears of the Aztecs and Incas in South America, where the plant originated. Archaeologists carrying out digs in Mexico's Tehuacán Valley have discovered fragments of fossilized fibre and boll (the fluffy fruit) believed to be at least 7,000 years old. No surprise, then, that South America and the southern states of the USA remain among the key cotton-producing areas. But there's a place where cotton production is equally important: India.

The ultimate super-crop

India produces more than a third of the world's cotton, creating a double income stream for the country's low-income farmers – from the fabric (the boll) and from the food (seeds and stems). Cotton fabric is natural and renewable, and people like it: after polyester, it's the world's most popular textile. It's used to make staple garments that just about everyone owns, among them jeans, t-shirts and pyjamas, as well as stuffing for mattresses, mattress covers, and the bedding that goes on top.

But cotton is not the easiest plant to grow. It's prone to blight, while the fluffy bolls provide cosy nests and food for

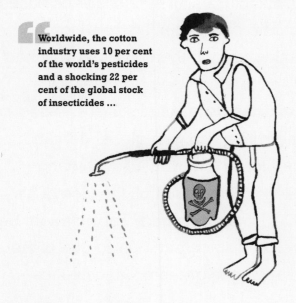

"Worldwide, the cotton industry uses 10 per cent of the world's pesticides and a shocking 22 per cent of the global stock of insecticides ...

insects, both of which can render cotton useless. Before cotton became widely used, this wasn't a serious problem because the demand for cotton clothing was low and livestock gobbled up the damaged crop; now, however, with the increased importance of cotton as a cash crop, it is. Blight and pests can reduce a farmer's entire livelihood to ruins and, for many, the only way to deal with the problem is to use chemicals – and in vast quantities.

The dark side of cotton

In India, cotton accounts for just 5 per cent of total agricultural land but uses a staggering 54 per cent of the country's stock of agrochemicals. And it isn't just India. Worldwide, the cotton industry uses 10 per cent of the world's pesticides and a shocking 22 per cent of the global stock of insecticides – on a crop that takes up just 3 per cent of the world's agricultural land.

And it gets worse. According to the World Health Organization (WHO), chemical pesticides kill 20,000 farmers a year, of whom 99 per cent are from the developing world – where health and safety equipment simply doesn't measure up to the advanced gear used in First World nations. But what about the environment? Appalling as the effect of growing the plant is on human health, the impact on the natural world is worse.

The poisonous impact of pesticides

In 1962, the American marine biologist and conservationist Rachel Carson published a book called *Silent Spring*. The book caused a storm because of

THE HUMAN COST OF COTTON

With such focus on the environmental impact of cotton production, little attention is paid to the effect on the human population. And yet it can be equally devastating. From China to India, pesticide-related deaths among cotton workers are spiralling, with an estimated 20,000 losing their lives due to agrochemicals every year, according to the WHO. Pressure on water sources, including pollution, adds to the misery, while small farmers are crowded out or resort to genetically modified (GM) crops to compete. Although the physiological effects of the latter remain unknown, there's no escaping the fact that it contributes to the debt-spiral many find themselves in and, in India, plays a part in the suicides of 1,000 farmers every month, according to Indian government statistics.

the revelation that not only was pesticide use dangerous to human health, it was also wiping out the birds, animals and insects that populate agricultural land. So critical was the impact of the book, it resulted in the banning of DDT, a particularly noxious pesticide, in Europe and the USA. However, DDT remains in use throughout the Third World – particularly to tackle malarial mosquitoes in Africa. It is also employed by cash-strapped cotton producers, who regard it as an inexpensive way to keep their crops healthy. But why should cotton crops need the protection of chemicals such as DDT? The answer lies in the way the cotton bush is cultivated.

The silent farm

The average cotton plantation – anywhere in the world – consists of field after field of neat cotton bushes in easy access straight lines. There are no other plants, whether they be weeds, trees or other crops. Cotton, like coffee, tea, palm oil and many other commodities, is grown in monocultures – a relatively modern agricultural innovation that makes life easier for farmers but much, much harder for biodiversity.

As with any form of intensive farming, large-scale monocultures take a serious toll on soil fertility, upset the local ecological balance and necessitate the use of extra fertilizer to replace nutrients usually obtained from animal dung and surrounding plants. For farmers, monocultures aren't an unmitigated boon either – diseases can spread far more quickly through a lone species. In order to fight these disease outbreaks, farmers are forced to apply more pesticides and herbicides.

Competition for resources

Local people, especially in the Third World, also suffer as their own defenceless crops are ravaged by

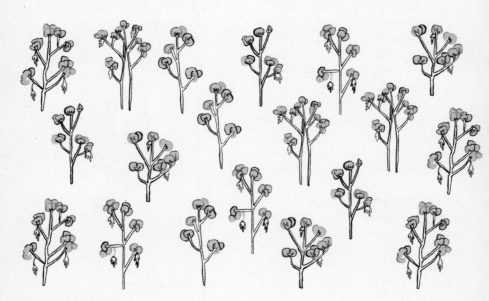

diseases emanating from nearby plantations, causing hunger and poverty. Equally problematic is the competition for resources brought about by large-scale monocultures of thirsty plants such as cotton. As a result, small-scale farmers are confronted with water and other shortages, as well as contamination from pesticide spraying and from genetically modified crops.

Quite clearly, these large-scale monoculture plantations have an appalling environmental impact, no matter what species is being cultivated. Pesticide use, the loss of biodiversity and contamination from GM crops are all problems associated with cotton production, but it's the impact of cotton monocultures on the local water supply that could turn out to be the most serious problem of all.

> Cotton, like coffee, tea, palm oil and numerous other commodities, is grown in monocultures – a relatively modern agricultural innovation ...

DDT: THE ORIGINAL CHEMICAL KILLER

One of the earliest pesticides to be widely used, DDT (dichloro-diphenyltrichloroethane) was hailed as a wonder chemical in the years following WW2 – especially in the cotton industry. It was only later that people realized it was killing more than just insects: it was having an impact on human health as well. The problem with DDT is that it doesn't break down in the soil, with the result that traces are still to be found in many food crops grown in fields once treated with the chemical, according to the Pesticide Action Network. Worse, the chemical has been linked to serious illnesses such as cancer and problems such as thinning eggshells among bird populations. Yet despite this, and although alternatives are now available, DDT is still in use in malarial countries as a cheap way of wiping out malarial mosquitoes.

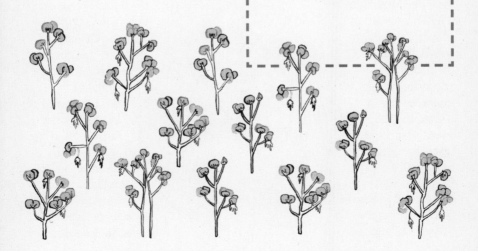

WATER: IT MATTERS

Half a century ago, people approached their wardrobe with respect. With the privations of World War Two still fresh in the collective memory, the 1940s and 50s were the age of make do and mend, with the majority more familiar with a darning needle than the inside of a fashion boutique. Today, however, fashion is the ultimate disposable treat.

Throwaway nation

Every year, more than 1.5 million tonnes of clothing are thrown away in the UK alone – the equivalent of 30 kg (66 lbs) for every man, woman and child. In the USA, the annual figure is 13.1 million tonnes, according to the US Environmental Protection Agency, of which just 2 million tonnes (2.2 million tons) are recycled. Much of the discard pile is cotton and, while it degrades quickly, it's an appalling waste, particularly given the amount of water that is needed to make each cotton garment and the impact that this has on the planet.

Peak water

Cotton production requires shocking amounts of water. According to *Thirsty Crops*, a 2009 report produced by the World Wide Fund for Nature (WWF), just 1 kg (2.2 lbs) of cotton takes a staggering 20,000 litres (5,300 US gal) of water to grow. Together, cotton and the world's two main food crops, wheat and rice, consume 58 per cent of water used in agriculture – itself a whopping 1 per cent of the world's fresh water every year. But why does it matter?

It is swiftly becoming clear that water is no longer the ultimate renewable resource, due to the twin impacts of climate change and a growing global population. Although 'peak oil' – the point at which oil production reaches its maximum capacity and begins to decline – is a buzz phrase among environmentalists, it could soon be replaced by a new phrase: 'peak water'. Shockingly, the amount of water available for human use is in decline, with leading science journal *Nature* describing demand as 'unsustainable'.

When you consider the specifics of water use, the reason for this becomes considerably clearer. Water scarcity is a relatively recent phenomenon, the result – in part – of climate change but due largely to huge demand from the world's growing population. Water is expected to be the next natural resource to become the subject of increased competition and even a future trigger for conflict. Already Egypt and Ethiopia have come to blows – thankfully diplomatic – over who controls the Nile, with Ethiopia threatening to dam the Nile in order to provide extra water for local agriculture. Unsurprisingly, Egypt, with an economy that depends heavily on the ability to grow cotton, disagrees.

> **Supplies are beginning to run out – most strikingly in the Aral Sea [pictured left and right] in central Asia, which is now just a quarter of its original size.**

WATER: THE FACTS

According to the Water Project, a staggering one billion people do not have access to clean, safe drinking water. The reasons for this are twofold. First, climate change has resulted in arid regions becoming increasingly dry, compounded by skyrocketing demand from growing populations, agriculture and manufacturing. Second, pollution has put many water sources out of action, worsening the crisis. Despite fresh water accounting for less than 0.03 per cent of the world's total water, according to the International Association of Hydrogeologists, it is the world's most extracted resource. As a result, in some areas, supplies are beginning to run out – most strikingly in the Aral Sea in central Asia, which is now just a quarter of its original size. This is the result in no small part of the surrounding cotton industry. Worse, because water supplies have dwindled so much, psephologists predict that H_2O could become the next resource to follow in the bloodstained footsteps of diamonds and oil and become a source of international conflict. Already, Egypt and Ethiopia have come to blows – thankfully diplomatic so far – over who controls the Nile.

As precious as gold

'We believe water is turning into the new gold,' Ziad Abdelnour, president of US private equity firm Blackhawk Partners, told news agency Reuters. And as climate change and the world's rising population is making water increasingly unattainable – and, therefore, valuable – so it becomes more difficult to justify using such vast quantities to produce t-shirts and other garments with life spans that can be measured in months.

A combination of economic pressure and shortsightedness – as well as a lack of knowledge about the impending water crisis – has meant that cotton farmers have yet to find a way around the problem. Worse still, the pesticides and other agrochemicals required to sustain the monocrop have led to the pollution of the very water that cotton farming depends on to survive.

In India, currently the world's biggest organic cotton producer, the impact is already being felt due to a worrying combination of water scarcity and climate change. Over 50 per cent of agricultural land in India depends entirely on groundwater – much of which is now polluted as a result of heavy pesticide use. In north and north-east India, where perennial rivers sustain the agricultural land, farmers have to deal with issues such as flooding caused by climate change, the result of – for example – speedier glacier melt and erratic monsoons. All of this directly affects the cotton crop. Tragically, it also takes a heavy human toll.

The human toll

According to the WWF report *The Impact of Cotton on Freshwater Resources and Ecosystems* (2000), a quarter of the world's freshwater supplies were lost to pollution and overuse between 1970 and 1995. Unsustainable cotton farming, with its massive inputs of water and pesticides, has already been responsible for the destruction of large-scale ecosystems and is known to have had a deleterious

effect on the health and livelihoods of people living there. Intensive cotton production is now threatening the populations living around the Indus River in Pakistan, the Murray-Darling Basin in Australia, and the Rio Grande in the USA and Mexico.

A less-known threat to local farmers, and even to local people with no involvement in cotton production, is the impact of competing with big producers for scarce water supplies – and nowhere has been more adversely affected than

Cotton production now has a well-deserved reputation for being one of the world's dirtiest crops. How ironic that a natural fibre, championed for years as a green alternative to polyester, should have become just as big a disaster for the planet as fabric produced using crude oil. As a result, more brands are experimenting with alternative textiles as well as cotton fabric grown organically. The question is, just how much of an improvement are they?

India. According to figures from the Indian Ministry of Agriculture, more than 1,000 small farmers commit suicide every month – a total of 250,000 between 1995 and 2010. The vast majority are from climate change afflicted states such Andhra Pradesh and Maharashtra. Most are trapped in vicious cycles of debt caused by failed monsoons, increasing droughts and the high cost of GM seed – much of it purchased with the aid of unlicensed money lenders.

GREENER COTTON?

1

While the environmental and social impact of conventionally grown cotton is huge, it has become such an integral part of modern life that the prospect of doing without it is almost unthinkable. Enter organic cotton, the perfect solution to the world's cotton addiction. But is it really? The Soil Association, which certifies organic cotton for use in the UK, argues that it is – for numerous reasons.

THE PROBLEM WITH PROCESSING

For many, the problem with conventional cotton begins and ends with agriculture. But this oversimplifies the issue, particularly in light of the fact that all stages of the production process – bleaching, dyeing and so on – use vast amounts of chemicals known to pollute both the atmosphere and water bodies. Defoliating, which removes extra leaves and makes harvesting easier, is done with herbicides – traces of which can remain in the finished product. During manufacture, other chemicals such as formaldehyde, bromine, sulphuric acid and halogen are used to bleach the cotton bolls, remove wrinkles from the finished fabric and get rid of any agricultural smells. Although the fabric is washed several times, the softeners and detergents used are equally chemical heavy and often contain skin-irritating surfactants.

Ditching the chemicals

Identical to conventional cotton in texture, feel and durability, organic cotton offers the same quality but without the pesticides and other chemicals. This means that biodiversity is encouraged on cotton plantations, allowing complementary species of plants and animals to exist alongside cotton bushes. This enriches the soil naturally and creates organic compounds that lock in carbon dioxide (CO_2) – a positive boon for the planet. Furthermore, water used on the cotton crop will not pick up dangerous toxins, thus reducing pollution.

Factories wishing to work with organic cotton also have to avoid potentially harmful substances such as heavy metals, formaldehyde and aromatic solvent, all of which are regularly used during the cotton production process, and many of which are classified as hazardous by the WHO. Links between these substances and medical issues such as cancer and birth defects have also been noted by some scientific researchers. The Soil Association, the US Food and Drug Administration (FDA) and the majority of other organic bodies will refuse to certify a factory that is using any of these substances.

However, there is a catch to organic cotton – it is just as thirsty, and uses just as much water, as any other variety. This has prompted a backlash from some in the green movement, who regard it as a 'greenwashed' fabric little better than bamboo – a similarly thirsty plant, championed by some as a good alternative to regular cotton.

Does it make a difference?

So who is right? Can choosing organic cotton really make a difference? Eco designer Minna Hepburn thinks not. 'If you buy an organic cotton t-shirt and you just wear it once, then no, it's not ethical,' she argues. 'If you buy it, wear it for years and care for it, then yes, it is ethical.' The same could apply to conventional cotton or just about any other material that biodegrades. Polyester will go on polluting even after it's been worn to rags. But cotton aside, there are plenty of other options around that are becoming increasingly popular with green consumers – and which are precipitating a new, green industrial revolution in the process.

YOU MIGHT THINK I'M BETTER FOR THE ENVIRONMENT ... WELL, I'M NOT

THE FUTURE OF FABRIC

1

Ask the average eco-conscious consumer about the future of fabric and they'll have one textile in mind: hemp. Hemp is hardy, so doesn't require chemical protection. It doesn't require much water and it's easy to grow. The fabric it produces is sturdy and lasts a very long time. Like cotton, it can even be eaten. But there's a problem: the material it produces doesn't look or feel good, and it suffers from a serious image problem. Luckily, the fashion industry has been quietly working on other eco-friendly alternatives, ranging from manmade fabrics such as Tencel® to vegan-appropriate animal derivatives. The big question is: do they live up to the hype?

Natural alternatives

Like its close cousin, flax, hemp has been out of fashion for a very long time. It is coarse and, as a result, few consumers are willing to touch it. Not surprisingly, brands with an eye on their bottom line won't go near it either. So what's being done to make it more palatable to the public?

Blending is one answer, with 'hemp silk' – usually 60 per cent hemp to 40 per cent silk – now available along with hemp versions of traditional fabrics such

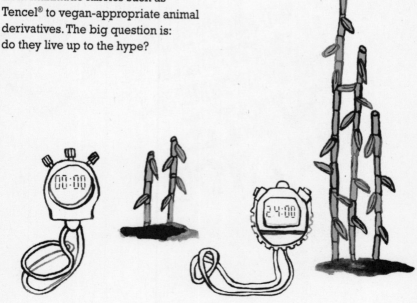

as corduroy, although cotton still makes up around 40 per cent of the blend. However, the silk and cotton elements of these blends aren't always as eco-friendly as they could be. Other blends involve bamboo, an eco textile that has been hailed as the green alternative to cotton. But though bamboo has been welcomed by many, some green groups are concerned. Why?

The case for bamboo

Bamboo produces a gorgeously soft, jersey-type material with antibacterial and insulating properties that make it comfortable to wear all year round. 'I think it's important for people to understand that they are doing something useful for themselves and for the environment [when they buy bamboo],' explains Alice Asquith, founder of Asquith London – a bamboo-based yoga wear line. 'It's not just about how soft it feels, but about how well it wears and how versatile it is and how practical.'

Bamboo, like cotton, is a thirsty crop, but it grows extremely quickly – sometimes as much as 1.2 m (4 ft) in a single day. It regenerates within six months,

making several harvests a year possible, which is good news for farmers. Its high silica content makes it unappetizing for termites and other pests, thus reducing the need for agrochemicals, and its thick root system is believed to help prevent soil erosion – great news for the planet. In short, it's the perfect alternative to cotton. Or is it?

Has bamboo been 'greenwashed'?

There's a dark side to bamboo – the use of sodium hydroxide (caustic soda or lye) during the manufacturing process. Like other corrosive acids, it can cause severe burns and even blindness, if it gets in the eyes, as well as producing hydrogen – a greenhouse gas – should it come into contact with metals such as aluminium. Concerns have also been raised by Greenpeace and others about the possibility of bamboo monocultures if its popularity increases enough, although it's likely these wouldn't have the detrimental effect of cotton plantations due to the smaller amounts of agrochemicals required. So is this enough to rule it out? Perhaps a new manmade fabric, Tencel, can do better.

Man-made solutions

Tencel (lyocell) has natural origins – like viscose, it's made from dissolved wood pulp. However, pulpwood forests are yet another type of monoculture, subject to pesticides, GM and so on. The manufacturing process that turns wood pulp into cloth requires an industrial solvent called N-Methylmorpholine N-oxide, derived from crude oil, to dissolve the wood chips. The process requires huge amounts of energy to complete, much of it derived from fossil fuels. The dyeing process uses more chemicals – often petrochemical derivatives – just to get the fibres to accept the dye.

Nevertheless, Tencel, unlike polyester, does biodegrade, and wood is more sustainable than crude oil. Better still, it's cheap to produce, can be used to simulate a whole range of different textiles including leather and suede, and feels comfortable to wear.

Animal magic?

Fibres of animal origin have the power to polarize opinion like nothing else. Some animal-derived textiles – wool and cashmere, for instance – are widely accepted, as harvesting the fibre doesn't result in the death of the animal. However, materials such as leather, sheepskin or rabbit skin are often a by-product of meat production. They are subject to all the associated welfare issues, though many argue that using them means no part of the animal is wasted – unlike fur (see page 30), often produced for the pelt alone.

Significant amounts of toxic chemicals, such as chrome salts, are needed to process animal skins into a usable fabric. That said, not all leather and skins are treated the same way. Vegetable-tanned leather is an increasingly important sector of the fashion textiles manufacturing industry, and uses no chemicals to treat the leather at all. In short, it's a relatively green option for those who are happy to use animal skins.

So which is best?

As renewable materials such as wool, silk and (organic) cotton become increasingly popular (and widely available), it is becoming easier to shop with a clear conscience. While the emergence of ethical alternatives to conventional fabrics – such as peace silk – is a positive step forward, there are still serious problems associated with many textiles.

Choosing upcycled, recycled and vintage pieces can help to tackle this, although the expense of designer works and curated vintage puts these options out of reach for many. But whether you choose to splash out on a hemp blend or a peace silk blouse, or stick to vintage, you're still doing something to help the planet's beleaguered ecosystem.

Silk

Another serious, but less well-known, issue is created by the production of conventional silk, which kills the worm as the thread is extracted, making the fabric unsuitable for vegetarians and vegans. In this instance, however, there is a viable alternative in the shape of wild or peace silk. Producers of wild silk wait until the silkworm has left its chrysalis before removing the silk fibres. The resulting textile is less smooth (the worm chews through some of the fibres while making its escape) and is more expensive than the conventional version, but it does have the advantage of being entirely animal friendly.

> **Producers of wild silk wait until the silkworm has left its chrysalis before removing the silk fibres.**

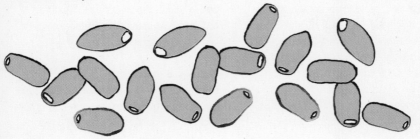

GREEN JEANS

When even a big brand like Nike admits that non-organic cotton is a bad thing, you know the message is finally getting through. 'Organic cotton is definitely better than non-organic,' said Hannah Jones, vice-president for sustainable business and innovation at Nike in an interview with *The Sunday Times* in London. And she's right. But while Nike has focused on producing collections made from recycled plastics, the big news is the increasing importance of organic cotton for makers of denim.

A sustainable staple

Organic jeans might seem insignificant in the great scheme of things, but they are not. In the UK alone, each person owns on average seven pairs of jeans – a total of 432,544,000 – and in the USA, 450 million pairs are sold every single year. Each pair, taking the manufacturing process, repeated washes and disposal into account, produces around 415 kg (915 lbs) of CO_2 over the average lifespan of around four years. Choosing organic denim reduces this exponentially and, although it doesn't help hugely when it comes to water scarcity, anything that reduces the amount of chemicals used in manufacturing and agriculture can only be a good thing.

So who's doing it, and why? One of the best companies for sustainable denim is Sweden's Nudie Jeans, which, along with producing entirely organic pieces, also operates a zero waste policy and makes a point of creating denim that lasts – in short, the antithesis of fast fashion. Launched in 2001 by Jonkoping native Maria Erixon Levin, the brand underpins its 100 per cent organic denim with a corporate social responsibility (CSR) policy that embraces other eco-friendly essentials such as ethical production, living wages and avoiding air freight. Now one of the world's top brands, it's proof that stylish and sustainable are not mutually exclusive concepts.

Hemp denim

But Nudie isn't the only one turning the enormous denim industry upside down. Jackpot, a Danish label specializing in

DENIM: THE FACTS

Most denim is made from conventional cotton, which is bad news for the environment. In terms of water, an astonishing 6,819 litres (1,800 US gal) are required to produce enough cotton to make just one pair of denim jeans – and that's without taking into account the manufacturing process. Interestingly, jeans continue to pollute long after they've been purchased. According to jeans manufacturer Levi, consumers can reduce the impact of their jeans by 50 per cent, simply by washing them in cold water and line-drying them – both of which reduce energy use.

green jeans

organic casual wear, works closely with the Dutch organization MADE-BY, which encourages fashion brands to improve sustainability and working conditions right along their supply chain. Howies, a Welsh label, also uses organic cotton, but, uniquely, also boasts several styles made entirely from hemp. Although the hemp styles aren't cheap, they are proof that hemp has a future in the fashion industry – even if only as a hard-working pair of jeans.

Elsewhere in the UK, Derbyshire-based Monkee Genes put major brands such as Wrangler and Levi's to shame with their 100 per cent organic policy across their entire range. In Australia, elsom. also focuses on sustainable design. Working closely with organic cotton farmers in India, all cotton and denim used is chemical free, and the label also sources unusual materials such as canvas woven from horsehair by small, artisanal producers.

FUR: AN ETHICAL DILEMMA

1

Not so long ago, fur was almost universally shunned. A raft of initiatives led by People for the Ethical Treatment of Animals (PETA) saw it pulled from the catwalk and high street stores, while production was banned in many countries – including the UK. But recently, fur has staged a comeback, with the British Fur Trade Association reporting that sales are now better than ever.

Has fur been 'greenwashed'?

Fur has even had a green makeover, with a special website, furisgreen.org, set up and promoted by the Fur Council of Canada, which says: 'Fur is a natural, sustainable, renewable resource. We only use part of what nature produces each year without depleting wildlife populations or damaging natural habitats that sustain them. The goal is to maintain long-term ecological balance.' The question is: do the claims really stack up?

On the face of it, they appear to. After all, if you remove considerations such as animal welfare, and look at it purely as a fabric, fur is renewable, natural and biodegradable. It's also warm and long-lasting, as the craze for vintage fur proves. Interestingly, fur tanning uses significantly fewer chemicals than leather tanning, while nearly 5 litres (1.3 US gal) of petroleum are required to make just three fake fur jackets.

Yet there's no escaping the fact that a living creature had to die to produce a real fur coat. Certainly, not all furs come from animals raised purely for their skins. Some, such as sheepskin and rabbit fur, are by-products of the meat industry. Some skins come from

animals raised for both. But the real problem arises with animals that are bred solely for their skins. Is it right to kill animals for fur and discard the rest, no matter how sustainable the practice?

An ecological disaster

'The term ["renewable material"] is misleading and the fur industry needs to come up with a better communications tool to support their claims that fur supports the environment and ecosystems – especially farmed fur,' says the Ethical Fashion Forum's Elizabeth Laskar. She believes animal welfare remains a big issue, particularly as standards vary from country to country, while sourcing skins from wild animals also remains contentious. Currently, 80 per cent of fur is farmed, with the rest coming from the wild.

PETA co-founder Ingrid Newkirk says the farming element has proven particularly hard to square with the industry's eco-friendly claims: 'Fur is an ecological nightmare. The fur industry has been identified as a major polluter by government agencies around the world. Many of the mordants used to keep the pelts from decomposing [...] are highly toxic and have been shown to poison rivers and streams, killing off fish and other water life, as well as raising rates of testicular and other types of cancer in those living near tanneries.'

Is fur really green? The answer, clearly, is no.

ROADKILL COUTURE

Roadkill couture, a small but growing part of the fur industry, makes use of animals that were killed on roads, died of natural causes, or were trapped and killed by the wearer – the grounds for this being that it's no different to killing a deer for food. Brighton-based designer Jess Eaton, one of the UK's leading proponents of roadkill couture, makes use of a huge range of animal-derived textiles, including pheasant feathers and fox pelts, all sourced from the roadside. While this does at least ensure the carcasses don't go to waste, some may find it hard to stomach.

THE BAAND

Copenhagen might be better known as the Scandinavian capital of cool but the city is also building up quite a reputation for its focus on all things green, from travel by bike to renewable technology. Not surprisingly then, in a country where style and sustainability have long had equal cachet, the Danish fashion industry is forging ahead on all things ethical. From all-natural fabrics to ethical manufacturing, Danish brands are world leaders in combining an eco ethos with desirable ready-to-wear. And top of the wishlist right now are pieces by one of Copenhagen's most hotly tipped young design duos: **Stine Bauer Boskov** and **Julie Villumsen**, aka THE BAAND.

> **I wanted to make clothes but I wanted to make them in a better way. And then I learnt that it was possible to do it in a better way.**

Eco fashion made cool

Launched in 2009, The Baand specializes in seriously cool basics with a quirky fashion edge alongside sound eco credentials. 'From the very beginning when I went to school I was taught about how the clothing industry was affecting the climate and the environment,' says Stine. 'It was one of the things that I wanted to do. I wanted to make clothes but I wanted to make them in a better way. And then I learnt that it was possible to do it in a better way.' For Stine and design partner Julie Villumsen, the epiphany came on a trip

COTTON PRODUCTION IN PERU

Although not one of the top ten cotton producing countries, Peru is swiftly making a name for itself in the organic cotton world. The country specializes in 'pima' cotton, a long-fibre variety that lends itself well to organic cultivation and has been described as 'the cashmere of the cotton world'. According to the US Department of Agriculture (USDA), Peru produces around 45 million tonnes of the textile every year, of which roughly 20 per cent is pima – which is only grown in three other countries: the USA, Israel and Australia – and 80 per cent the bog-standard Tangüis variety. Much of the pima cotton is grown in the northern Piura region, which benefits from a mild cotton-friendly climate and a growing tradition that dates back as far as 3100 BC.

for many seasons, and it's not just on trend: it's something you can use forever. We used to do a complete collection and we never really felt: "this is what we want to do for the rest of our lives." […] Now it's all fallen into place. It feels so much more relaxed, so much more confident, it's who we really are.'

> **The quality of the cotton was amazing. So, it was so easy to say "okay, we will move all of our production to Peru" …**

Smaller & more sustainable

The Baand does do seasonal collections, but they are smaller and less frequent than most high street and designer brands. 'We still do a collection every season [but] a lot of the styles are the same; it's just the colours that change,' says Stine. 'But that's just because that's how the fashion industry works. We don't do a collection every six weeks or every two weeks like H&M but we do one every six months, and that works for us. And it also feels right because you can change the colours, but you can still combine them with the colours you had from last season or the season before. Like today when Julie is wearing a t-shirt that's two and a half years old, but still feels right, the colour is still in fashion.' The biannual collections take up less than a single rail and most are entirely

to Peru. 'We had an opportunity to go to Lima and it was a really, really fantastic trip,' says Stine. 'The quality of the cotton was amazing. So, it was so easy to say "okay, we will move all of our production to Peru" because this is really unique.' Peru also had a network of ethically sound family-run co-operatives that could turn the duo's designs into Fairtrade fashion that outlasted the high street competition.

'What we like to do is create clothes that can last for a really long time,' explains Stine. 'It's important for us that the quality is so good so we can use it

> **You have to deliver a new collection: you have to understand how the business works because a lot of our customers also go to H&M and buy some things that are just here now.**

focused on t-shirts and sweatshirts in muted shades of white, dove grey and a soft pink similar to the colour of China clay. It's not the riot of wildly different shapes, textures and hues that most high street shoppers have come to expect but it's fabulous quality – as a quick feel of the fabric swiftly proved – and extremely wearable.

Quality basics

That, as Stine is at pains to emphasize, is the point. 'We have to play by the rules of the fashion industry, otherwise you get no customers,' she explains. 'You have to deliver a new collection: you have to understand how the business works because a lot of our customers also go to H&M and buy some things that are just here now. Then they also try our t-shirts and maybe that's when they start thinking a little bit more: "OK maybe I can buy my basics maybe last longer and I can combine them with something that's a little bit more just for the moment."' The idea of longevity in fashion isn't new, with vintage, eco-friendly and luxury labels all

pushing the concept of the investment piece, but it's something that's so far eluded most of the high street – and its core clientele.

'We think it's a big shame that H&M also make basics because they make it in such bad quality that it doesn't last for a very long time,' says Stine. 'So people just throw it out and it's just such a waste of cotton and also the energy to make it. We think that customers should just buy something that will actually last for at least three years – that would be better for the environment. Also you have to remember organic cotton is not better than, for example, polyester. Polyester uses less energy, lasts longer but high quality organic cotton is a lot better than poor quality conventional cotton. And that's what we like and we really like the fact that you can just focus on high quality – good quality – that lasts for a long time. It's not something that you need to put away for many years; it can really become your favourite.'

> **You have to remember organic cotton is not better than, for example, polyester. Polyester uses less energy, lasts longer but high quality organic cotton is a lot better than poor quality conventional cotton.**

The Baaand

2 Workers' rights

INTRODUCTION

Fashion has come to be regarded as one of the worst employers of Third World workers. But is the industry as black as it's painted? The answer is yes… and no.

In Bangladesh, fashion accounts for 78 per cent of the country's total exports and employs 3.5 million people. In Cambodia, the industry employs 400,000. Both countries struggle with large rural populations living below the poverty line. Although garment workers are paid a pittance by Western standards, they are at least lifted out of poverty.

But, as the 2013 collapse of a Bangladesh factory producing garments for high street labels demonstrated, the industry doesn't exactly have a stellar track record on workers' rights. The answer for many consumers is to turn to Fairtrade, but this remains a small – if growing – part of the business. Is the answer a complete boycott of high-street brands? Some would say yes, but that could potentially mean the loss of jobs for those who can afford it the least.

Instead, this chapter looks at what consumer pressure can achieve – whether through Fairtrade or by forcing retailers to clean up their act.

A THIRD WORLD TRAGEDY

2

While Edna Ruth Byler and Ruth Lederach were setting up the world's first Fairtrade company, big business was occupied in doing the opposite. With World War Two fading into memory, the USA and Europe were convulsed by a new industrial revolution, which saw rapid advances in technology, fabric and transport. The effect of this was twofold. First, prices for ready-to-wear fashion dropped sharply, benefiting millions of lower-paid people for whom clothes had previously been unaffordable. Second, thanks to advances in transport – particularly aviation – and ever-improving technology, a large proportion of manufacturers moved abroad to take advantage of the cheaper labour and flexible tax conditions available outside of Europe and the USA.

Manufacturing goes global

This combination of factors set the scene for what would come next. Under pressure to produce ever cheaper fashion, the big retailers – Arcadia, the Walmart group and many others – had to reduce their costs in order to stay profitable. This was achieved by introducing more cheap man-made fabrics such as rayon and polyester and by keeping labour costs to the absolute minimum. Cheaper clothing helped to create an appetite among Western consumers for trend-led fashion, which required the speeding up of production cycles in order to satisfy demand.

These two factors were a recipe for an ethical disaster. Today, although Fairtrade and greater consumer awareness of labour issues and conditions in developing countries are beginning to drive change, working conditions for many garment workers remain grim. In Bangladesh, one of the biggest producers of ready-to-wear in the world, wages are pitifully low, while the working environment is substandard and industrial accidents are common.

'If you pay a little more, we can live a little better'

People Tree boss Safia Minney has spoken of the conditions endured by Bangladeshi workers and is campaigning to ensure all workers – not just those who work for Fairtrade co-operatives – are paid a 'living wage'. Currently, the minimum wage in Bangladesh is a pitiful 2,800 taka (£22) a month. Not surprisingly, this has seen manufacturers flood into the country, which is now the source of the majority of cheap clothes found on Western high streets. But 2,800 taka isn't enough. Bangladesh is an extremely low-cost place to live but even the thriftiest will struggle to survive on a wage that puts them on the poverty line – defined by the UN as living on a dollar a day.

Workers who get involved in campaigns to improve their wages risk losing their livelihood, as retailers may switch production away from Bangladesh or choose different factories in response to consumer pressure.

With that in mind, Minney is against a total boycott of Bangladeshi-produced garments. Instead, she argues, consumer pressure is needed to encourage brands to introduce a 'living wage' of 5,000 taka (£39), which would lift the country's three million garment workers over the poverty line.

Although still well below what any Western worker would accept, it does, nevertheless, represent an improvement. Consumers would have to pay around 80p more for their clothes but this shouldn't be an insurmountable hurdle. As Sharti Arta, one of the workers quoted in Minney's book *Naked Fashion*, explains: 'Come and see where I live. If you pay a little more, we can live a little better.'

The scandal of our times

But wages are often the least of garment workers' problems. Working conditions can be extremely hazardous, particularly in tanneries, where toxic chemicals such as chrome salts are regularly handled by workers who lack proper protection. The problem isn't confined to Bangladesh – from Brazil to Belarus, the developing world is full of low-skilled labourers willing to accept low wages, who are exploited by unscrupulous corporations.

'Multinational corporations, which exercise more power than many governments and make increasingly large profits, have the responsibility to ensure human rights are upheld for people who produce and sell their goods,' says Anna McMullen, campaigns coordinator at Labour Behind the Label. 'The right to decent wages in the fashion industry is systematically abused both here and abroad. It is the scandal of our times.'

In 2000, there was an even more shocking scandal that hit the fashion industry when a report to the European Parliament revealed that two Indonesian factories used by German sportswear conglomerate Adidas employed child labourers. Workers stated that they were expected to work more than 70 hours a week, were penalized for taking sick leave and had their wages of $60 per month docked for the most minor of infractions.

Although willing to admit that quotas at the factory had been set too high, Adidas say

> **Working conditions can be extremely hazardous, particularly in tanneries, where toxic chemicals such as chrome salts are regularly handled by workers who lack proper protection.**

their factories aren't universally grim. Spokesman Peter Csanadi told the British newspaper the *Guardian* at the time: 'We have factories where the conditions are very good and we take this whole issue very seriously. [...] We work closely with factory management and demand that they ensure good conditions for workers. We also have a team of our own people who go to factories to sort out problems.'

Keeping the West equipped

But this scandal is by no means the worst. Just before the 1998 football World Cup, it was discovered that footballs were being made by child labourers in India, working for as little as 6p an hour. An investigation by

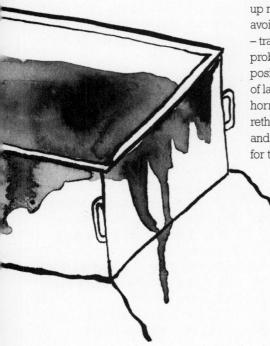

Christian Aid also found that children, some as young as seven, were regularly employed in the production of a wide range of sports goods in India. Most of the goods went to the West. The problem was not limited to India, though. In 1999, an underage worker from a Bangkok factory told Christian Aid that, for less than £1 per day, she worked 12-hour shifts seven days a week, producing sportswear, shoes and replica kits for the West.

But are the retailers entirely to blame? Many orders submitted to factories by big name brands are subcontracted at local level, with the result that many companies have little idea of where and how their goods are produced – leaving workers vulnerable to unscrupulous factory owners. Although this is changing and retailers are stepping up monitoring in factories – if only to avoid PR catastrophes such as these – transparency in supply chains remains problematic. But there has been another positive side effect of the succession of labour scandals. The revelations horrified consumers, forcing many to rethink the way they purchased fashion and, in so doing, helped pave the way for the Fairtrade boom.

WHY FASHION HAS TO CHANGE

From Topshop's 'Made in Britain' range to Tom Ford and Gucci's embrace of the Green Carpet Challenge eco initiative, there are signs that things are changing in the fashion world – particularly on the high street. But despite the green shoots, not everyone is doing enough.

No rights for workers

A report by campaign group War on Want revealed that the vast majority of garments from Bangladesh sold in major high street chain stores are made by women aged 18 to 32, who struggle to survive amid poor pay and working conditions. Sewing operators' pay is approximately 3,900 taka (£30) a month, against average household spending on basic needs of around 8,900 taka (£70). Conditions are terrible, and serious industrial accidents are rife.

In April 2013, the collapse of a building housing several garment factories producing clothes for Primark, among other brands, made headlines worldwide. The implosion of the rickety eight-storey concrete building, Rana Plaza, killed more than 1,129 people and injured thousands more. Primark subsequently released a statement declaring itself 'shocked and saddened' and revealed that it would push for a review of building safety standards and

pay compensation to the victims and their families. Others, including Mango and Benetton, initially denied any links to the Rana Plaza workshops. Workers, meanwhile, told the press they had warned owner Mohammed Sohel Rana of the precarious state of the building but had been forced to enter anyway.

So what can be done to protect workers? One group that thinks it has the solution is Labour Behind the Label, a collective made up from trade unions, charities and consumer groups, which has helped name and shame the worst offenders in the fashion world, and actively works to raise awareness of the plight of garment workers.

Ringing the changes

A recent Labour Behind the Label documentary exposed the appalling conditions endured by Cambodian workers creating garments for a major high street retailer. 'The documentary revealed the reality behind the glamorous veneer of fast, cheap fashion,' explains Klaus Melvin Jensen, Coordinator of Clean Clothes Campaign Denmark, part of the Labour Behind the Label movement. 'I fear many customers will lose their appetite for cheap clothing after seeing this film.'

Among Labour Behind the Label's many campaigns is one that aims to provide all garment workers with a decent living – the very same living wage espoused by People Tree's Safia Minney. But are the major high street brands prepared to pay it? According to the Clean Clothes Campaign and Labour Behind the Label, Debenhams, Topshop, Hobbs, Levi's and the Peacock Group – among others – refuse to reveal what they pay their garment workers, while at the same time refusing to deal with local trade unions. As a result, it's very difficult to determine whether any of them have really made progress on overhauling their production processes – as numerous brands have promised to in the past.

Despite the progress made, there is still a problem – made plain by the appalling tragedy in Bangladesh. But could the horrified reactions that followed the collapse herald the beginning of a sea change in attitudes towards garment workers? Rana is now behind bars and brands such as Marks & Spencer and Next are working towards providing workers with a living wage. Zara has signed up to the ethical framework outlined by the International Textile Union Federation. It might not all be plain sailing, but signs of positive change are afoot.

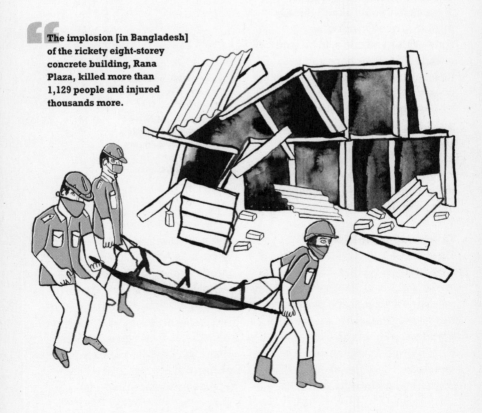

> **The implosion [in Bangladesh] of the rickety eight-storey concrete building, Rana Plaza, killed more than 1,129 people and injured thousands more.**

THE FAIRTRADE REVOLUTION

2

Although Fairtrade has been around since the end of World War Two, it has only existed as a mainstream concept since 1989, when the first Fairtrade label, Max Havelaar, was launched by Dutch economist Nico Roozen, his compatriot Frans van der Hoff and a Dutch NGO called Solidaridad. The independent certification would allow ethically produced goods, including comestibles and crafts, to be sold outside NGO-run shops and in mainstream outlets, thereby reaching more consumers and – they hoped – boosting Fairtrade sales in the process. The initiative would also allow customers and distributors alike to track the origin of the goods to confirm that the products were really benefiting the producers at the end of the supply chain.

" …Fairtrade continues to grow … more than a million small-scale producers, organized into 3,000 grassroots groups in 50 different countries, are benefiting from it.

Fairtrade takes hold

The concept caught on and, within a year, Fairtrade-labelled coffee had a market share of almost 3 per cent. In the ensuing years, similar non-profit Fairtrade labelling organizations were set up in other European countries and in North America, and in 1997 the worldwide association, Fairtrade Labelling Organizations International (FLO),

was created. FLO is now responsible for setting international Fairtrade standards, for certifying production and auditing trade according to these standards, and for the labelling of products.

Today, Fairtrade continues to grow. Despite the recent recession, sales of Fairtrade products remain buoyant – more so than in the organic sector – and more than a million small-scale producers, organized into 3,000

Fairtrade & the environment

Unlike coffee and cocoa, Fairtrade fashion can have a positive effect all the way along the supply chain. With comestibles, Fairtrade principles apply almost exclusively to those producing the raw material – small farmers. The raw material is then bought by a Fairtrade company, such as the chocolate-maker Divine, who have responsibility for processing it. But while many Fairtrade companies are environmentally responsible, this is not a requirement. Either way, the supply chain for Fairtrade food and drink is short and relatively uncomplicated. With fashion, it's a different story. The average garment begins as a raw material, either cotton or another natural fabric, or as a man-made fabric. Because Fairtrade incorporates environmental principles, the UK's Fairtrade Foundation and others don't have certification schemes for polyester, viscose and other man-made materials. For cotton, conventional or organic, it does. The most recent figures from the Fairtrade Foundation show that Fairtrade cotton currently has a retail value of £100 million in the UK, a huge amount, even though it amounts to just 0.6 per cent of total UK cotton sales.

grassroots groups in 50 different countries, are benefiting from it. Clearly, it is a concept that works, whether in food, drink or fashion. But although Fairtrade comestibles have become a regular feature of the weekly food shop, Fairtrade still has some way to go in fashion. Yet Fairtrade fashion really can make a tremendous difference, and it isn't just garment workers who benefit. The environment does as well.

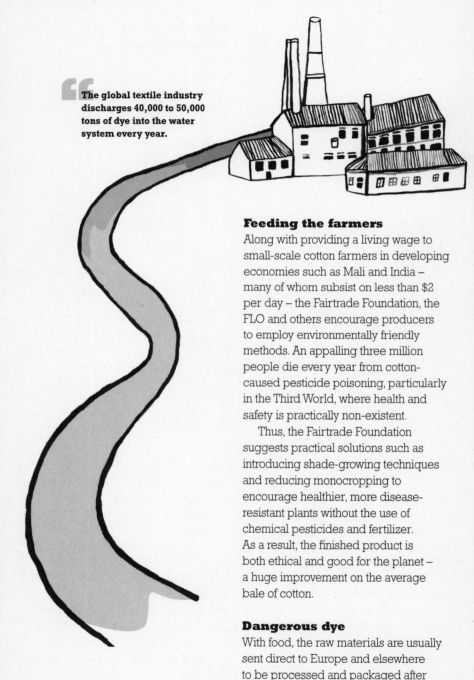

The global textile industry discharges 40,000 to 50,000 tons of dye into the water system every year.

Feeding the farmers

Along with providing a living wage to small-scale cotton farmers in developing economies such as Mali and India – many of whom subsist on less than $2 per day – the Fairtrade Foundation, the FLO and others encourage producers to employ environmentally friendly methods. An appalling three million people die every year from cotton-caused pesticide poisoning, particularly in the Third World, where health and safety is practically non-existent.

Thus, the Fairtrade Foundation suggests practical solutions such as introducing shade-growing techniques and reducing monocropping to encourage healthier, more disease-resistant plants without the use of chemical pesticides and fertilizer. As a result, the finished product is both ethical and good for the planet – a huge improvement on the average bale of cotton.

Dangerous dye

With food, the raw materials are usually sent direct to Europe and elsewhere to be processed and packaged after being harvested. But with fashion, there's another stage: dyeing and manufacturing. Many of the dyes used to colour fabric are highly toxic and can have a catastrophic effect on both workers' health and the environment. 'During the dyeing process an average t-shirt will use 16 to 20 litres of water,' said a report produced by the University of Cambridge. 'Eighty per cent of the dye is retained by the fabric and the rest is flushed out. The global textile industry discharges 40,000 to 50,000 tons of dye into the water system every year.'

Fairtrade helps to tackle this, particularly in terms of cotton processing, eschewing dangerous synthetic dyes and championing the use of natural plant-based colourants in their place. Pioneering Fairtrade organizations such as Aranya in Bangladesh have been quick to adapt natural dyes, creating beautiful, jewel-like colours, and directly improving the livelihoods of artisans and the health of the planet in the process.

Small-scale manufacture

Finally, there's the manufacturing and weaving of the cloth itself, much of which is done by small collectives in workshops supported by the Fairtrade system. Workers are paid a Fairtrade premium and receive a living wage – none of which happens in standard factories – and other benefits such as healthcare and support groups are facilitated.

With three different stages where Fairtrade can make a difference, it's clear that the movement is of real benefit both to deprived communities and to the environment. But although some big retailers have begun to stock Fairtrade

pieces, there's still a considerable way to go until Fairtrade fashion has the same market presence as Fairtrade food and drink.

TEXTILE DYE

Historically, natural dyes such as bark, bugs, saffron and indigo were used in textile production, and while some – cochineal beetle blood, for instance – are still in use, most have been superseded by synthetics. Anionic dyes – the commonest – are often used in conjunction with fluorescent brighteners in textile production. The majority of finished dyes are non-toxic, but the chemicals needed to process them can be extremely dangerous to dye workers. In environmental terms, incorrect disposal of water-soluble dyes poses a problem when they're washed into river systems. Once in the water, dye is hard to remove and can seriously affect photosynthesis in algae, causing a knock-on effect on the rest of the ecosystem.

'IT'S THE DIFFERENCE BETWEEN HEAVEN AND HELL'

While the lot of a Third World garment worker is often a grim one, things are different in Fairtrade factories, according to Kulsum Begum, a Bangladeshi mother of four. Kulsum works as an embroiderer at Thanapara Swallows garment makers' collective, which produces clothes for British brand People Tree. Her Fairtrade fashion job has proved a lifeline for her and her family.

Making a difference

'Life in a rural village isn't easy for Bangladeshi women,' she explains. 'But Fairtrade really can make a difference […]. Swallows is a comfortable, airy, friendly, well-paid workplace where women can earn enough to support their families without having to leave their villages in search for work in a garment factory in the cities. They can live in a beautiful village, eat healthy food and [drink] clean water, rather than live in a slum surrounded by pollution wondering when they will next see their children. It's the difference between heaven and hell.'

Skills & training

For Kulsum, working for a Fairtrade business has meant gaining extra skills and having access to childcare. 'Most of the 200 women [employees] walk to work at 8.30am, dropping their children at the day care centre or at the Swallows school,' she says. 'We start at 9am and work to 5pm […]. Work involves hand embroidery work, bobbing and sewing, or tailoring. People Tree has funded tailoring, pattern cutting and quality management skills development workshops. With better quality products, order sizes have trebled in the last five years, providing more regular work for more women in the villages. This means that more than 1,000 people benefit directly from People Tree orders. Also the profile of Swallows products is much higher in fashion and international press. It makes us feel proud!'

Social change

The brand has also supported a Swallows initiative aimed at tackling domestic violence, a huge social problem in Bangladesh. 'We work with 250 women at Swallows, of which I'd imagine between 20 and 50 per cent have, in one form or another, experienced domestic violence at a serious level,' reveals People Tree founder Safia Minney. 'The anti domestic violence program has helped to build awareness that domestic violence is NOT acceptable,' adds Kulsum. 'Laws have been passed and a network of trained female village-based lawyers help to arbitrate and prosecute if any cases come to light.'

Sadly, many still do. 'Last week there was a case of an 18-year-old wife who was so badly beaten with a stick that her skull had been cracked open,' says Kulsum. '[She has had] three expensive and painful operations but she will never be physically and psychologically the same again. Women need to know that domestic violence is not acceptable, however 'traditional' and male-dominated society is in Bangladesh. Women were seen to be half the value of a man. We have to be seen as equal.'

This is the difference that buying Fairtrade can make. Not only does it pay a living wage, it also helps to engineer social change, as Kulsum is eager to point out. 'Buying Fairtrade clothing brings change and helps women escape poverty and discrimination. It helps bring strong, peaceful, educated communities that can become leaders for the future. It might just seem like a nice dress, but a Fairtrade dress brings about a transformation in the society where it is made.'

BUY ONE, GIVE ONE AWAY: TOMS

Everyone is familiar with the concept of 'buy one, get one free' (BOGOF) and none more so than **Blake Mycoskie**, founder of American accessories brand TOMS. However, Mycoskie's take on the traditional BOGOF deal comes with an ethical twist: instead of two pairs of shoes for you, when you buy TOMS one goes to you and one to someone who really needs them. From Argentina to Uganda, TOMS have now given away more than two million pairs of their classic canvas shoes and have helped to tackle problems from hookworm to school attendance in the process.

> **Ninety per cent of [people suffering from visual impairment] live in developing countries, where untreated cataracts and infectious diseases are the leading cause of visual impairment.**

Fashion that makes a difference

'We looked at why people need shoes,' says Mycoskie. 'People ask if it's our goal to give shoes to everyone and that's absolutely not the goal. We look to where people need shoes the most desperately.' But Mycoskie hasn't stopped at shoes. In 2012, TOMS eyewear was launched, and the company has rolled out a new version of its 'One for One' model, this time aimed at tackling sight problems.

According to the WHO, 285 million people worldwide suffer from visual impairments of some sort – including 39 million who are totally blind. Ninety per cent of these people live in developing countries, where untreated cataracts and infectious diseases are the leading cause of visual impairment. Even more shockingly, WHO figures suggest that 80 per cent of all cases of blindness or visual impairment can be either cured or avoided altogether. In many countries, tackling them requires money that sufferers simply don't have.

Enter TOMS: 'We go to a lot of different places and meet a lot of different NGOs and non-profits doing work in the field,' explains Mycoskie. 'One of the groups that I was most impressed with was people doing cataract surgery and setting up eye clinics. Whether in Ethiopia or South Africa or in Nepal, they bring in eye surgeons and change people's lives, literally in 48 hours. I was thinking about what we could do with the one for one model to address additional needs in the field and the most powerful thing I could imagine is giving someone their sight back.' But can buying a pair of sunglasses really help?

According to Mycoskie, it certainly can. 'Basically, for every pair of sunglasses we sell, we help give sight to one person. We work with one organization [in Nepal] called the Seva Foundation. Originally we were thinking to sell a pair of sunglasses, give a pair of prescription glasses, but what we found was that only really serves a third of the people because some people who come to the clinic need treatment. Other people who come to the clinic actually need surgery and we never want to have to turn anyone away, so what we decided was that one pair of sunglasses sold equals one

> **...what we decided was that one pair of sunglasses sold equals one person gets sight. If that means we have to do surgery then we do surgery, if that means we can give them prescription glasses, we give them prescription glasses.**

person gets sight. If that means we have to do surgery then we do surgery, if that means we can give them prescription glasses, we give them prescription glasses.'

Repeat giving

Starting with Nepal, the anti-blindness campaign will eventually take in Ethiopia, Guatemala, Argentina and Zambia among others, with TOMS using the same NGO partners as it does for shoe giving. What's more, as with the shoes, TOMS will keep going back for as long as it's needed.

'What a lot of people don't realize is that the most important parts of what we do is what we call sustainable and repeat giving. We don't just give shoes to kids as a one-off: we make a commitment to that community to repeatedly provide the shoes to the kid as they grow out of them and as they need them. We feel that on average each child that we're serving we give

> **What a lot of people don't realize is that the most important parts of what we do is what we call sustainable and repeat giving. ... on average each child that we're serving we give shoes to three times a year ...**

shoes to three times a year and that way they're constantly getting the new shoes that they need and it's one of the most important parts of our model. There's no reason to do it if there's no long-term sustainable way, adds Mycoskie.

'Ideally I want to work myself out of a job, so we don't want to be giving to them. I think there is a time for aid, but what we're really trying to do is empower the people so they don't need our aid anymore. My long term goal, and this is a 20, 30, 40 year goal, is that

> **My long term goal, and this is a 20, 30, 40 year goal, is that we're also creating a lot of jobs in these communities over time with local production ... so that can help the local economy as well.**

we're also creating a lot of jobs in these communities over time with local production and things like that, so that can help the local economy as well. Aid is important at a certain time for health and education, but it's definitely not something we want to do forever.'

Staying sustainable

Mycoskie has raised an interesting point – for all that 'One for One' is a lovely idea that has helped a lot of people, it doesn't look – superficially at least – like the most sustainable idea for a business. After all, TOMS shoes start at £34.99 per pair, from which Mycoskie has to pay overheads not on just one pair of shoes, but on two. So how is he making it work?

The answer, says Mycoskie, is slashing advertising. 'First thing is we use high-class factories that are very specifically monitored and given checklists in terms of what we expect,' says Mycoskie. 'We don't spend any money on traditional advertising, so if you look at most companies, like Converse or Nike, any of our shoe competitors, they're doing print advertising and billboard advertising, celebrities, professional athletes, TV commercials... TOMS doesn't do any of that and it [advertising] can be anywhere from 10 to 15 per cent of the cost of a sole.

'We take all that and put that into the manufacturing and distribution of the giveaway shoe. We're very disciplined in our overheads so we have very controlled costs for our staffing and especially with the no advertising, it gives us a lot of extra money that other companies wouldn't have.'

Blake Mycoskie

THE WORKER'S CHAMPION: SAFIA MINNEY

'Just not being a sucker is really important!' Blunt words from a woman who has built a career on the back of exposing injustice and trying to do something about it. And what People Tree founder Safia Minney has done is nothing short of exceptional. What began as a small boutique has become a Fairtrade empire that's changed the face of fashion.

Campaigning for a 'living wage'

The brand is already a household name in the UK and Japan, and has just been rolled out in Scandinavia and Germany too. But while profit is important to Minney, it's what she does with it that consumes her – driving social change, empowering workers, transforming lives with new skills and trying to encourage politicians to back a new sort of 'ethical economy'.

'Fashion is a very dirty and un-transparent business,' she explains. 'I think the exploitation of workers and the environment is absolutely unacceptable. In garment factory production, something like a living wage would lift absolutely millions of people out of poverty so that's something we feel very passionately about.'

People Tree is one of the few ethical brands that genuinely competes with the high street, with prices unusually low for the green fashion sector. This, reveals Minney, is all part of the master plan. 'We've been very much wanting to be

a solution in mid-market womenswear,' she explains. 'We really, really do have a massive problem to solve and the only way we can do that is by providing fabulous fashion that is affordable. OK, so People Tree isn't as red carpet as I'd like it to be, but that won't employ a great number of cotton farmers.'

Empowering workers

While Minney likes a glamorous gown as much as anyone else, it is how that gown can change someone's life that really motivates her. 'I think in terms of money, we're anything between 30 per cent higher income and double the usual level,' she explains, when asked how People Tree benefits workers. 'In a rural area, we might be ten times the amount they might otherwise earn, and that's because there's very little employment for women in those areas. But I think money is an increasingly poor indicator of the benefits that Fairtrade brings, because

it's also about the confidence and the skills that allow the artisan to access new international markets.'

Clearly, Fairtrade benefits both workers and consumers – so why, then, don't more brands get involved? 'I think the reason most fashion companies don't bother is because it means taking a much longer term view,' says Minney, ruefully. 'Unfortunately, over the last seven years fashion has become much more short term, so things like long-term development of new factories, new skills with producer groups, which is what People Tree has done, does take time, does take money and I don't think many want to do that. We're still developing and evolving it.'

So much has Minney invested, her company is yet to see a profit. 'Most of our profits are going into creating a supply chain for Fairtrade. And it's not that we don't want to make a profit, it's the reality of creating a business model that will create a product of good quality that people want to continue buying.'

3 Recycling

INTRODUCTION

Recycling used to be a fairly simple affair and it has been going on for centuries, albeit from necessity rather than desire. But in recent decades, this thriftiness has been lost, with people happy to consume and throw away without a second thought.

Things are beginning to change though – and the fashion industry with it. More and more retailers are reducing the amount they send to landfill, with some encouraging customers to return old clothes for recycling. Vintage clothing has soared in popularity creating a market for second-hand clothes.

But more exciting plans are afoot. Upcycling – the art of turning old fabric into fabulous new things – is gathering momentum, thanks to cool young designers such as Christopher Raeburn using so-called waste textiles such as parachutes discarded by the British army.

It isn't confined to clothes, either. Accessories made from 'junk' are everywhere, among them ReLuxe's neon necklaces crafted from old plastic bags. As a result, the fashion industry is fast becoming one of the most excitingly green places to be.

DEALING WITH WASTE

3

As with food and just about every other sort of manufacturing process imaginable, the fashion industry generates a vast amount of rubbish. While the level of waste varies, every single stage of fashion production results in significant quantities of rubbish – much of which could easily be recycled. From the waste water created by growing cotton and bamboo and during cloth manufacturing to the discarded textiles and leftover swatches resulting from the design process, fashion has plenty of scope for cleaning up its act – and it's up to the consumer to help make it happen.

Quantity not quality

Prior to the rise of mass-manufacturing, clothes were treated with respect, mended, cared for and loved – all because they cost a lot to buy and were thus a valuable commodity in the eyes of the buyer. In the age of the lunchtime Topshop splurge, fashion has been devalued and clothing is now regarded as cheap, cheerful and eminently discardable. As a result, more than one million tonnes of waste fashion goes to landfill every year – more than half of which could be recycled instead.

All of this has had a catastrophic effect on the environment, whether because of the vast quantities of pesticides needed to grow cotton on an industrial scale or the human misery created by the retailers' need to make everything as cheaply and quickly as possible. It has also had a huge impact on quality, with clothes

that would once have been expected to last a lifetime now surviving for months at best. So what is being done to tackle the problem of waste clothing?

Cutting out the chemicals

At the beginning of the supply chain, the challenge is in minimizing the use of harmful chemicals and water. Once again, hemp emerges as the most glowingly green natural material around, thanks to the small quantities of water and fertilizer required. Cotton is as problematic as ever, whether it's organic or not, because of the intensive irrigation needed to grow it. It does, however, score highly in one respect: unlike many other textile plants, the whole of the cotton bush is used.

The next stage, manufacturing, creates yet more problems with regards to waste. Because of the synthetic chemicals used during the dyeing process, the enormous amount of water used has to be thrown away and cannot be reused. Here natural dyes could make a difference, although because they cost more and cannot produce neon or fluorescent shades, many brands still choose not to use them.

Finally, there's the garment-making process itself. Hugely wasteful, it results in thousands of tonnes of offcuts – most of which goes direct to landfill. Although some brands, such as From Somewhere, do use them, it's an interesting paradox that the majority don't. On the face of it, making the most of offcuts would seem to be the economical choice – after all, less waste should mean more profit. So why don't they? Luckily for us all, a stable of new brands is emerging to blaze a creative trail for the rest of the fashion industry to follow.

RECYCLING IS COOL

3

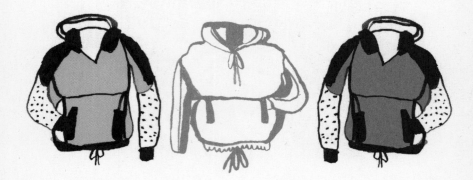

At a time when even the richest nations experience financial woes, austerity measures and spending cuts, waste is becoming more and more unacceptable as old-fashioned values stage a comeback. Recycling is a huge part of that. From government-sponsored recycling collection to greater awareness of climate change, reducing the amount we throw away has become an increasingly normal part of life. So why shouldn't the same principle apply to fashion? The answer is that it does – and thanks to a host of creative newcomers, recycled textiles are becoming more fashionable than ever.

The designers taking offcuts to the high street

Along with Orsola de Castro and her From Somewhere brand (see pages 72–75),

Nin Castle and Clare Farrell's label, Goodone, was among the first to turn offcuts and textile waste into high-end, original design – a process commonly known as 'upcycling'. Goodone's statement pieces are created from material that already exists, saving money, energy and water in the process. 'It's already been dyed, washed, finished and fabric tested,' says Farrell. 'Everything has already been done on it and then it just sits there gathering dust. I just think it is totally ready to go on someone's back.'

Standardization & other problems

But taking spare material and turning it into wearable designs isn't as easy as it looks. 'The problem we have is our fabric resources are un-standardized,' explains Castle. 'Buyers will be okay if it is a slight variation of grey but if

Discarded tents, for instance, are among the more unusual fabric waste that has found its way into Goodone collections.

it goes from a really blue-grey to a really dark grey – that is for them two different products. It has got to be really standardized.' Not that standardization and limited materials have stopped the duo from producing some spectacular pieces, or from taking aim at seasonal trends.

Interestingly, the fabric they use isn't just the standard leftovers from fashion textiles that you would expect. Discarded tents, for instance, are among the more unusual fabric waste that has found its way into Goodone collections. 'Over the years we have had to train ourselves to be very much design led,' says Castle, 'while having an understanding of what we've got as well. We try and get the two to meet in the middle and we're quite good now at going "this is what we have got, so what can we get out of it?"'

So far, what Castle and Farrell are getting out of it is considerable. In the years since it was launched in 2006, Goodone has gone global, been showcased at London Fashion Week and joined forces with mega brands such as Topshop and Tesco to take the eco message to the high street. With that in mind, you'd be forgiven for assuming that the pace would be slowing for the duo, but as Castle says, there's still plenty more to do. 'It feels like it [recycling] is so far behind where it should be,' she laments. 'We are in just quite an interesting place at the moment with the business.'

Sustainable smalls

Castle and Farrell aren't the only designers to have made a career on the back of recycling waste fabric. Along with the likes of feted eco designer Christopher Raeburn, other brands are turning unusual bits of textile waste, such as old coffee sacks, into pieces that are totally unique – a huge selling point given the current trend for one-offs and limited edition pieces. But while creating a dress from recycled fabric might not be the most ground-breaking idea, turning it into underwear most certainly is. Despite the phenomenal growth of recycled fashion over recent decades, one area where few have dared to go is the underwear drawer. When it comes to upcycling, it seems, lingerie is truly the final frontier – unless, of course, you

> **... while creating a dress from recycled fabric might not be the most ground-breaking idea, turning it into underwear most certainly is.**

happen to be the sisters behind eco lingerie label Holloway Smith Noir.

Launched in 2010 by Alice Holloway-Smith and her sibling, Sophie Holloway, the brand produces ridiculously pretty nipple tassles and knickers, all of which are made from recycled fabrics. Most of Holloway Smith Noir's output taps into the burlesque aesthetic and has a vintage feel. But although their designs are retro, their approach to the environment is decidedly progressive.

'[The environment] is part of our whole brand ethos; not because we're greenies but because that's the way we were brought up,' explains Sophie. 'Our mum was a bit of an eco warrior (a trustee of Traidcraft) so it's just normal for us and it's what we've always wanted to do. After all, why wouldn't you recycle or care about the environment?'

'So many people are just oblivious [about environmental issues],' Alice chimes in. 'It's so much more fulfilling when we know that what we do isn't damaging anything.'

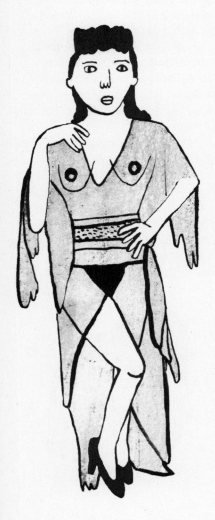

'Our USP is burlesque, vintage glamour,' continues Alice. 'People buy into burlesque because it's new but also retro. It's not about 'look at my body'; it's about the tease so it's intimate and translates better to the bedroom. Both men and women can buy into it.' The big challenge for Holloway Smith Noir, as with many eco labels, is turning their green ideas into a viable business. After all, how big can the market for eco-friendly nipple accessories really be? 'It's still niche,' admits Alice, 'but people really like pretty things and it's nice to have something fun and playful. You can't always wear a bra either, so in that case, it's nice to have something like this underneath. It's about incorporating it into the experience – all of it is about making the wearer feel really special.'

The Ford Cortina goes fashion

Lovely though the product is, what makes Holloway Smith Noir really stand out is the materials. Here, the pair have gone beyond Goodone and From Somewhere and have managed to incorporate not one, but two varieties of waste textile into their pieces: vintage silk and, rather wonderfully, old car seats. Just in case you were wondering how a bit of old Ford Cortina is supposed to make you feel great in the boudoir, the answer is in the backs of the nipple tassles, which are crafted from ultra-soft recycled car seat leather. It's possibly the quirkiest element of a quirky business but one of the cleverest too – and, along with finding a new use for shreds of leftover silk, one of the greenest. 'We practise what we preach,' says Sophie. 'Ethics are important to us.'

RETHINKING RUBBISH

3

One of the most positive developments in the modern fashion industry is the way creative designers have pioneered turning rubbish – real rubbish – into fashion. Accessories designers in particular have found a whole new way to recycle, from turning bottle tops into fabulous bags – even Mulberry launched a deluxe version, albeit lined with less than eco-friendly leather – to making purses from obsolete plastic cassettes.

The fire hose solution

But no designers have turned old junk into fabulous fashion quite as creatively as Brighton-based label Elvis & Kresse. Few fabrics are as challenging for would-be recyclers as thick rubber fire hose – but not only are the brand's unique bags, belts and iPhone holders made from recycled fire hose, they're so cool even Cameron Diaz has one.

So how are Elvis & Kresse doing it? 'It's such an amazing material to work with,' enthuses Kresse Wesling, who founded the label with her boyfriend, James 'Elvis' Henrit, in 2005. 'It seems mad to throw it away.'

'Because it's a composite material, it couldn't be recycled,' she explains. 'Tonnes of old fire hose went straight to landfill.' Happily, all that changed when Kresse made a chance visit to a London fire station.

'I saw all this old fire hose piled up on the roof; the sun was shining on it and it looked beautiful,' she recalls. 'That's when I found out about the hose problem and decided to take ownership of it. I carried a length of hose home with me; I had no idea what I was going to do with it. Originally I wanted to make roof tiles out of it – the material

is waterproof and fireproof so I thought that it would be perfect – but there wasn't enough of it to sustain a roofing business.' Accessories made from welded strips of the fabric were her ingenious solution.

Rubbish to riches

Kresse, however, is certainly not the only designer to have arrived at accessories as a uniquely stylish way to tackle the problem of waste. Ethical jewellery brand ReLuxe makes wonderful collars and chokers from old plastic bags and scraps of leftover jersey, while Mimosa Style makes beautiful fabric-covered notebooks from rags.

And it doesn't end there. Accessories designers have shown an almost infinite capacity for creating gloriously fashionable pieces from just about anything imaginable, including old guitars, yogurt pots and even discarded seatbelts. When it comes to recycling, fashion has the power to be a force for immense good. Best of all, although it has taken a long time, some big brands are finally getting in on the act.

HOW FIRE HOSE BECOMES FASHION

Because fire hose is a composite material made from a blend of rubber, cotton and synthetic fibres, it cannot be melted down like polyester, or its fibres picked apart and rewoven like wool. Dyeing is similarly impossible. To recycle fire hose, brands that use it – such as Elvis & Kresse – pull it into strips and weld or sew the resulting pieces together. Too heavy and rough to be used for clothing, the fabric does lend itself well to bags, iPhone cases and purses, which benefit from its hardiness.

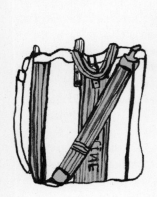

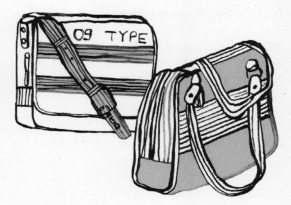

FANTASTIC PLASTIC

3

Polyester and plastic are derived from crude oil, and the manufacturing process requires toxic chemicals, produces toxic gases and needs vast amounts of energy and water for heating and cooling. Once made, they're practically indestructible and do not biodegrade. So how can plastic ever be fantastic? The answer is when it's recycled.

Transforming polyester

One of the few saving graces of polyester is the ease with which it can be melted down and turned into something else. It's far from perfect – the recycling process still requires a plentiful supply of energy and water. Nevertheless, this is better than sending it to landfill or making a fresh supply from dwindling oil reserves. But what's really interesting about recycled polyester is the identity of the company pioneering its use.

A giant solution to a giant problem

With an annual turnover of $16 billion, American sportswear giant Nike is one of the biggest fashion companies in the world. The company has faced its share of criticism for both workers' conditions and environmental impact in the past but, unlike some of the other major global players, it is now trying to do something about it.

Nike is behind one of the most intriguing environmental initiatives of the last decade and is at the forefront of a pioneering new scheme that transforms unethical polyester into something very green indeed. Launched in 2005, the leisurewear giant's Considered Design range uses discarded plastic bottles and waste polyester to make football shirts. Each shirt contains the equivalent of eight bottles and the company has recycled a staggering

HOW TO RECYCLE POLYESTER

Polyester is the world's most popular fibre, accounting for 65 per cent of the textiles produced each year. Given that production requires a staggering 70 million barrels of crude oil every year, recycling polyester isn't just eco-friendly – it has become essential. There are two methods of recycling polyester or rPET (recycled polyethylene terephtalate): mechanical and chemical. The mechanical method involves melting down the polyester and spinning fresh fibres from the melted plastic. Chemical recycling – 'depolymerization' – is less energy intensive, but involves breaking down the polymer into tiny molecules with solvents and using them to reform the yarn. The process is enormously expensive and rarely used.

13 million bottles so far. And as another plus, the recycled shirts also use 30 per cent less energy to produce than conventional polyester.

Setting a new standard

That's quite some achievement, particularly taking into account that the Considered Design range now makes up a whopping 15 per cent of the company's output. But perhaps more important than Nike's recycling of plastic bottles is the example it sets to other big retailers. The company has shown that recycling isn't something purely for small eco concerns – it's for everyone, from Tesco and the other fashion juggernauts down. Although Nike is by no means perfect, it deserves praise for its work on Considered Design and for becoming the world's third largest retailer of organic cotton (after US supermarket giant Walmart and Belgian fashion chain C&A), using about 5 million kg (11 million pounds) of the textile every year. Doing so provides considerable support for organic agriculture.

Could they do more? No doubt. But Considered Design has been a step in the right direction and, along with finding a new use for old polyester that doesn't involve a one-way trip to a landfill site, has set a standard that other fashion businesses could and should measure up to.

THE PIONEER:
ORSOLA DE CASTRO

From launching her own eco-fashion label to campaigning on environmental issues and providing a platform for new, young, green designers, **FROM SOMEWHERE's Orsola de Castro** has done much to raise the profile of British eco design. What's more, as the brains behind the British Fashion Council's Estethica initiative, she's helped champion young green design talent, all while working on her own label. But de Castro's work doesn't stop there.

Green collaborations

From Somewhere is known for its collaborations, most famously with supermarket giant Tesco (the label created a dress made from pre-consumer waste for the supermarket's Florence & Fred brand), but more recently with swimwear giant Speedo. Now, de Castro has launched Reclaim to Wear, which she describes as 'the collaborative arm of my label' and works with up-and-coming talent from London's premier fashion school, Central Saint Martins, as well as green-oriented A-listers such as Livia Firth. So is this the future of eco design in action?

> **Now, de Castro has launched Reclaim to Wear, which she describes as 'the collaborative arm of my label' and works with up-and-coming talent from London's premier fashion school, Central Saint Martins ...**

Reclaim to Wear

'We [Reclaim to Wear] started with a series of collaborations and Central Saint Martins is the first we're doing within education,' says de Castro. 'It has proved so successful that we're hoping to make it an annual appointment for Estethica. Reclaim to Wear is really a way of showing our knowledge and

> **Reclaim to Wear is really a way of showing our knowledge and taking it to another level and to as many people as possible, whether it's to students, the high street, established designers, young designers, and so to do it with Central Saint Martins was an incredible opportunity for us.**

taking it to another level and to as many people as possible, whether it's to students, the high street, established designers, young designers, and so to do it with Central Saint Martins was an incredible opportunity for us. The creativity has been amazing and the results are wonderful!' Like de Castro's From Somewhere label, Reclaim to Wear works mostly with pre-consumer waste – textile offcuts. The question is how sustainable upcycling really is for a label, because, surely, working with offcuts means losing consistency, which can be an issue for the consumer. But de Castro insists that it can work on any scale.

'No, that's not true,' she exclaims. 'We are doing a Reclaim to Wear project with a high street brand and it's a completely different scenario. It depends on what you're working with.

I mean if you're working with liability stock [spare fabric] you can achieve any amounts of reproduce-ability. The collection we did with Livia Firth (launched under the Reclaim to Wear banner and sold on Yoox.com) was also fully reproducible. So it's a designer choice whether you want to make it reproducible or unique, and entirely [depends] on where you're going to sell it. So, as I said, it's perfectly commercial. It makes a lot of sense. It saves a lot of money as well as water and energy to have good housekeeping in terms of your textile use.'

Spreading the word

But there is still one very pertinent question that needs to be answered: if it's cheaper and the quality is good, why don't more designers do it?

> **Upcycling is a novelty; in the sense there is no chemical or other industrial intervention in terms of recycling and shredding and all of that.**

De Castro says: 'It's a little more time-consuming and the cutting is different. But it's also very much of a signature and in the industry most young designers do it now. But it's only really in the last 25 years since over-consumption has created such a massive problem – the textile industry generally has operated a very successful system of recycling itself. Upcycling is a novelty; in the sense there is no chemical or other industrial intervention in terms of recycling and shredding and all of that. It's a relatively new technique that will become more and more commercially viable in the future.'

So what is in store for eco fashion over the next 20 years? Should it stay niche? Should green fashion become the mainstream? Is that even possible? And most importantly, are we seeing a real shift in consumer attitudes towards fashion, or is this just another trend?

De Castro is optimistic. 'I think particularly at a time like this when people just don't have the money to go and spend on an extra t-shirt, it becomes very interesting. People are thinking about the community price of what five t-shirts would have cost and [instead] are buying just one, which they know is the one that they want. So not only are people beginning to re-engage emotionally with what they're buying because they're buying better – they're buying because they want to rather than because they can, which is a very, very different attitude.' This, she believes, will have positive results for the greener end of the fashion spectrum.

Upcycling

'Upcycling is very powerful because it speaks – you will recognize something is upcycled – so it has the same value as a slogan t-shirt in terms of what you actually want to say about yourself.

'It's very intriguing to the younger generation – kids coming out of colleges are absolutely hell-bent in using upcycling as part of their collection. And of course as you know, we have Christopher Raeburn, who is green and an upcycler, being named the Emerging Talent for Menswear at the 2011 British

> **I also believe that it is the responsibility of the industry to change and I am also very much a believer that the uncool, kind of hippy-dippy image of eco fashion was on the way out before it started ...**

Fashion Awards. That has a profound impact on the way that young people see upcycling.'

So is de Castro proud of what her initiative has achieved? 'It [eco design] is very cool right now and I do believe that Estethica has very much changed the stakes in terms of eco fashion, so I'm very proud and delighted to have been a part of this.'

She adds: 'I also believe that it is the responsibility of the industry to change and I am also very much a believer that the uncool, kind of hippy-dippy image of eco fashion was on the way out before it started, because inevitably, you have to look at the full industry to see what fashion is.' Wouldn't she say eco fashion still has a whiff of homespun about it as far as many consumers are concerned? According to de Castro, eco fashion's once unstylish image has been consigned to the history books. 'I don't think the people in any way, shape or form associate it with hippy-dippy any longer,' she argues. 'I think it's much more cutting edge and I think it has earned its place in the fashion industry for good.'

Orsola de Castro

THE POWER OF VINTAGE

3

Another retail trend that has provided the fashion world with a positive step forward is vintage, which now accounts for almost $3.9 billion of annual clothing sales in the USA alone. Vintage boutiques are springing up on shopping precincts all over the world, while eBay has consolidated its position as one of the world's biggest retailers, all thanks to the popularity of the second-hand goods auctioned on the site.

The second-hand renaissance

Oxfam and other charity shops have also seen sales of second-hand garb soar – and it's not all because the recent financial troubles have limited spending power. Like offcuts and unique pieces made from recycled materials, vintage also panders to humanity's quest for looking unique and individual. Even the fashion industry has provided a boost to the vintage clothing industry, with its constant nods to the not-too-distant past.

'If you wanted to, you could go to a car boot sale every day of the year, except Christmas,' says Funmi Odulate, a vintage expert and author of *Shopping for Vintage*. 'Seventy-five per cent of my wardrobe is vintage but people don't always know it.' And thanks to celebrities such as Kate Moss and Alexa Chung, not only does second-hand no longer come with a stigma attached, it's moved into the mainstream.

The rise of vintage is good news for the planet, and a big part of the Environmental Justice Foundation's (EJF) vision. One of the world's leading environmental campaigners, EJF is unequivocally pro-vintage – high praise indeed. And there's another planet-friendly spinoff from the vintage craze – 'swishing'.

Retro retail

Swishing, or shwopping, is all about bartering. Despite no money changing hands, the mainstream fashion industry has come on board, with Marks & Spencer teaming up with Oxfam to launch shwopping boxes in-store. Drop your old clothes in one of the boxes, says the company, and they'll send them straight to Oxfam to be resold and reused. But Marks & Spencer certainly don't have the monopoly on this. Websites such as posh-swaps.com have sprung up, allowing consumers to swap clothes with one another at the click of a mouse.

With bartering and vintage staging a 21st-century comeback, the high street fashion industry has real competition on its hands. Not only is swishing free and vintage low cost, the quality is generally superior to high street output. Will swishing encourage retailers to change their ways? Whatever happens next, the vintage renaissance is a positive step forward for fashion.

TOP FIVE SWISHING WEBSITES

Swishing.co.uk is an eco-friendly version of eBay, where clothes are swapped rather than sold. Also a good resource for those who want to try swishing but aren't sure where to start.

Swishingparties.com lets you advertise gatherings to like-minded people, as well as pointing you in the direction of swishing parties in your area.

Swishing.com is packed with information on swishing, including what it is, how you can get involved and why it's brilliant news for the planet.

Bigwardrobe.com stages swishing roadshows and has a 'shopping' function for those who wish to swap their old clothes for something from someone else's wardrobe.

www.wakeupcampaign.co.uk has details of upcoming swishing events in the UK.

MINNA HEPBURN:
THE DESIGNER WHO MADE VINTAGE COOL

Along with Michelin-starred restaurants and top quality TV, Scandinavia is swiftly building a reputation for fabulous fashion with an ethical twist. From Denmark's A Question Of and The Baand to Sweden's Camilla Norrback and Nudie Jeans, Scandinavia might be small but it packs a powerfully green punch. Now, there's a new brand on the scene, Finland's MINNA. But don't expect to find organic cotton t-shirts and hemp jeans here – designer **Minna Hepburn** is all about vintage and finding new ways to use it.

Clothes that last

'I had a previous label called SE1 London and I saw how the world operates in terms of fast fashion,' explains the eco convert. 'I didn't like it. I saw how customers were responding to clothes; they bought, wore, returned and threw things around. You know how long it takes to make something, and I just thought: "I don't want to be part of something like that."' Her solution was to take the idea of the quick pick-me-up and turn it on its head, making vintage fabrics and traditional manufacturing central to her work.

As a result, the gorgeously girly pieces she makes are crafted from recycled textiles picked up at antique markets and handmade Scottish lace woven on looms a century old, while trimmings are made from vintage ribbons and offcuts. Everything is made according to Minna's strictly enforced 'zero waste' policy, which is why, should you be lucky enough to pay a visit to her south London studio, you'll find basket after basket of curiously shaped pieces of lace and short ribbon.

Much of this is channelled into Minna's bohemian bridal collection and, rather charmingly, ensures that what could have been landfill fodder instead becomes a treasured memento of someone's special day. 'In the bridal range, all veils and headpieces are 100 per cent made from offcuts,' Minna explains.

> **Much of this [offcuts] is channelled into Minna's bohemian bridal collection and, rather charmingly, ensures that what could have been landfill fodder instead becomes a treasured memento of someone's special day.**

Teabag dyes

Even the dyeing process at Minna is a nod to the world of vintage. Based on a simple palette of white, ivory, black and pale grey, lace and other fabrics are hand dyed when needed, and some are dyed using old teabags. 'In general, the overall look [of each piece in a line] will be the same – same but also different,' says Minna.

Although that can pose a problem for bulk buyers who want items to look identical, for Minna's customers it's all part of the charm. 'I accept it's hard to do on a mass production scale but I like that we treat each garment individually,' adds the designer. 'Clients all say positive things about it. Although it took years to find the right fabrics and the right suppliers for them, the business does make money – and the bridal range has been a real hit.' Wedding plans in the offing? For a dress that doesn't cost the earth – in any sense of the phrase – you could do little better than look to Minna.

Minna Hepburn

4 Slow fashion

INTRODUCTION

'Slow fashion' refers to clothing that lasts a long time and is often made from locally sourced or Fairtrade material. It might sound like an oxymoron, but it's rapidly becoming a force to be reckoned with.

As with slow food, the emphasis is on quality, which means dispensing with mass-produced petrochemical-derived textiles and instead using traditional methods and fabrics such as Harris Tweed. Made by hand in the Outer Hebrides of Scotland, manufacturing processes have barely changed in the past 200 years, and the cloth is now protected by an Act of Parliament.

Another benefit of local, traditionally made garments is the shorter, more transparent supply chain that accompanies them. This makes ensuring ethical and quality standards are adhered to much easier than the labyrinthine fast fashion system.

What slow fashion really needs to survive though, is investment, and this is where consumers from the Far East with an appetite for quality goods come in. Can consumption ever really be a force for good? If it's slow, then yes it can.

SLOWING DOWN THE FASHION CYCLE

Originating in the late 1990s, fast fashion is modelled on the American 'quick response' business model. As the global economy boomed and cheap credit became ever more widely available, the fashion industry – led by Spanish high street giant Zara – tapped into a pool of consumers, hungry for trends and passionate about fashion. Mostly young and overwhelmingly female, this new breed of shoppers wanted catwalk looks but at high street prices. And they wanted them now. Scenting an opportunity, the high street swung into action, producing more fashion and selling it at ever diminishing prices. Pile 'em high, sell 'em cheap was the buzz phrase – and it worked.

Cheap, but at what price?

Consumers loved it, with clothes – once a pricey investment – becoming a lunchtime treat. But cheap fashion came at a price. Shorter lead-in times meant turning a blind eye to unethical practices and increased the need for air transport, while lower prices meant screwing textile producers and workers further down the chain. It also meant more man-made fabrics such as polyester – a cheap by-product of crude oil.

'Fast fashion isn't really about speed, but greed: selling more, making more money', comments eco-textiles consultant Kate Fletcher. 'Time is just one factor of production, along with labour, capital and natural resources that get juggled and squeezed in the pursuit of maximum profits. But fast is not free. Short lead times and cheap clothes are only made possible by exploitation of labour and natural resources', she adds.

Quality, not quantity

Along with prioritizing quality over quantity, the rise of slow fashion has helped bring about one very positive change. As discussed in previous chapters, after years of t-shirts that don't last more than a couple of washes and shoes that fall apart on their first outing, consumers are fed up. With the global economic boom a distant memory, few have the money for a £10 sartorial 'treat' and fewer still are prepared to shell out for clothes that don't go the distance.

As a result, people are looking to handmade traditional items and textiles such as Harris Tweed, gabardine and silk, all of which last longer and wear better than polycottons and oil derivatives.

Like the increasing numbers turning to the Slow Food movement's rare breed meat and locally grown sprouts, there is growing momentum behind these traditionally made fabrics – all part of the slow fashion effect.

But it isn't just concern about quality that's driving the trend. Scandals surrounding labour issues have forced brands to look again at their supply chains, with many repatriating production to traditional factories in their own countries – providing a double benefit of boosting local industry and cutting down on transport emissions. Consumers pay a little more but the piece they buy lasts, and lasts, and lasts.

'Of course, quality costs more,' adds Fletcher. 'We will buy fewer products, but higher in value. A fairer distribution of the ticket price through the supply chain is an intrinsic part of the agenda. Jobs are preserved as workers spend longer on each piece. Slow design enables a richer interaction between designer and maker; maker and garment; garment and user. A strong network of relationships is formed, which permeates far beyond the garment manufacturing chain.'

> **People are looking to handmade traditional items and textiles such as Harris Tweed, gabardine and silk, all of which last longer and wear better than polycottons and oil derivatives.**

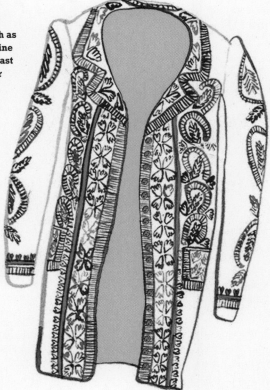

TRANSPARENCY & THE SUPPLY CHAIN

4

Transparency and supply chains have become an increasingly pertinent issue in recent years. Supply is a complex, opaque business, particularly where fast fashion is concerned – the average cotton top will have gone through at least seven pairs of hands before reaching the shop floor. But what do convoluted supply chains have to do with the environment, and by extension, the slow fashion movement? The answer: more than you think.

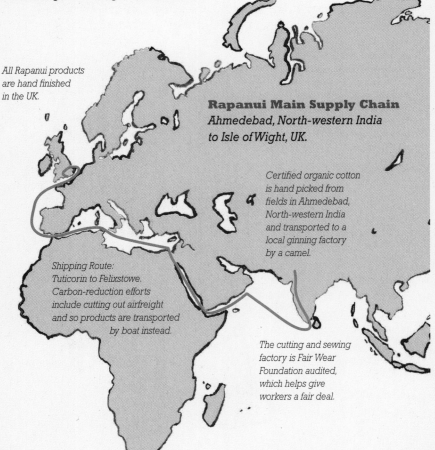

All Rapanui products are hand finished in the UK.

Rapanui Main Supply Chain
Ahmedebad, North-western India to Isle of Wight, UK.

Certified organic cotton is hand picked from fields in Ahmedebad, North-western India and transported to a local ginning factory by a camel.

Shipping Route: Tuticorin to Felixstowe. Carbon-reduction efforts include cutting out airfreight and so products are transported by boat instead.

The cutting and sewing factory is Fair Wear Foundation audited, which helps give workers a fair deal.

Keeping track

For a start, complex supply chains tend to result in cutting corners and a lack of accountability. Can any brand, however big, be expected to keep track of every single garment produced for them? No, of course they can't. But for slow fashion brands, where the onus is on producing quality classics rather than responding to trends, casting a critical eye over the supply chain is part of the business plan. Typical is Rapanui, a young company attracting attention thanks to its 'traceability' map – an interactive tool that allows shoppers to see the story behind their clothes. Type a garment code into the website and follow the trail of that item from seed to shop.

'When we started, we wondered why it was that electrical appliances and food had information on exactly where and how products were made, but clothing didn't,' explains co-founder Rob Drake-Knight. Elizabeth Laskar, an ethical fashion consultant and one of the Ethical Fashion Forum's founders, believes that this type of tool can benefit everyone: 'Traceability systems are good news for the fashion sector. Organizations like Rapanui are accountable to the environment, their suppliers and their customers.'

Getting the big boys on board

For bigger brands, however, the task of bringing transparency to their supply chains is tougher. Not that Drake-Knight thinks they should be allowed off the hook. 'If you consider how much power large brands and high street stores have and how much their suppliers want to keep them happy, it's just about asking for the information. It does obviously get harder for larger brands because there's a lot more information they need to get hold of.'

And help is at hand. MADE-BY, a not-for-profit organization working to make sustainable fashion common practice, used to run a Track&Trace system, available to any brand that asks, and now works to help implement similar systems at companies across the world. But, says spokesman Ulrich van Gemmeren, even with help, getting it right isn't easy. 'It's a system based not on a brand declaring how its products are made but on information given by each individual supplier in the chain,' he explains.

'It's important to have this independence, but also one of the challenges. Small brands, for example, have less impact and less ability to pressure their suppliers to enter data in time and deliver certificates.' This is why some brands signed up to MADE-BY's system decided to leave it again. 'How can you guarantee sustainability in the chain if only one supplier enters data?' asks van Gemmeren. 'You have to get everyone to do it.'

Whatever the difficulties of setting up a system like this, Laskar is confident the movement is a convincing one. 'The concept is needed and will stay,' she says. 'It may develop into a legal requirement over time, especially if carbon reduction plans come to fruition. My hope is that more retailers will pick up the baton to become accountable and transparent about everything they put in their shops.'

WOOL: A VERY BRITISH TRADITION

4

> **Natural, endlessly renewable and sustainable: the three reasons wool is making a comeback among eco-fashionistas.**

Long-wearing, cosy and incredibly versatile, wool can be spun into anything, from the softest felt to the toughest gabardine. Yet, despite its versatility, wool fell out of favour in the 1950s and 60s and has never entirely recovered. But the Campaign for Wool, initiated by The Prince of Wales and lauched in 2010, has endeavoured to change this.

Endlessly renewable

Using and wearing wool benefits more than just sheep farmers, as John Thorley – veteran sheep farmer and the campaign's Honorary President – explains: 'Wool is wonderful because it's a naturally produced fibre and is ecologically superior to all its competition. In addition, it provides a new crop every year [which can be used for anything] from softer fabrics that can be worn, to homeware such as carpets and furniture.'

Natural, endlessly renewable and sustainable: the three reasons wool is making a comeback among eco-fashionistas. Among them are Ada Zanditon, whose gabardine coats and felt jackets regularly receive plaudits from the fashion press, and William Tempest, whose championing of all-natural materials have made him an under-the-radar eco-fashion star. But wool is also beginning to reappear on the high street, at Topshop, Marks & Spencer and & Other Stories, to name but three. So why now and why wool?

'People are realizing that wool is a better choice,' explains Thorley. 'Unfortunately, wool suffered with the advent of man-made oil-based fibres which could be produced at lower prices initially, and appeared to be easier to deal with during manufacture and in aftercare. The cost of wool does affect the decisions that retail store buyers make […] but they are starting

CAMPAIGN FOR WOOL

Few fabrics merit their own campaign but wool isn't any old textile – and neither is the movement aimed at promoting it. Bringing together a polyglot mix of sheep farmers, manufacturers, designers and craftspeople, the campaign, launched in 2010, aims to educate people about the diverse benefits that using, wearing and buying wool can bring.

footprint in the shape of air miles, particularly if you happen to be a British consumer purchasing Australian or New Zealand wool. PETA also warn of unethical practices such as 'mulesing' – a gruesome hide-trimming technique that involves cutting loose chunks of flesh from the animal's back in order to prevent fly-strike. The organization describes Australian merino as 'the cruellest type of wool' and warns unwary buyers to steer clear.

Happily for those in search of a wool coat or jumper that lasts, 'mulesing' is limited to Australia, which means that the majority of wool products can be purchased with a clear conscience. And buying wool people most certainly are, with the UK alone now producing 60,000 tonnes of the stuff every year. All of which is good news for the planet, and for consumers, who benefit from a long-wearing textile that doesn't cause the pollution or use the chemicals that cotton and other natural fibres do. All that's left to do is to fight for more of it – the environment will thank you.

to understand wool and its real benefits a little better now […].'

'Mulesing'

But not all wool is created equal, and there are some environmental problems associated with the fibre. The most obvious is transport. Unless you choose wool produced in your own country, the textile can rack up a huge carbon

THE RENAISSANCE OF HARRIS TWEED

For a type of cloth exclusively made on a tiny island in the Scottish Outer Hebrides, **HARRIS TWEED** has had a disproportionately big impact on the fashion world. Loved by royalty and worn by everyone, the fabric has a long history and a future that has just taken a turn for the exotic. But why is Harris Tweed popping up in a book about eco-friendly fashion? The answer is that it is a wonderful example of how green, locally produced textiles can not only survive in the modern fashion industry, but flourish.

The history of 'Clò Mór'

Produced on the islands of Lewis, Harris, the Uists, Benbecula and Barra, the history of Harris Tweed, or Clò Mór [the big cloth] as it's locally known, is a long one. Although the origins of the cloth are thought to be Iron Age, it wasn't until the Industrial Revolution that the fame of the textile spread. Unlike the rest of the UK, the Outer Hebrides retained their traditional processes, continuing to produce cloth by hand long after the rest of the country had turned to new-fangled machines such as the spinning jenny.

In 1836 Alexander 6th Earl of Dunmore inherited the North Harris Estate from his father. At that point, the virgin wool used to produce the tweed was still being washed in soft, peaty water and dyed using local plants and lichens. It was then processed and spun, before being hand woven by the crofters in their cottages.

When the 6th Earl died in 1843, responsibility for his estate on the Isle of Harris passed to his wife, Lady Catherine Herbert, who was quick to spot the potential of the cloth being produced. She had it made into clothes for her gamekeepers but quickly realized that it would also be ideal for aristocratic friends who wanted to enjoy outdoor sports, and promoted it at every opportunity, with the result that it swiftly became the fabric of choice for the landed gentry and aristocracy of the time. It marked the beginning of the Harris Tweed industry, which at its peak in 1966 was producing 6.9 million metres of the cloth every year.

> **Fashion changed ... The fabric [Harris Tweed] virtually disappeared from the high street, found only in small specialist stores and worn only by the old-fashioned and eco-minded. But Harris Tweed wasn't to remain in the doldrums for long.**

But like other traditional fabrics such as gabardine, felt and silk, sales of Harris Tweed plummeted in the face of competition from cheaper man-made textiles such as polyester. Fashion changed and tweed lost ground among 1970s' fashionistas, who wanted loose poplin blouses and wide denim flares instead of starchy, old-fashioned tweed. The fabric virtually disappeared from the high street, found only in small specialist stores and worn only by the old-fashioned and eco-minded. But Harris Tweed wasn't to remain in the doldrums for long.

Protected by law

After spending 20 years in the fashion wilderness, Harris Tweed received an important boost in 1993, when an Act of Parliament – the Harris Tweed Act 1993 – established the Harris Tweed Authority in law and gave the new governing body a mandate 'to promote and maintain the authenticity, standard and reputation of Harris Tweed; for preventing the sale as Harris Tweed of material which does not fall within the definition...'.

As a result, all Harris Tweed now has to conform to the following criteria: 'Harris Tweed means a tweed which has been hand woven by the islanders at their homes in the Outer Hebrides, finished in the islands of Harris, Lewis, North Uist, Benbecula, South Uist and Barra and their several purtenances (the Outer Hebrides) and made from pure virgin wool dyed and spun in the Outer Hebrides.' It was the beginning of a new future for Harris Tweed, this time as a heritage fabric.

A Far Eastern future

Harris Tweed finally proved it was back to stay with the news in 2013 that a tranche of shares in one of the last three surviving Harris Tweed producers, Carloway Mill on the Isle of Lewis, had been bought by one of the world's largest textile companies, China's Shandong Ruyi Technological Group. China, while hardly the greenest world power, has proved a driving force behind the renaissance of British heritage fabrics and brands and currently purchases a staggering 40 per cent of all Harris Tweed produced.

Saving a cottage industry

Now producing more than a million metres of cloth every year, what was once a stuttering cottage industry is returning to its pre-1970s best. As spokesman for Carloway Mill, Bruce Armitage put it: 'This [the Chinese deal] is very important not only for the

> 'With international investment and an increasing international appetite for the fabric [Harris Tweed], the cloth is a slow-produced, environmentally friendly textile that is now displacing non-green alternatives – all without becoming a niche product for green shops.

investment and an increasing international appetite for the fabric, the cloth is a slow-produced, environmentally friendly textile that is now displacing non-green alternatives – all without becoming a niche product for green shops. This is in itself hugely important. Imagine if the story repeated itself with gabardine, wild silk, wool and Scottish handmade lace. Not only would the future fashion industry be a less wasteful place, it would be a much greener one too.

Carloway Mill, but for the Harris Tweed industry and the future economy of the Western Isles. Although the industry has developed and grown appreciably over the past three years, this new association with a global textile company is a first for Harris Tweed and will allow the Carloway Mill access to a potentially massive platform to expand its volumes and profitability.

'Shandong Ruyi has a home marketplace of 1.3 billion people, but it also has a sales presence in 51 countries across the world. This and their extensive knowledge of the textiles industry, together with their ambitions for Harris Tweed, make them a highly desirable partner.'

What is clear is that the future of Harris Tweed and the Carloway Mill looks assured. With international

A BOON FOR THE PLANET

The newfound success of Harris Tweed is particularly fascinating because it has turned the prevailing fabric trend of the last half century on its head. Until recently, textiles were becoming increasingly detrimental to the environment, with top-speed techniques combining with toxic chemicals to create an environmental horror story. By contrast, Harris Tweed, which uses the same hand-weaving techniques and lichen dyes as it has always done, is a positive boon for the planet.

HARRIS TWEED

TAMING THE DRAGON: WHY SLOW FASHION NEEDS THE EAST

4

From accusations of slave labour in Zimbabwean diamond mines to smog clouds that would put Victorian London to shame, China, and its rapacious appetite for natural resources, has become synonymous with careless capitalism. And yet that very appetite for consumption is proving something of a saving grace in the fashion world. While the 1990s were dominated by rich Russians hungry for furs and Balmain, the 2000s saw the rise of the Eastern oligarch with a taste for heritage, tradition and, yes, eco fashion.

Investing in China

While big brands, Prada and Chanel among them, floating on the Hong Kong stock exchange have made headlines in the business press, the luxury fashion houses aren't the only ones to have benefited from oriental largesse. British labels, too, are angling for a share of this newfound Chinese prosperity.

So important has it become that Mulberry's share price took a tumble when the Chinese economy experienced a slowdown in the early part of 2013, while heritage brand Burberry already has 57 outlets on the mainland and expects that number to increase by 43 within the next five years. Included in the current Burberry tranche is the Beijing flagship at Sparkle Roll Plaza, the British brand's most high-tech store to date.

Status and slow fashion

Equally popular with Chinese consumers are labels that produce garments made with tried and tested eco-friendly techniques. Harris Tweed (see pages 90–93) is one such beneficiary, with a massive input of capital from the Shandong Ruyi Technological Group ensuring that the fabric will continue to survive well into the 21st century. Likewise the American denim brand rag & bone, which relies on the time-honoured techniques and natural dyes used in its Tennessee factories, has an ever increasing client base in the Far East. French

heritage handbag maker Hermès, which still makes its leather goods by hand in its Paris atelier, is also benefiting, with the brand's Kelly and Birkin bags proving just as popular in the East as they are at home.

But what's particularly interesting about the Chinese impact on fashion is that it is reversing the impact of the Russians and their appetite for the shiny, new and bling. For Chinese consumers, it's all about quality and status – and that's good news for slow fashion. Because of the time it takes to make things by hand, slow fashion will never be able to compete with the high street on price. But on quality, it's a different story, which is why the trend for quality plays so beautifully into its hard-working hands. It's ethical luxury, and China – which overtook Japan as the world's top consumer of luxury goods in 2012 – is now the perfect market.

> **For Chinese consumers it's all about quality and status – and that's good news for slow fashion.**

> **... [soy's] luxurious and soft 'cashmere' texture mean it's popular in the production of a range of garments, from underwear and socks to dresses and t-shirts.**

Ethical luxury

The Chinese market is also an incredibly fast-growing one, with total sales of luxury goods reaching more than £9 billion in 2012, fuelled by the rapid growth of the Chinese economy. Better job opportunities and higher wages, particularly for women, have seen the demand soar for designer shoes, 'it' bags and high-end fashion. There are more than 150 female Yuan billionaires (close to £95 million) in China, and 11 of the world's 20 wealthiest self-made women live in the country, which in retail terms equates to an awful lot of disposable income to spend on Hermès Birkin bags and British-made trench coats.

It also means there's increasing room for eco designers such as William Tempest, Christopher Raeburn and Minna, all of whom produce the sort of luxurious, stealthily green fashion so adored by the Chinese consumer. What's more, beneficial though the Eastern fashion boom is to the Western slow fashion fraternity, China – and its neighbours – is home to a small but growing band of home-grown slow fashionistas. Among them is Gong Jia Qi, winner of the inaugural China EcoChic Award in 2012, and a passionate believer in sustainability and quality.

Sustainable style

'I'm very interested in sustainable fashion design because it combines fashion design with environmental and social development,' Gong explains. 'It's about more than the designer's aesthetic expression or about meeting the needs of a typical group of customers and instead it allows design to become an effective solution to environmental social problems. Personally, it makes me feel that it's not difficult or impossible to share environmental and social responsibilities as an individual.' And Gong isn't the only Chinese fashionista to pay more than lip service to the environment. The country is also becoming increasingly open to green business initiatives, all of which spells better days for eco fashion.

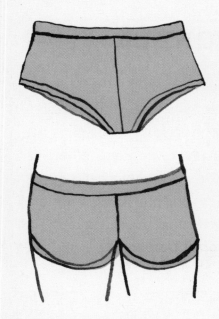

Overhauling industry

Along with revamping its manufacturing processes to take into account ethical and environmental concerns, China is also stepping up production of green fibres, including soy, hemp and organic cotton. Soy, in particular, is considered a sustainable fabric because it is made from the by-products left over from processing tofu, soybean oil and other soy products – all of which the Chinese consume in their millions of tonnes – and its luxurious and soft 'cashmere' texture mean it's popular in the production of a range of garments, from underwear and socks to dresses and t-shirts. According to the Organic Exchange, China is now the third biggest organic cotton producer after Turkey and India. Clothing labels belonging to the MADE-BY network have been importing Chinese organic textiles since 2007, while Dutch NGO Solidaridad has also been investing in finding reliable partners in the cotton province of Xinjang. As a result of this initiative, one big farmer turned 220 hectares of soil into an organic cotton field.

While China's own green garment industry remains a work in progress, its impact on eco fashion abroad has been considerable. From rescuing Harris Tweed to saving Savile Row, Chinese consumerism can be a real force for good in the world, particularly where eco fashion is concerned. All that's needed is to persuade the Eastern consumer that no, ivory isn't a great accessory, and the future of some of the greenest brands in the world will be left looking infinitely brighter. But regardless of whether China stays the course, slow fashion is here to stay – and that can only be regarded as a huge step forward for the planet.

THE WOOLLY WONDER:
IZZY LANE

Wool is undisputedly one of the greenest fabrics available, but it does have a dark side, particularly if you are vegan or vegetarian – because no matter who owns them, or how well they're looked after, the fact remains that most sheep end their days in a slaughterhouse. But one British flock of sheep will never see a slaughterman up close, and they belong to IZZY LANE founder **Isobel Davies**.

Welfare for wool

Prior to launching her label, Davies ran a box scheme called Farmaround – which she still controls – selling slaughter-free eggs and milk. 'The most important thing is animal welfare,' says Davies. 'Why is it OK to have different levels of welfare for meat and not wool? This is something the British Fashion Council and DEFRA should be addressing.'

Farmers are currently obliged to sell the wool they produce to the British Wool Marketing Board, which pays a set price and then sells to the highest bidder. This prices smaller manufacturers out of the market, Davies explains, and also makes it impossible for green consumers to buy wool raised, for instance, according to organic or slaughter-free principles. While the textile itself remains green, choice and traceability are poor.

Davies' battle with the Wool Board to get a licence to sell her own product took some time, but the result of her titanic struggles is an important one: Izzy Lane, the world's first slaughter-free fashion business. Every single piece produced by the label, from thick woollen jumpers to cosy tweed coats, is made from wool

> **Farmers are currently obliged to sell the wool they produce to the British Wool Marketing Board, which pays a set price and then sells to the highest bidder.**

Izzy Lane

SLAUGHTER-FREE WOOL

Like chickens and cows, the vast majority of sheep end their days in a slaughterhouse, even if their primary purpose is to produce wool. Davies' approach differs because she allows her sheep to live out their full natural lives. While this makes her product more suitable for vegetarians, she is one of the few farmers to do so: most choose not to because of the prohibitive costs of keeping unproductive animals.

shorn from Davies' 500 Swaledale sheep and crafted in traditional textile mills to help keep the UK's old-fashioned family-run enterprises alive.

Making the most of slaughter-free wool

'My approach to fashion was two-pronged,' explains Davies. 'First, I wanted to help revive the [British] textile industry in general and wool in particular. I used to spend a lot of time with farmers who would tell me all these stories about having to burn wool because transport had become more expensive than the value of the wool. To me, this seemed appalling.' What's more, adds Davies, wearing wool makes more sense now than ever before. 'People are struggling these days so it makes sense to wear wool,' she says. 'There really is no comparison between something synthetic and a natural fibre. It keeps

you cool when it's hot, warm when it's cold and it even cleans itself. It just goes hand in hand: wool and British clothes.'

And the efforts of Davies and the Campaign for Wool are finally beginning to pay off, although Davies is keen to move on to the next stage: rolling out slaughter-free wool across the industry. 'It's the only fibre we produce here. Any revival of "made in Britain" is good and the results are encouraging. Wool prices are finally climbing.

'[But] the Wool Marketing Board needs reform,' Davies reveals. 'I wanted to introduce the first ever animal welfare certification on wool but the board was dead against it and said it undermined other wool. So many sheep are exported for halal slaughter, which is just not right. And young designers cannot go to farms, verify the sheep, meet the farmer and buy the wool direct. [...] Changing that would make a huge difference to animal welfare and to the wool trade.'

> There really is no comparison between something synthetic and a natural fibre. It keeps you cool when it's hot, warm when it's cold and it even cleans itself. It just goes hand in hand: wool and British clothes.

5 Retail revolution

INTRODUCTION

Consumerism. The number one target of anti-globalization campaigners and green activists the world over. But consumerism can create jobs, throw a lifeline to dying industries and make manufacturers and retailers change their ways.

As wealthy Western consumers have become less willing to accept unethical practices, so companies have begun to clean up their act in response. Witness Zara and its adoption of an ethical code of practice. Witness the burgeoning number of eco brands that are not only greening the face of fashion but making a profit as well. Then there are the Far Eastern consumers with their appetite for quality and willingness to pay for high-end slow fashion.

Of course, you can't overlook the role of the internet in all this. As ASOS proves, it's possible to dispense with boutiques and still be a success, as its 'Green Room' and 'Marketplace' initiatives show. And greening the high street isn't a pipe dream either. Whether it's Topshop's embrace of 'Made in Britain' or H&M's Conscious Collection, going green is not only popular but profitable too.

GREENER CONSUMPTION

5

Consumption is a topic that polarizes opinion in the green movement, with some arguing that it should be sharply reined in, and others taking the pragmatic view that it's a necessary evil. Certainly in terms of conserving resources, the former group has a point – after all, wearing more vintage and toting new purchases until they fall apart helps reduce pressure on the planet. And yet, those in favour of that argument are essentially spitting in the wind. Despite the impact of recent recession, inflation and economic slowdown, people are buying as much as ever. The answer, therefore, is to make fashion retail greener.

Responsible retail

Green retail doesn't just mean buying hemp and wearing out your clothes. There needs to be an end to clothing made by low-paid workers from cheap, energy-hungry textiles. Retailers need to think local, reduce energy consumption, and – most importantly – help educate consumers on the merits of buying green. Happily, on this latter point in particular, there are signs that the message is getting through.

'Big retailers do have a responsibility to pay attention to the planet and make ethical decisions […],' explains green retail expert Christian Smith. 'All industry is based on the ability of the earth to produce the goods we buy and sell. If we destroy the earth's ability to rejuvenate itself and continue to live in a world that promotes quantity over quality, then we will have no ability

to build businesses and create employment for people. Companies need to be aware of their impact on crucial things like water, soil and people's health and collaborate to reduce those impacts.'

Every garment counts

Among those beginning to change their ways are Topshop, whose 'Made in Britain' range supports traditional garment-making, while H&M's Conscious Collection makes products from green fabrics such as organic cotton and Tencel available to all. Internet retailer ASOS has introduced a 'Green Room', stocking an ever increasing array of eco brands including People Tree, Fleur of England, Wildfox and Danish label A Question Of.

Smith, who was instrumental in setting up the ASOS Green Room, says it is an important step towards raising awareness both of green brands and the issues at hand. 'I think the best thing we did at ASOS was the Green Room,' he reveals. 'It now exists and if it were to disappear they [ASOS] would have a lot of questions to answer. Even though it might ebb and flow, it's there, waving the flag and showing what is already possible today, right now.'

He also has a message for those consumers considering making a switch to green fashion, even if it's just one organic cotton t-shirt. 'It's a start,' he says. 'The fact is that every little change that individuals make has an impact. In buying that organic shirt, you are recognizing that organic is at least as good and as desirable as non-organic. It's the start of something and we have to look at it in the wider context of long-term behaviour change. But each organic item bought disproves a lot of preconceived notions that people aren't interested or that it's too expensive.'

More importantly, for beleaguered traditional manufacturers, highly skilled artisans and eco-friendly textile producers, every green garment bought is a much needed lifeline – and another nail in the coffin for fast fashion.

THE LOCAL REVIVAL 5

Since 1966, the family-run Michael Edward Ltd factory in Walthamstow, London, has been turning out fashion for the world's top designers. Renowned for its attention to detail and fast turnaround, it's now at risk of closure due to decades of dwindling orders – the result of overseas competition and an increasingly globalized fashion industry. And Michael Edward isn't the only one. From Scottish lace makers to Peruvian batik artists, artisan producers are in real trouble, wherever they're based.

Decline & reinvention

The decline of the London factory is a story being repeated all over the developed world. At its peak, Michael Edward employed 110 staff. Now there are just 12. Where it once had two or three big clients signed up for the long haul, it now has four or five smaller brands putting in orders month-to-month for much smaller collections.

But it's not all bad news and, for others, reinvention has been the route to survival. Manchester's Cooper & Stollbrand, known for making outerwear for Paul Smith, Topshop, and All Saints among others, was once at the centre of coat making. It too has felt the knock-on effects of the slowdown

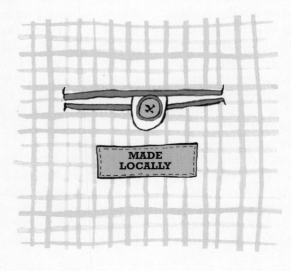

MADE LOCALLY

MADE LOCALLY

in British fashion manufacturing but remains busy – the only factory along the River Irwell (a manufacturing area that once employed 70,000 people) still open. Now Cooper & Stollbrand is producing its own menswear collection, Private White VC, to keep heritage tailoring and skills alive.

This kind of passion is what's driving the fashion industry's new appreciation of British craftsmanship, raw materials and textile expertise. London-based textiles design studio Wallace Sewell turned its attention to bygone industrial techniques to produce textiles designed by hand.

Founders Harriet Wallace-Jones and Emma Sewell use yarn sourced from UK companies and produce and finish at two Lancashire mills, and they've noticed a sea change in the way British manufacturing is seen. 'A lot of mills closed when manufacturing went to Asia but the UK has a good reputation for quality and we've noticed a lot of customers happy to see our products are made exclusively here,' says Sewell.

THE PERSONAL TOUCH

Sara Kelly and Paul Vincent, founders of S.E.H. Kelly, a timeless menswear brand, scour the UK for mills that are in decline and put them back to work. They share a passion for Britain's hidden gems and love manufacturing in the UK, using only British materials. 'It is more expensive so our products cost more but our customers seem to understand the value of UK made and appreciate knowing the provenance of their garments,' says Vincent. This approach is the antithesis of fast fashion as production runs can be as low as five or six pieces and even the history of the buttons is available to the customer. 'These mills rely on loyal and continuous custom,' he adds. 'We've lost two makers since we started but there are still some really great places left. I like being able to visit the makers, I like the stories they have to tell and the history behind the mills.'

Homegrown talent

While cost has driven many brands out of the UK, quality has kept many at home and brought many flocking back. Heritage brands such as Barbour, which has been trading since 1894, are also helping to drive the trend, with the company now producing 140,000 classic waxed cotton jackets in its South Shields factory every year.

But cost isn't the only issue facing British manufacturers. When UK designers and brands headed to China, Turkey and Poland en masse, lower costs were only part of the attraction. In 2009, the Centre for Fashion Enterprise (CFE) published a government-funded report, *UK High-end Manufacturing*, to find out why Italian and French rivals had such a competitive edge. Was it because they, unlike the British, had fashion factories on their doorstep? What was it about the vision, products and processes that was holding the British textile industry back? The answers that emerged from the report were illuminating. In the UK, the specialist skills needed to maintain consistently high standards had faded, finance was hard to come by and infrastructure was weak. Investment in new technology was limited, especially from smaller fashion manufacturers, and knowledge about products and product cycles was poor on all sides.

But change was in the air. Along with funding from the European Regional Development Fund came a new initiative, the Designer-Manufacturer Innovation Support Centre (DISC), established early in 2012 to address these needs. 'It's all about innovation,' says Wendy Malem, Director of the CFE and of DISC. 'Making is innovating. We have really fantastic creative designers in London who rightly have had the focus, but let's support them with innovation through manufacturing now.'

Wanted: young blood

DISC will support fashion manufacturers and designers in the luxury sector and help them improve their business models, products and services. This will help people like Marissa Montgomery, designer and founder of lingerie brand Pussy Glamore, who moved her production from the UK to Morocco – for cheaper prices and 'the high quality and finish achieved in Morocco and the machinery required for certain details.'

British producers are getting older too. In the report *The Value of the UK Fashion Industry* (2010), the British Fashion Council points out that more than 60 per cent of the workers in the textiles and manufacturing sectors are aged over 40. The industry needs to attract more young blood to retain its skills base and worldwide reputation.

Bringing fashion home

In 2012, the UK Fashion and Textiles Association (UKFT) launched the Let's Make It Here campaign, aimed at making it easier for the two sides of the fashion coin – design and manufacturing – to meet and make. UK manufacturers can publicize their details to UKFT members and the system covers all stages of the supply chain. If word of mouth helps grow the database, the resource could help keep UK manufacturing alive.

There is also more interest in UK-made on the high street. Topshop has announced it will double its lines produced in Britain over the next few years (although it declined to specify any figures) and ASOS is rumoured to be expanding its UK base too. The Made in Britain tag may have disappeared for a while but it's still important for UK jobs, skills and the environment, as well as for consumers who put quality and principle over price.

THE FIGHT FOR TRADITIONAL CRAFTSMANSHIP

5

One of the more interesting anomalies the fashion industry throws up is that despite being a byword for Third World exploitation and cheap labour, it also employs more highly skilled artisans than any other. France alone is home to more than 5,000 'petites mains' – seamstresses – who spend hour after hour laboriously assembling some of the world's most expensive gowns. Yes, couture might be considered a synonym for excess by some, but it's also helping to keep traditional craftsmanship alive.

Petites mains and couture

From Dior to Chanel, 'les petites mains' play a critical role in producing the couture collections that thrill fashion insiders and give birth to the trends that high street consumers will wear in seasons to come. The opulent shows have produced some of fashion's most iconic looks, including Yves Saint Laurent's 'Le Smoking' trouser suit and Dior's fit 'n' flare post-war 'New Look'. But although the eccentric creative brains of Christian Dior and Yves Saint Laurent produced the vision, it was the skilled artisans who turned their visions into reality. However, lower down the fashion food chain and with more brands shipping their production overseas and cutting costs, France's 'les petites mains', the USA's denim experts and the UK's lacemakers are all at risk of extinction.

Keeping craft alive

Despite the expense of traditionally made crafts, there are, however, a number of up-and-coming designers who are beginning to produce pieces that combine

craftsmanship with the principles of Fairtrade: garments made in their own factories with good working conditions, where staff are trained and supervised by the designers themselves. These are independent designers, not all of whom define themselves by green production, but who have nevertheless redefined the concept of couture fashion with their own brand of artisan garment-making – creating a niche between high street and the high fashion of Paris and Milan in the process.

Among them is Malaysia's Bernard Chandran, who launched his career at home and built up an impressive client base (including royals from Malaysia and Brunei) before heading off to London. Despite being an unknown when he arrived, within a few seasons he made his mark by reinterpreting traditional Malay garb for a modern, fashionable audience.

Garments are made in Bernard's atelier in Kuala Lumpur, where he manages a technical and creative team of 70 people, comprising both local and foreign workers (mainly from India). Every member of staff goes through rigorous training before they are, in Bernard's words, 'allowed to touch the real stuff.' 'I have always believed in quality craftsmanship,' he adds. 'I believe that's our strength even though ours is a ready-to-wear presentation. We emphasize quality, good cut and craftsmanship.' All materials for the collections are sourced from reputable suppliers.

Sourcing new talent

One of the biggest challenges for Bernard is to find staff with the potential to develop their skills and who are able to cope with the creative challenges of the prêt-à-porter market. For those with a 'passion for excellence', the rewards are great: fair working conditions, wages commensurate with commitment, paid annual leave and equal treatment of local and foreign workers – in a nutshell, the opposite of the horror stories about sweatshops in developing countries.

The most talented staff work on the catwalk show in London, including Fazlur Rahman, who arrived from India four years ago without qualifications and in search of employment. Chandran gave him a chance and unearthed an artisan, whose beadwork is the equal of anything produced by a Parisian petite main.

Another ethical designer currently making it big is British talent Jas Sehmbi. His biggest claim to fame is the 'DJ bag'. Radical when he first made it, the bag responded to the needs of the then dominant 1990s dance scene and became as ubiquitous as the music

itself. Eventually, in 2000, the bag's success developed into a fully fledged fashion label, Jas MB, which is now as big internationally as it is at home.

So what's the secret of the label's appeal? The answer is that it's all made in Britain. Everything is produced in east London, albeit using Italian leather ('the best'), zips from Switzerland and cotton for linings sourced from a green supplier in Taiwan. His colourful team, including workers from the local community, über-cool graduates from Central Saint Martin's, interns from local colleges and family members, sums up the label's cosmopolitan, British feel.

Reversing the decline

Given that Sehmbi lives and works in the city that's home to some of the world's best fashion schools, you could be forgiven for thinking that usable skills come as standard – but, paradoxically, he faces the same problems as Chandran when looking for craftsmen. 'Colleges create talent but there is no craftsmanship to help production-wise.

A craftsman is someone who's broken their hands to learn and put together a product. You got to feel how to twist and turn leather, how to manipulate it… We lost that craft. In this country, we have no ateliers and factories left.'

The high cost of production in the UK generally means that the moment designers reach critical mass, they come under commercial pressure to move production abroad in order to respond to demand from the international fashion buyers' market. Big London Fashion Week names who developed organically, including Ashish and KTZ, have their ateliers in India and Indonesia respectively. Like Chandran, they have trained their staff but are forced to shuttle backwards and forwards when production starts.

Life for independent designers is precarious and it has had a knock-on effect on craftsmanship, both in London and Paris. 'In the long-term, France's position as a leader of fashion and creativity is at risk,' says Clarisse Reille, a luxury-goods consultant, who notes that orders placed with French artisan garment workers have dropped by 30 per cent since 2008. The same can be said for the UK – and that is bad news for both people and the planet. But with the likes of Chandran and Sehmbi leading the fight back, all is not lost for traditional craftspeople.

BRAND WATCH:
WILLIAM TEMPEST

The word 'phenomenon' is used all too frequently to describe people, places and objects that aren't really phenomenal at all. But in **William Tempest**'s case, the accolade is deserved. His rise to fashion's top table has come at lightning speed, with celebrities, colleagues and critics queuing up to tell the world how wonderful he is. What's more, with a passion for natural fibres and an impressive social conscience, he is part of a new generation of designers for whom sustainability is almost as important as style. But like many other mainstream designers, Tempest rarely discusses this part of the business.

Sustainable fashion

Tempest is diminutive, unassuming, approachable and charming, and has a soft, northern twang when he speaks. Nonetheless, Tempest is no lightweight. His A/W13 show was the ninth in a career that has seen him dress the likes of Emma Watson and create bespoke pieces for Madonna. He has even made a foray into make-up in the form of a limited edition collaboration with ethical beauty brand The Body Shop. An unexpected twist in the tale? Not quite.

'I'm a vegetarian, so it's really important to me to know that no animals were hurt making these products,' Tempest explained, speaking about the make-up range. 'The ingredients are 100 per cent natural too. For me, make-up is what completes the look,' he added. 'The Body Shop's sustainable and cruelty-free make-up range allows us to create the fresh, effortless and glowing feel we wanted and I'm so happy with the results.'

Making eco chic cool

Unlike contemporaries such as Henry Holland and Giles Deacon, the cerebral, modest Tempest eschews the limelight. He takes a considered view of tough issues surrounding sourcing and production, and has been quietly making what most of us would

> **The Body Shop's sustainable and cruelty-free make-up range allows us to create the fresh, effortless and glowing feel we wanted and I'm so happy with the results.**

William Tempest

call eco fashion for years. Not that he makes much of it.

'With my own brand, all the fabrics are natural and are produced to high ethical standards but it's not something I focus on getting across [to people],' he says. 'People tend to expect that green fashion will be ugly but it's something that we all could do. You can do really creative things with natural materials.'

And it's this progressive attitude that has seen him searching for new ways to get his message across, whether via the medium of video or online. 'I've been doing some work with Vogue.com,' explains Tempest. 'The whole online thing is huge and you have to get it right every time. It's a really different way of doing things and everyone wants to explore it.'

Exploring and pushing the boundaries with each new venture, scheme or collection has become something of a signature for Tempest, whose design references have been as diverse as the Queen of Sheba and Islamic architecture. Tempest is certainly not a man who does things by halves.

But then, this kind of uncompromising dedication is exactly what you'd expect from a young phenomenon. William Tempest might be only a few years into his career, but on current form, there's plenty more to come from Cheshire's favourite son.

THE QUEEN OF GREEN:
KATHARINE HAMNETT

'What does it mean becoming part of the establishment?' splutters **Katherine Hamnett**. 'Shutting up because you want a medal? [...] Does it mean you're obeying laws?' Hamnett is reacting to a question about whether she, and fellow national treasure Vivienne Westwood, might have finally joined the fashion establishment. 'I think you'd have to question everything always,' she adds firmly. 'If you see something wrong and you don't do anything about it, you're finished.'

Beyond the slogans

Best known for her slogan t-shirts, most famously the '58% Don't Want Pershing' [missile system] t-shirt she wore to meet British Prime Minister Margaret Thatcher in 1984, Hamnett never shies away from standing up for what she believes to be right. But there's far more to her than political sloganizing, both in fashion terms – she is, after all, the woman who brought us stonewashed, distressed and stretch denim – and campaigning terms.

Hamnett's 1989 A/W collection, 'Clean up or die', was the fashion industry's call to arms. In the early 1990s, following debate surrounding this collection, she commissioned a report into the textile industry, which found that cotton agriculture was responsible for

> In the early 1990s Hamnett commissioned a report into the textile industry, which found that cotton agriculture was responsible for 10,000 (now 20,000) deaths per year from accidental pesticide poisoning.

10,000 (now 20,000) deaths per year from accidental pesticide poisoning. She was also among the first to expose the squalid conditions in which millions of these people were forced to work.

But, says Hamnett, despite the success of initiatives such as the British Fashion Council's Estethica, fashion still isn't doing enough to clean up its act. 'Just look at the CO_2 [produced] by shipping and unnecessary travel [thanks to] fast fashion – people wanting shorter and shorter lead times and the whole fashion circus; you know, trade show, fashion show, trade fair with tens of thousands of people flying all over the planet to do stuff they could probably do online.'

> **Consumers are actually concerned about how their clothes are made, how people are treated, [the impact of] what they're buying for the environment. That's the only thing that's forcing the industry to change ...**

Cleaning up fashion

But shouldn't we be taking comfort from the numbers of designers and brands – both large and small – making a shift towards greener textiles and manufacturing? Hamnett is cynical. 'They offer this service because consumers are becoming increasingly informed and alarmed and this has been reflected in their buying patterns,' she says. 'Consumers are actually concerned about how their clothes are made, how people are treated, [the impact of] what they're buying for the environment. That's the only thing that's forcing the industry to change – I think most textile clothing manufacturers would be really, really happy if it was business as usual. They could pollute without paying any fines, they could use slave labour and it would mean that they can make more money.'

Hamnett's point is an interesting one, particularly in light of the debate among parts of the green movement about whether any consumption at all is good for the planet. For the majority, though, Hamnett included, conscientious consumption really can help change the world. 'I mean if you look at M&S [customers], 83 per cent are concerned about the impact of the goods that they buy on the environment,' says Hamnett. 'Thirty per cent are actually not buying something because they're afraid. It's huge. Those reports from these accountancy companies now say that people have either gone environmental or they're out of business. It's not a path being tried; it's a long-term trend.'

One that, according to some of eco-fashion's leading lights, is due to changing perceptions of what eco-fashion looks like.

Giving eco fashion an image makeover

'Nobody is going to buy clothes out of pity,' says Hamnett. 'People buy clothes because it cheers them up, makes them feel great and makes them look great. So the whole concept that environmental has got to be sort of porridgey coloured, I hope it's gradually fading.

> **People buy clothes because it cheers them up, makes them feel great and makes them look great. So the whole concept that environmental has got to be sort of porridgey coloured, I hope it's gradually fading.**

The choice of materials now is phenomenal. You've got the most beautiful long staple cottons, you've got the finest muslins and beautiful jerseys. There are things obviously that you've got to avoid like hell and there will always be a lot of things that are horrendous for the environment, so you do have to steer around those and have some degree of self-discipline.'

But no one has done as much to promote green fashion as Hamnett, with the result that her own label, once made in the same factories as everybody else's, is now 100 per cent eco-friendly in everything from materials to manufacture.

'I think I talked myself into a situation where I would completely lose credibility if I didn't put my money where my mouth was,' she says. 'Like it or not, I had to do it and in the beginning it was difficult because we were the first people doing it. It was hard, but it's easy now.' Could that be why more designers aren't making the switch, despite consumer pressure and the huge range of eco textiles available? Hamnett's response to this question is typically forthright.

'Well, some of them just really don't care, which I think is pretty disgraceful. But more than the designers it's really the decision of the CEO. They've got their heads in the sand. It is more difficult initially to do it because you've got to change your supply chain, you've got to research different suppliers and fabrics […] but it is the CEO's decision more than the designer's. Designers can try. I tried, I would research fabrics and one Italian manufacturer said to me, "if you carry on with this environmental shit, you can take your collection and get lost."'

What's next for Britain's Queen of Green?

Not that Hamnett's worried. Along with her own line and projects for the Environmental Justice Foundation (EJF) and Climate Week, she has launched a collaboration with a leading Italian supermarket. The Italian market, she

> **If we care about extinction of species, if we care about life on earth, if we care about survival of the human race, if we care about a habitable planet, we just have to adjust our lifestyle.**

says, is changing enormously, but that doesn't mean she's finished. 'I did a Climate Week t-shirt that just says "Save The Future",' she remembers, ruefully. 'I mean there's not much time left to do it. I think the t-shirts…you can't *not* read them. There's no way you can look at someone and not read what it says. It passes all the filters, gets into your brain and makes you think and actually take some positive action.'

'If we care about extinction of species, if we care about life on earth, if we care about survival of the human race, if we care about a habitable planet, we just have to adjust our lifestyle. […] If we all tried to buy organic cotton whenever we could, if that would be our first choice in cotton garments, it would have an enormous impact.'

Katherine Hamnett

6 Green future

INTRODUCTION

Not so long ago, eco fashion was seen as thoroughly uncool.
It was about hemp, about hippies, about lumpen grey
garments that looked terrible and felt worse. But what did
that matter so long as it was 100 per cent planet-friendly? The
answer, as it turns out, is quite a lot. As Katharine Hamnett so
pithily puts it, people don't buy clothes out of pity. And while
some brands have fallen by the wayside, many more have
risen to the challenge: fashion that combines looking good
and wearing well with emerald green eco credentials.

As previous chapters have shown, the last decade has
seen the rise of a legion of talented eco-friendly designers.
Whether that means the Duchess of Cambridge's favourite
Beulah, who plough their profits into turning trafficked Indian
women into highly skilled garment workers, or Minna, who
has hit upon a way of making vintage fabrics and antique
lace into some of the prettiest bridalwear around, eco fashion
is fast catching up with its mainstream competitors.

Conversely, mainstream designers such as William
Tempest are embracing natural fibres, while Gucci has
thrown its not inconsiderable weight behind the Green
Carpet Challenge – an initiative aimed at promoting high-end
eco wear. Could this mean that, one day, eco fashion will be
synonymous with mainstream and vice versa – that, in short,
all fashion will be made according to green principles?
So far, the signs are good.

GREEN IS THE NEW BLACK

6

According to Pantone, the fashion industry's authority on colour, it's not black – the shade most of us associate with the fashion world – that's got designers talking in the past few years, but green. Whether pistachio, eau de nil, emerald or mint, the planet's style-setters just can't get enough of the colour. Green as a concept has also been gaining ground – whether that's finding ways to incorporate more natural products such as vegetable dyes and wild silk or overhauling corporate social responsibility policies.

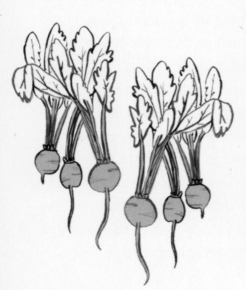

Increasing localism

Thanks to Chinese consumers' growing appetite for traditional British brands and heritage clothing, 'Made in Britain' is enjoying a renaissance internationally, while British brands – Mulberry and Aquascutum among them – are repatriating production from the Far East. Speaking of the localism movement, Topshop's Sir Philip Green told the UK's *Times* newspaper: 'Arcadia as a group would make more in the UK if there was more capacity. We've got to start the machine up. Because of the cost of doing it, there has to be a real commitment.'

'What I've seen in my voyage within the industry is one factory after another just closing, closing, closing and closing and [the UK] losing a huge chunk of jobs and skills,' comments From Somewhere designer Orsola de Castro. 'So reintroducing this industry within the UK and Europe is incredibly important and will have a massive effect on the younger generations. Not just in providing jobs and skills but also confidence. In Europe we innovate and then we export, so if we innovate sustainably and then export that back to China and India and the developing countries, then that in itself is equally impactful.'

Scandinavian lessons

While New York and Milan lag behind in the eco-chic stakes, one other fashion capital is running London close. In Copenhagen, the Danish fashion industry has made marrying sustainability with style into a fine art. 'I've worked in the industry for years as a Fairtrade and organic certification consultant,' explains Danish eco label Walisuma's Anders Nash. 'There is almost nowhere in the world where sustainability is so high on the agenda as it is in Denmark.'

Despite the economic downturn, the sales of Fairtrade certified products are growing at an estimated 30 to 40 per cent each year and sales of organic products are mushrooming too. Many shops are setting minimum quotas for [organic and Fairtrade] certified goods and many products, despite commanding higher prices, are still being purchased in Denmark in spite of having little other competitive advantage over [conventional] replacement products.'

Sustainably stylish

On the Danish catwalks, a succession of designers have switched focus to pieces crafted from sustainable textiles such as angora, wool and organic cotton, while, behind the scenes, some of the Danish industry's biggest names are working to make their businesses greener. 'We do try to work with naturals in our choice of silks, wools and so on,' says Rui Andersen Rodrigues Diogo, one half of design duo SPON DIOGO. 'The recycled poly-based fabrics are opening a great new chapter both in [design] structure and in environmental sustainability.' 'I think in many ways [Danish designers] are leading the industry,' adds Nash. 'Companies such as [scarf specialists] Elvang Denmark and Walisuma are putting sustainability at the forefront of their agendas and marketing. Numerous groups are pressing on with organic fibres.'

Making it work

In Denmark, where green issues have topped the political agenda for decades, incorporating sustainability into all aspects of the fashion industry has been a natural progression. 'Denmark has a tradition for "soft" values,' says Maryam Azmayesh Terp, corporate social responsibility manager at high street eco brand Jackpot. 'When you add the fact that we are a small country with equally small clothing businesses, it is only natural to be thinking of ways to differentiate ourselves.' But, she adds, there's still more to be done – both inside and outside Denmark. 'We need to clean up our production overall,' she comments. 'In addition, there has been an overload of brands offering [green] clothes. Now you have to really bring something to the consumer: forgettable brands won't survive.'

Majbrit Weidemann, the designer behind 'ethicool' childrenswear label New Generals, agrees that making sure collections are sustainable can be tough. 'Navigating the multitude of regulations, organizations and certifications is difficult with too little and often conflicting information available. Sourcing raw materials, finding suppliers and making sure they comply with our standards is time-consuming. Not least of the problems is the cost. The fabrics can be up to three times more expensive as a similar fabric produced with little regard to sustainability; the costs of certifying the entire supply chain are enormous, as is the cost of managing the processes involved. Yet we, as the owners of New Generals, have decided that we must persevere – it is simply too important to take the easy route. And it works – consumers love our products.'

Facing forwards

Orsola de Castro, too, thinks that the efforts of green designers are helping to change the way people consume fashion. 'Eco fashion is introducing a whole new breed of young designers to the market and introducing a whole new concept,' she says. 'Upcycling is the perfect example. For very, very large companies, it's just going to be a nuisance – a complicated way of going about things. But for a young designer this is a challenge and so what the big guys can't do, the new guys are attempting. Ultimately, as consumer demand increases for what the new guys are doing, that will strengthen demand for younger labels. Fashion is very cyclical and I feel that we are moving towards a shift. We're beginning to readdress what we see in London, what we see in New York.'

So does that mean localism and sustainability will become the norm? For de Castro, that's exactly what we're looking at. 'People constantly talk about global and local and I feel that one of the big changes is that people will be shopping [for clothes] in their local market as they are doing when they buy Abel & Cole and Riverford,' she says. 'They will be doing this more so in terms of design, not just fashion design but design in general, and this is because we are beginning to provide a background in the industry for young designers to be able to work locally.'

HOW CAMPAIGNING GOT COOL

6

From the suffragettes chaining themselves to railings in the early 20th century to Greenpeace activists promoting nuclear disarmament, the last hundred years have seen campaigning move out of the political sphere and into the mainstream. But the 2000s saw a campaigning revolution, and where once it was the preserve of the passionately committed, it's now something that everyone is into – and that includes fashion brands.

Reforming zeal

Among the campaigners are Fairtrade brand People Tree, whose founder Safia Minney has been at the forefront of campaigns for workers' rights and against fast fashion. 'The reason that policy is where it is in developing countries is because the large factory owners are brothers of politicians or they're the politicians, so there's no accountability or traceabilty,' she explains. 'We do a lot to try and get them to produce legislation and actually implement legislation, so we shouldn't be naive about what we're up against or the need to level the playing field.'

Minney's campaigning streak extends beyond Fairtrade, and she's currently supporting the IF campaign, which encourages fashion brands to behave at a corporate level. 'I think the IF campaign is really interesting because it's calling for transparency and proper accountability in terms of tax,' she adds. 'There are a few things that could help create a level playing field where Fairtrade and ethical labels are concerned, where things aren't subsidized by massive pollution of waterways or the exploitation of children and adults. You would then start seeing Fairtrade as a reasonably priced product with integrity in terms of design and how it's been produced and I think that's key.'

The Green Carpet Challenge

Fashion brands have also been getting into bed with eco campaigns that encourage green practice outside their own industry. Among them are H&M, which teamed up with the Environmental Justice Foundation and Katherine Hamnett to sell slogan t-shirts with 'Save the Future' splashed in stark black and white across the front, and department store Selfridges, which staged fund-raising events for Project Ocean and the Fish Fight campaign led by TV chef and environmental campaigner Hugh Fearnley-Whittingstall.

But arguably more interesting – and effective – from a fashion perspective is the Green Carpet Challenge led by actor Colin Firth's wife, Livia. Her idea, a simple one on the face of it, was to wear green fashion to every red carpet event she was invited to. Although her solo campaign has helped raise awareness of eco brands such as the USA's Prophetik, it has also encouraged mainstream designers to show that they too can design with green principles in mind. Among those who have already contributed are Tom Ford and Gucci, with the result that green fashion is at last beginning to shake off its fusty image in the minds of consumers.

While each campaign has made a difference in its own right, the multiplying number of initiatives prove that public pressure and green campaigners can come together and, as one, make the fashion industry a greener place to be.

POLLUTION SOLUTION

Campaigns such as the 2010 Clean Clothes Campaign's Killer Jeans initiative have helped end the environmentally damaging practice of sandblasting in most countries, while Greenpeace made such a success of their Dirty Laundry effort that the majority of high street brands have now taken steps to tackle water pollution caused by the garment manufacturing process.

> **...the Green Carpet Challenge [is] led by actor Colin Firth's wife, Livia. Her idea was to wear green fashion to every red carpet event she was invited to.**

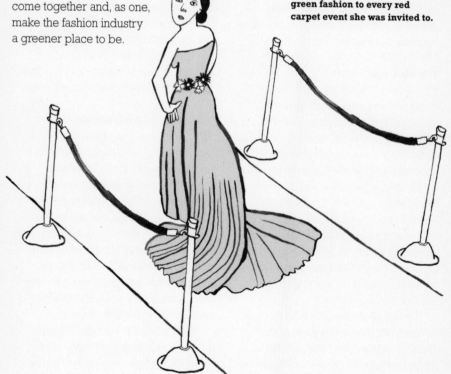

ECO FASHION: A GROWING TREND

6

From the organic cotton clothes lining H&M's rails to the burgeoning People Tree Fairtrade empire, you don't have to go far to find eco-friendly fashion. Increasing distrust of huge global conglomerates and growing awareness of the appalling conditions and pay suffered by Third World workers has encouraged a real appetite for change among consumers – and the rise of the internet has made it easier than ever for genuinely ethical companies to make fair fashion pay.

On the up

Eco fashion is becoming increasingly prevalent and, as a result, green consumption is booming. 'There's an increasing democratization of fashion, meaning that smaller players can survive and give the bigger companies a kick up the backside,' explains eco-fashion expert Christian Smith. 'Trust in big companies is at an all-time low, one of the reasons "Made in Britain" or "Made in New York" or LA resonate so much. We can at least claim to know where the money is going and that impact is close to home.'

Retailers have responded in a variety of ways, with some embracing slow fashion and localism, while others choose to take an organic or Fairtrade

approach. Some have even devoted entire sections of their shop floor to green fashion, among them ASOS, one of the e-tail world's biggest success stories to date. What began life as a cheap and cheerful knock-off shop has burgeoned into a retail empire.

ASOS provides a platform for eco brands in the shape of its dedicated Green Room and a sub-site called ASOS Marketplace, which allows vintage sellers and small designers to peddle their wares to the e-tailer's 4.7 million regular customers. What's particularly interesting is the way ASOS has embraced ethical initiatives in line with its youthful, socially aware client base.

Thinking long term

'ASOS invest [in corporate social responsibility] because it's part of fashion,' explains Smith, who was instrumental in setting up the brand's eco policies. 'ASOS caters to many different types of people and knows that some of those people are interested in shopping better. At a deeper level, it also understands the role it plays within fashion and, done the right way, it can have a very positive impact in the industry in the long term.'

'Brands need to understand their products and think long term,' adds Smith. 'The short-term nature of our

economic model is the element that makes change so difficult for companies. This pressure to deliver results every quarter distorts how businesses operate so that anything not deemed as crucial gets left behind very quickly and that's very often anything to do with being cleaner or greener.'

And yet, despite his warnings, Smith believes that eco fashion is one trend that's unlikely to have a short shelf life, thanks to a combination of campaigning, media awareness and the wealth of information available to consumers online. 'Information is one of the main reasons green fashion has become such a huge trend,' he reveals. 'It's hard to

[Eco-fashion expert] Smith believes that eco fashion is one trend that's unlikely to have a short shelf life, thanks to a combination of campaigning, media awareness and the wealth of information available to consumers online.

hide so supply chains are less mysterious than they used to be. [...] The information age has also made it easier for smaller companies to develop. Those who feel either let down by the industry or feel it's not moving fast enough can challenge the incumbents without the massive start-up costs that existed before.'

BRAND WATCH:
TOPSHOP

Loved and worn by everyone from the Duchess of Cambridge to Jennifer Lopez, **TOPSHOP**'s cheap and cheerful charms are a ubiquitous part of the British fashion scene, with a presence in malls from Dubai to Los Angeles. And although it's had its share of labour scandals, Topshop has begun to clean up its act in recent years. Is this a sign that consumers have finally had enough of fast fashion and shoddy, poor quality catwalk rip-offs? It seems they have.

> **With shorter supply lines, local factories and minimal air miles, [Topshop] offers a version of slow fashion, albeit at high street prices ... And yet ... Topshop still doesn't pay a living wage to the workers in its Bangladeshi garment factories ...**

A change for good

Like ASOS, which has evolved from red carpet rip-off merchant to serious fashion player, Topshop has diversified and improved its output, introducing designer capsule collections by the likes of J.W. Anderson, Mary Katrantzou and Kate Moss, and showing its own Unique collection during London Fashion Week. It also has a premium line, Boutique, which focuses on high quality natural textiles and is mostly made in the UK. With shorter supply lines, local factories and minimal air miles, it offers a version of slow fashion, albeit at high street prices.

So has Topshop changed for good? According to the company's corporate social responsibility policy, it has. 'We have long-term relationships with our suppliers,' it reveals. 'We work with them to make lasting improvements to working, social and environmental conditions. Our programme is based on the Universal Declaration of Human Rights, the International Labour Organization (ILO) core labour standards and other relevant guidance, good practice and regulations. Our programme deals with issues important to our stakeholders, such as working conditions […] and the reduction of the environmental impact resulting from the manufacture, distribution and sale of our products.'

Green or greenwash?

And yet, despite the fine words, Topshop still doesn't pay a living wage to the workers in its Bangladeshi garment factories, according to reports by workers' rights organization Labour Behind the Label. It has also been the focus of demonstrations aimed at both its record on workers' rights and at its owner, Sir Philip Green – a resident of Monaco, the notorious tax haven.

What's more, despite the introduction of the odd Fairtrade or organic range, it is yet to sign up to the Ethical Trading Initiative, which insists on basic good practice such as outlawing child labour and providing a wage that allows workers to enjoy a decent standard of living.

Then is this still the same old fast fashion dressed up as an ethically sound retail business? Or is Topshop making a genuine effort to do the right thing? What is certain is that Green's commitment to manufacturing at home has made a huge difference to Britain's beleaguered manufacturing sector,

which employs 10,000 people while also helping to reduce the brand's massive carbon footprint. But is it enough? For many, although Topshop's 'Made in Britain' initiative is a start, there's still a long way to go.

BOOSTING LOCAL MANUFACTURING

Topshop's 'Made in Britain' line is made in 47 traditional British factories, and found throughout the brand's collections. What's more, it is, according to CEO Sir Philip Green, a growing part of the brand's output. 'We've been pushing to see what we could do to keep [manufacturing] nearer home,' he revealed during a recent press conference. 'This is something we are permanently looking at, every day, every week. UK manufacturing gives us a different capability.'

THE FUTURE OF FASHION:
BEULAH

Rarely can a brand just a few years old count the likes of the Duchess of Cambridge, Livia Firth and model Rosie Huntington-Whiteley among its fans. **BEULAH** can. It's rarer still to find a brand that was set up, first and foremost, to provide jobs to some of the most deprived people on the planet. But **BEULAH** founders **Lady Natasha Rufus Isaacs** and **Lavinia Brennan** did exactly that, when in 2009, having met a group of women trafficked for sex in Delhi, they made the decision to try to help them via fashion. And so, **BEULAH** was born.

> **We spent three months in Delhi in India, and having heard about human trafficking, the aim is to try and involve those [trafficked] women in production.**

A brand & a cause

'We are a luxury British brand and, first and foremost, a fashion brand,' explains Rufus Isaacs. 'We sell silk dresses perfect for any occasion, whether it's a wedding or Ascot, and lots of people come to us for special occasions. But behind it is the charity and cause for which we set up Beulah in the first place. We spent three months in Delhi in India, and having heard about human trafficking, the aim is to try and involve those [trafficked] women in production.'

Fit for a (future) Queen

Unlike other Fairtrade brands, most of which focus on converting high street consumers, Beulah are unashamedly focused on the luxury end of the market, although it's worth pointing out that prices don't scale the heights of Prada and co. The clothes, mainly dresses, have a timeless appeal, featuring flattering billowing sleeves and modest hemlines, and come in a host of

> **What's particularly good about the future queen, and other celebrities, being papped out and about in Beulah, say the founders, is the way it has helped raise awareness of trafficking.**

gorgeous jewel bright colours. Everything looks as if it could have been designed with the Duchess of Cambridge in mind: subtle, chic and utterly wearable. What's particularly good about the future queen, and other celebrities, being papped out and about in Beulah, say the founders, is the way it has helped raise awareness of trafficking.

'I think [celebrity fans in Beulah] has definitely got us amazing sort of brand awareness and we have been incredibly fortunate that such a young business has had someone like Kate wear our dresses,' says Rufus Isaacs. 'In terms of ethical fashion, I think it has maybe got our message out more than it would have done so on that front I think it has definitely raised awareness. Whenever we are mentioned in the press the word "ethical" comes in front of us.' But although the future Queen of England has regularly been spotted out and about in the label, there's much more to Beulah than celebrity endorsements, as Rufus-Isaacs is only too keen to point out.

Helping trafficked women

'I suppose it has grown a lot faster than we anticipated,' she explains. 'I think people love an idea of a brand with a story. Essentially, what we're trying to do is to give these women a new start via fashion,' she continues, angrily brushing off the notion that this is just another label that relies on star power to succeed. 'It is quite frustrating, as that was the initial vision and we're trying to implement it and involve the women despite their lack of skills.' Upskilling their Indian staff is the main thrust of the designer pair's immediate plans, despite – as they're willing to admit – the challenging nature of building a workforce from scratch.

A greener future for fashion

It's a wonderful project, made all the more so by the fact that neither Natasha nor Lavinia had any kind of formal fashion training. What made the opportunity to start Beulah so wonderful, they say, is that their passion for fashion dovetailed neatly with their humanitarian ambitions. 'It was initially going to be

> **Upskilling their Indian staff is the main thrust of the designer pair's immediate plans, despite – as they're willing to admit – the challenging nature of building a workforce from scratch.**

> It is so important for people to have a decent corporate social responsibility [CSR] and as well as being judged on their profitability, businesses in the future will be judged on their CSR.

'What we have realized is that we need, in order to help all these people, to be a profitable business […].'

But, she adds, there are signs that the fashion industry of the future will be an altogether more equitable, environmentally friendly place. 'Maybe as we [Beulah, William Tempest etc] as a group are the first to see things this [ethical] way,' she adds. 'But [fashion] will start to move in the same direction as Fairtrade food. I actually think fashion is slightly behind but hopefully it will catch up. It is so important for people to have a decent corporate social responsibility [CSR] and as well as being judged on their profitability, businesses in the future will be judged on their CSR. It is definitely the way that companies are going.'

shoes but dresses we started designing while we were out there [in India],' says Rufus Isaacs. 'We came across a factory and because both of us always loved dresses and dressing up, and Lavinia already made her own clothes, it was something we both loved and knew that the [trafficked] girls could get involved somehow. And being in India there was inspiration all around and we somehow got put in touch with a clothes manufacturer who made women's clothes, so things fell into place and it seemed like a logical step.'

Interestingly, despite being so obviously an ethical label, they're keen to be recognized as a fashion brand rather than a Fairtrade establishment. It's not entirely an unexpected step, particularly given the stance of other ridiculously cool eco designers such as Christopher Raeburn and William Tempest, who despite being wonderfully green, choose not to nail their colours to the environmental mast for fear of being shunned by mainstream consumers. 'I think rather than an ethical fashion label we are more luxury fashion with a humanitarian cause,' explains Brennan.

SAVING WOMEN FROM TRAFFICKERS

The Beulah duo is working hard to take care of the emotional needs of their staff, all of whom are victims of human trafficking. 'We are supporting two projects currently, one in Delhi and one in Calcutta,' reveals Lavinia. 'The one in Calcutta is making our canvas bags and that employs ex trafficked or ex prostitutes so it is based outside the biggest red light district. What we plan to do next is to give them bank accounts and health insurance. The idea is they get lots of benefits to enable them to live a free life so they won't have to go back to what they were doing before.'

BEULAH

Sources & References

TEXTILES
Introduction

Mary Schoeser, *World Textiles: A Concise History*
LONDON: THAMES & HUDSON, 2003.

NY FASHION CENTER,
www.nyfashioncenterfabrics.com

Killer cotton

Peter Aldhous, *'The World's Forgotten Crisis'*
NATURE 422, 2003.

Rachel Carson, *Silent Spring*
LONDON: PENGUIN MODERN CLASSICS, 2000.

Janet Hethorn and Connie Ulasewicz, *Sustainable Fashion: Why Now?: A Conversation Exploring Issues, Practices, and Possibilities*
NEW YORK: FAIRCHILD BOOKS, 2008.

Safia Minney et al, *Naked Fashion: The New Sustainable Fashion Revolution*
OXFORD: NEW INTERNATIONALIST, 2011

Josef G. Thundiyil, Judy Stober, Nida Besbelli, and Jenny Pronczuk, *Acute Pesticide Poisoning*
WORLD HEALTH ORGANIZATION, 2013.

Stephen Yafa, *Big Cotton: How A Humble Fiber Created Fortunes, Wrecked Civilizations, and Put America on the Map*
NEW YORK: VIKING BOOKS, 2004.

Water: it matters

Maude Barlow, *Blue Covenant: The Global Water Crisis and the Coming Battle for the Right to Water*
NEW YORK: THE NEW PRESS, 2004.

Tara Lohan, *Water Matters: Why We Need to Act Now to Save Our Most Critical Resource*
SAN FRANCISCO: ALTERNET BOOKS, 2011.

The Impact of Cotton on Freshwater Resources and Ecosystems
WWF, 2000.

Thirsty Crops: Our Food and Clothes: Eating up Nature and Wearing out the Environment?
WWF, 2013.

Greener cotton?

Exposure to Highly Hazardous Pesticides: A Major Public Health Concern
WORLD HEALTH ORGANIZATION, 2010.

Technical Information for Farmers
SOIL ASSOCIATION, 2013.

MINNA HEPBURN, minna.co.uk

The future of fabric

Janet Prescott, *Fashion Textiles Now*
LONDON: VIVAYS PUBLISHING, 2013.

Green jeans

Lucy Siegle, *To Die For: Is Fashion Wearing Out the World?*
LONDON: FOURTH ESTATE, 2011.

WORKERS' RIGHTS
Introduction

Tim Harford, *The Undercover Economist*
LONDON: ABACUS, 2007.

A third world tragedy

Safia Minney et al, *Naked Fashion: The New Sustainable Fashion Revolution*
OXFORD: NEW INTERNATIONALIST, 2011

The fairtrade revolution

Nancy Brocken, Soren Ellebaek Laursen, Cecilia Malvido De Rodríguez, *Well Dressed? The Present and Future Sustainability of Clothing and Textiles in the United Kingdom*
CAMBRIDGE: INSTITUTE FOR MANUFACTURING, 2006.

Ha-Joon Chang, *Bad Samaritans: The Guilty Secrets of Rich Nations and the Threat to Global Prosperity*
LONDON: RANDOM HOUSE, 2008.

Joseph E. Stiglitz and Andrew Charlton, *Fair Trade For All: How Trade Can Promote Development*
OXFORD: OXFORD UNIVERSITY PRESS, 2007.

RECYCLING
Dealing with waste

Luz Claudio, *Waste Couture: Environmental Impact of the Clothing Industry*
US NATIONAL LIBRARY OF MEDICINE, 2007.

Fantastic plastic

Sandy Black, *Eco-chic: The Fashion Paradox*
LONDON: BLACK DOG PUBLISHING, 2011.

Lucy Siegle, *To Die For: Is Fashion Wearing Out the World?*
LONDON: FOURTH ESTATE, 2011.

The power of vintage

Fummi Odulate, *Shopping for Vintage*
LONDON: QUADRILLE PUBLISHING LTD, 2008.

SLOW FASHION
Slowing down the fashion cycle

Elizabeth L. Cline, *Overdressed: The Shockingly High Cost of Cheap Fashion*
NEW YORK: PORTFOLIO 2012.

The renaissance of Harris Tweed

China Breakthrough for Harris Tweed,
HERALD SCOTLAND, 12TH MARCH 2013,
www.heraldscotland.com

Chinese Firm Buys Into Harris Tweed Mill',
BBC, 11TH MARCH, 2013
www.bbc.co.uk/news

Lara Platman, *Harris Tweed: From Land to Street*
LONDON: FRANCES LINCOLN, 2011.

RETAIL REVOLUTION
The local revival

High-end fashion manufacturing in the UK: product, process and vision
CENTRE FOR FASHION ENTERPRISE, 2009

The UK Designer Fashion Economy Value relationships – identifying barriers and creating opportunities for business growth
CENTRE FOR FASHION ENTERPRISE, 2008

The Value of UK Fashion
BRITISH FASHION COUNCIL, 2010

The fight for traditional craftsmanship

Charles-Roux E, *Théâtre de la Mode: Fashion Dolls: The Survival of Haute Couture*
NEW YORK: PALMER-PLETSCH ASSOCIATES, 2002.

GREEN FUTURE
How campaigning got cool

Dirty Laundry
GREENPEACE, 2011.

Further Reading

Safia Minney et al., *Naked Fashion*,
OXFORD: NEW INTERNATIONALIST, 2011

Lucy Siegle, *To Die For: Is Fashion Wearing Out The World?* LONDON: FOURTH ESTATE, 2011

Sandy Black, *Eco-chic: The Fashion Paradox*,
LONDON: BLACK DOG PUBLISHING, 2011

Michael Braungart and William McDonough,
Cradle to Cradle: Re-making the Way We Make Things, LONDON: VINTAGE, 2009

Annie Leonard, *The Story of Stuff: How Our Obsession with Stuff is Trashing the Planet, Our Communities, and Our Health - and a Vision for Change*, LONDON: CONSTABLE, 2010

Kate Fletcher, *Sustainable Fashion and Textiles: Design Journeys*, LONDON: ROUTLEDGE, 2008

Alison Gwilt and Timo Rissanen,
Shaping Sustainable Fashion: Changing the Way We Make and Use Clothes,
LONDON: ROUTLEDGE, 2011

Tamsin Blanchard, *Green is the New Black: How to Save the World in Style*,
LONDON: HODDER PAPERBACKS, 2008

About *The Ecologist*

The Ecologist is the world's leading environmental affairs title and has been setting the environmental agenda for over 40 years – bringing the critical issues of our time into the mainstream through cutting-edge reporting, as well as pioneering original thinking and inspiring action.

Founded in 1970 by Edward Goldsmith, the magazine shot to fame in 1972 for devoting an entire issue to its Blueprint for Survival, a radical manifesto for change that proposed, amongst other reforms, the formation of a movement for survival. This led to the creation of the People Party, later renamed the Ecology Party and finally the Green Party.

In the years that followed, the magazine continued to break new ground in the environmental debate, notably by pointing to global climate change during the African droughts of the mid-1970s, and exposing the extent of the slash-and-burn operations ravaging the Amazon rainforest during the early 1980s. It went on to unveil the fallacy of plentiful nuclear energy during the era in which the technology's future was thought to herald electricity 'too cheap to meter'.

During the last ten years, *The Ecologist* has continued to highlight the contradictions of economic globalization, the health effects of everyday toxins, and the huge environmental cost of industrial agriculture. Its continued coverage has pushed many of these issues into the mainstream.

The Ecologist aims to encourage its readers to challenge conventional thinking and tackle global issues at a local level. In 2012, *The Ecologist* merged with *Resurgence* magazine, creating a stronger voice for the environmental movement to inform and inspire change.

Index

Ruth Styles

Ruth Styles is a writer and journalist specializing in fashion, culture, travel and lifestyle. Currently a senior writer at the *Daily Mail*, she also writes for a number of national and international publications including *National Geographic Traveller*, the *Wall Street Journal*, the *London Evening Standard* and the *Telegraph*. She was previously the Green Living Editor of *The Ecologist* and has worked in the UAE and Uganda. Passionate about fashion, she's convinced that Fairtrade is the key to giving Africa's fortunes a boost and spends as much time as she can travelling around the continent. When not travelling, she lives in London and focuses on giving up-and-coming talent in art, theatre, film and fashion the platform they deserve.

Acknowledgements

Firstly, I would like to thank my many wonderful interviewees – it's safe to say that this book couldn't have been written without your generosity. In particular, I'd like to thank Safia Minney, both for the interview and the encouragement, and the kind people at the Campaign for Wool who patiently answered my (numerous) questions.

To my editors Jacqui Sayers, Jayne Ansell and Monica Perdoni, I'd like to say a huge heartfelt thanks for making the process of writing the book a pleasure and for keeping me on track and on deadline. Your support, help and advice has been invaluable and is much appreciated.

Lastly, I'd like to thank my family and friends for putting up with not seeing me for weeks on end while the book was being written and for all the support and encouragement. I couldn't have done it without you.

KING of CLUBS

ANTON JOHNSON

Grosvenor House
Publishing Limited

This book is published by
Grosvenor House Publishing Ltd
28-30 High Street, Guildford, Surrey, GU1 3EL.
www.grosvenorhousepublishing.co.uk

A CIP record for this book
is available from the British Library

ISBN 978-1-78148-528-6

Acknowledgments

My Thanks go to Andrew Greenaway – my mainstay behind the book; Gerry Lane – who got me started; Michael Anderson – for being with me through thick and thin; John Fordham – for helping my family; Iain Bayliss of Snapshadow Productions – for your help with the photos. To my family for their moral support, and to Jan my wife for her help over the last three years to decipher my hand-written notes and for making me finish this book.

On the production side, thanks to Neil Silver – for putting this book together for me; Sean Garnett – for your sub-editing skills; and to Lawrence Goldsmith, Christopher Davies, Mark Silver, and Michael Crocombe – all part of the team. And to everyone at Grosvenor House Publishing Limited.

Contents

Prologue

AS you may expect, much of this story revolves around football. Football's just a game to some, but it's a lifelong passion for me and millions of others. It's the source of millions of conversations – often heated – in pubs, cafes, offices, building sites, factories and homes across the land and one of the   reasons tabloids fly off shelves during the season as fans clamour to gather every scrap of gossip and information regarding their team.

No doubt millions of fans will have harboured a dream, no matter how far-fetched, of running a club at one point or another. For proof, just look at all the fantasy football leagues in newspapers and on the internet. I'm no exception. In fact, at one time, my love of the game ended with me owning three football clubs in the same league. And look where it got me...

I am sitting in a 6' x 8' room. There is a bench with a grey blanket on it and a toilet in the corner. I am in a holding cell under Chelmsford Crown Court in Essex waiting nervously for the jury to return a verdict on me – all through a situation I allowed myself to get into, and all because of football.

The case has been going on for three weeks, with me locked up every lunch-time. I still cannot understand why; every morning I come to court and return home again after the day's proceedings. I can only think things are going against me, and soon I may not be going back after lunch.

As I wait in the cell, the wardens have a habit of walking outside rattling their keys – just to see me get up and look out through the hole in the door. Each time I promise myself I will not allow that to happen again, but somehow I always forget and jump to attention.

In my forty years, I have never been in any trouble with the police. On the contrary, I have assisted them on many occasions. And they have always been welcome at the football clubs I owned - some in a working capacity, others just coming to see the game and get free drinks!

Years earlier, when I owned butchers' shops, I was young and foolish and sometimes listened to the wrong people. One of my shops was broken into. The guys who worked there wrote a list of everything that was nicked, and added a few extras. Later, I was contacted by a friend of my father's. He said he was a friend of the investigating officer, who wanted to talk to me alone. We met, and the detective said he thought the list was excessive, but he would turn a blind eye in return for half a pig for his freezer - which I duly supplied.

Many years later, there was an internal inquiry between various police departments over corruption in the force. Some of the police in question drank in one of my pubs.

I was contacted by officials from one of the forces, as they wanted to talk to me about these customers. I agreed to a meeting, where I was told the head of the inquiry would be coming along later. Sure enough, he turned up; you should have seen his face – and mine! It was the very same man who wanted half a pig.

Back at court, the jury has come back and I am led back in. The place is packed with lawyers, barristers and the media. It goes quiet as the judge finally asks the jury for its verdict. My hands are sweating, and I am in complete daze not knowing whether I am going home or back to a cell. The foreman stands up and declares I have been found not guilty on both counts. You would expect me to have breathed a massive sigh of relief and punched the air in delight. I cannot remember much after that, except for all the press and cameras outside the court.

Much later, I find out the detective who had originally arrested me had advised the people who instigated the action that there was not a case against me, but they had offered him the position of head of security at Southend United when he retired, so he pursued the case.

After the trial, Judge Peter Greenwood said he felt the whole thing had been a total waste of taxpayers' money. But that came too late for my reputation. They had achieved what they had set out to do.

But all of this is getting ahead of myself. I had a life before this...

Chapter 1

Kick-Off

The beginning's a very good place to start, I think, so that's what I'll do. I was born at Danbury Palace, near Colchester, on 12 February 1942. That sounds very grand, unless you know Danbury Palace; it was a run-down stately home that had become a maternity hospital during the Second World War; no silver spoons for me.

Dad was a 'wireless engineer' in the RAF. I don't have any early memories of him. I suppose a lot of people born then had much the same experience. Dads went off to war, while mums struggled to hold families together.

My earliest recollection is of mum carrying me to an air raid shelter. It was dark and cold, I know that. And I vaguely remember searchlights waving in the sky and the roar of planes and the noise of the anti-aircraft guns. Apart from that, my war memories are fuzzy to say the least.

The only other thing that stands out from those days was the memory of waiting on Piggs Corner (Piggs was a large grocers and bakery) with lots of mums and children too young to go to school. A lorry would stop and we would all climb into the back. We were then taken to a farm. One lady took care of the children, while the rest of the mums went to work in the fields. The ladies (most of whose husbands were away fighting) were working alongside German and Italian prisoners of war. There did not seem to be too much security for the POWs, and the thing that stuck out most in my four year old mind was lunchtime and seeing ladies and prisoners vanishing into the woods.

At the end of the war, dad took us back to the family business: Johnson & Sons, Family Butchers, in Grays, Essex. We lived over the shop. Dad did the butchery and mum worked in the shop, as well as delivering meat orders. She must have been very fit, because the deliveries were made using what was called a 'trade bike', which was very heavy and awkward, with a huge basket at the front. If you've watched the TV series Open All Hours, you'll remember David Jason, as G-G-Granville, wrestling with a 'trade bike'. The basket was so big that, fully loaded with weekend meat orders, it must have outweighed mum, who wasn't a large lady. Somehow, she managed. People just did back then.

By the time I was five, I had a job in the shop after school, cutting out the food coupons from customers' ration books. My other after-school job was boiling water in a 'copper', which was a very large cast-iron vessel, embedded in a brick surround with a fire grate underneath. I had to light the fire and keep it burning using newspaper and any old pieces of wood I found lying around, or scavenged from the area around the shop. The hot water was used for scrubbing the tools and benches in the shop.

Because mum and dad worked such long hours, I was often left to my own devices. As soon as I'd done my chores, I would go out into the alley behind the shop, where there was always a gathering of boys and dogs. Invariably, there were several games going on. Marbles were rolled and flicked, won and lost. Cigarette cards, too, were used to flick. If you flicked one and it landed on top of another player's card, you won the card you'd covered.

The cards were given away free in packets of cigarettes. Issued in sets, they had pictures and short pieces of information on all sorts of subjects, such as sports personalities, film stars, cars, trains and boats and planes. Some sets were regarded as priceless, and games involving them were always noisier and more exciting than others. Nowadays, those old cigarette cards are worth a small fortune.

Games with marbles and cigarette cards weren't our only pastimes. We had things called 'winter warmers', which were tins with holes punched in the bottom using a hammer and a big nail, and a loop of wire threaded through two more holes punched at the top. The tin would be filled with scraps of wood and paper, which would be lit. The tin would then be swung vigorously around the user's head to keep the flames burning and heating the sides, before being employed to warm the user's hands.

Of course, we played hide and seek and quite a few variations on games involving chasing each other around. All those games, though, would only go on until there were enough boys out to get down to the main pastime – football.

One alley would play the next alley. Boys of all shapes and sizes would compete against each other. In between the alleys there was the baker's shop, which had a light outside on the wall, so we could play in the dark on winter nights, even though visibility wasn't made any better by the fact we had only a tennis ball, and often one that was pretty bald.

Mum and dad almost always had to work very late, so when the other boys were called in by their mothers, shouting from the various back gates along the alley, I would be the only one left. I would go home, but when I was indoors, they were always still working in the shop. Even at five years old, I often made my own tea and went to bed unsupervised.

Chapter 2

Into The Valley

At Christmas of 1949, mum and dad started what was to become a family custom. They invited the entire family around, which meant everybody came for Christmas dinner. In the evening, somebody played the piano and everybody sang. As the evening wore on, the men made for the table to play cards. The kids played with their board game presents. The ladies all brought their knitting and started talking in earnest. There were hot drinks later, and then everybody found somewhere to sleep – some on the counters in the shop.

The next morning, all the men and boys went to watch the local football derby, Grays versus Tilbury. By the age of seven, all I wanted to do was play football. Other games just didn't interest me. Not surprisingly, Boxing Day was always the best part of my Christmas. I've discovered since that kick-off was at 11.00am with a crowd of about 2,000. But my lasting memory is that there were more people in the ground than I'd ever imagined together. I'd never been to a real football stadium before. How was I to know how small that crowd was, compared to what I would experience in later years? Right then, it was as if I'd moved into a different world of noise and excitement - and of real football, played by proper teams on a proper pitch.

I also remember all the dads had these mysterious bottles of something, which they passed to each other. The only thing for the boys in those days was the peanut man or the hot chestnut stand. When you queued at either of them, all you could smell was alcohol; no wonder the vendors braziers seemed to burn brighter than the ones you could see on other streets.

I have a pretty vivid memory of the rest of Boxing Day, after the match. We'd all go back to our house for a lunch of cold salt pork, ox tongue, chicken giblet pie and mashed potatoes, accompanied by various home-made pickles. I also recall the sounds of a lot of glasses clinking and corks popping. After lunch, all the men found a place to sleep. It was as if they were hibernating. By evening, when the men re-appeared, the ladies had cleared up and restocked the table. There were brown shrimp, winkles, cockles and assorted sandwiches, followed by a homemade trifle, Christmas cake and various sponges, all made by the aunties as their contribution to the family event.

When tea was over, people started to leave as most of the men had to go to work the next day. By mid-evening, everyone had left, dad was snoring in his armchair, mum was clattering the pots and pans in the kitchen, and I played Ludo on my own. Things gradually started to improve after the deprivations of the war years, and the shop became busier and busier. By Christmas 1952, mum and dad decided we could afford a television set. The family gathering that year seemed to be all about this new gadget, with the dads avidly listening to my old man, with his RAF experience as authority, talking about how television worked and how tricky it was to get a perfect picture on the bulbous screen. Everyone was enthralled by the Queen's Christmas message, and then a couple of variety shows. Much to my relief, though, the television didn't affect the Grays versus Tilbury excursion with the dads, which was much as it had been in previous years.

The television set made me very popular a few months later when the Boat Race, one of the sporting highlights of the year, was televised on Saturday morning in the spring of 1953. Mum and dad were working in the shop, but they let me have all my pals in from the alley. Their mothers made the boys have a really good wash and put on their best clothes, just to come to our house to watch television. Watching the Boat Race at the Johnsons' house became an annual event for a few more years, though numbers gradually dwindled as my pals' families got TVs of their own.

That spring, another televised sporting occasion that proved memorable for me was the FA Cup Final of 2 May. Directly across the alley from our house lived the Buttigieg family. Ida Buttigieg was from Liverpool, and husband Fred was Maltese. Their children were Beryl, who was in my class at school, and Brian, who was a year older, but one of my best friends in the alley. Because mum and dad were almost always working, I was invited to the Buttigieg house for tea quite often and sometimes, if mum and dad were working very late, I was allowed to sleep over.

If I was staying with the family on a Friday evening, I would be allowed to go with Fred, Brian and Beryl to Tyrell Hall Working Men's Club. Before we went, Ida would make sure we all had baths – in the kitchen. She would bring a metal tub in from the shed and, before Mr Buttigieg got home, she would boil up kettles and saucepans of water to fill it. Mr Buttigieg would have the first bath, followed by Beryl, then me and then Brian – all in the same water. Although we had a proper bathroom at home, I always felt cleaner after a bath in the Buttigieg kitchen.

Brian didn't like football, but his dad was fanatical about Charlton Athletic. He even organised coaches from Tyrell Hall WMC to go to their games. Fred wasn't able to go to the FA Cup final (something I was able to sort for him later in life), and the Buttigiegs didn't have a television, so I asked mum and dad if Fred could watch it on ours.

Because Fred and his family did so much for me, they were only too pleased to invite him to our house. I was excited, too, looking forward eagerly to watching Blackpool versus Bolton, with the great Stanley Matthews and Stan Mortensen playing for Blackpool. My own craftiness, though, was about to be my undoing. All year I had been practising country dancing at school, because it took me out of lessons once a week. I practised too well, as I was picked to be in a team to represent the school in a contest which, to my horror, was on the same day as the Cup Final! I tried everything to get out of it, but I had to go. So I missed what came to be called

'The Matthews Cup Final', with its dramatic 4-3 last-minute victory for Blackpool, and Mortensen's hat-trick. Fred watched it, alone, at our house. Meanwhile, miles away, I was prancing about keeping time with a fiddle and accordion, wearing a fixed smile.

A month later, it was Coronation Day, with street parties and all sorts of excitement. It was a public holiday, so the shop was closed. Our television did sterling service that day. All day until late afternoon, we had a couple of dozen neighbours, mainly entire families, crowded into our house, sitting on dining chairs they'd carried round from their own houses. Kids sat cross-legged on the floor between the adults and the flickering, fuzzy, black-and-white picture on the 14 screen. Plate after plate of sandwiches and cakes were passed around, and I drank so much pop I felt pretty queasy. Still, it could have been worse. One of my pals went with his family to stand along the coronation route. They stood for hours, much of the time in drizzling rain, then, just as the coronation coach came into view, dozens of large policemen appeared and stood in front of the crowd, so my pal didn't see much more than the top of the coach as it passed by.

When we lived behind the shop, the school summer holidays were very quiet for me. One week into the holidays, removal vans and lorries would arrive on nearly every corner in working-class areas like ours. All my friends and their mums and dads, sometimes even their nans and granddads, would be seen clambering on the back of lorries or disappearing into the back of removal vans. Like thousands of other working folk in that part of England, they were spending their annual holidays going hop picking, which meant I didn't see those friends for the rest of the summer. The summer holiday of 1953 was no exception, and I spent quite a bit of time mooching around aimlessly.

When the football season started again, Fred came round to the back gate of the shop and asked my dad if I would like to go with him on the coach to watch Charlton Athletic. Although my granddad's brother, Jack Johnson, had played for one of the

Sheffield clubs, dad wasn't really interested in football. But he was quite happy for me to go with Fred.

On the day of the first match, Brian and I went to Tyrell Hall with Fred. He went in for a drink, while we waited in the garden for the coaches to appear. Six arrived together, and people poured out of the club. They'd all climbed aboard before Fred came out to us with two empty beer crates in his hands. He put us in the front seats of the coach, with the crates on the floor in front of us, before going off with a paper in his hand to check that all the paid passengers were present before we moved off.

We left Tyrell Hall and went via the Blackwall Tunnel to Charlton. When we arrived, Fred led us out of the coach carrying the crates. The crowd at the Grays versus Tilbury match hadn't prepared me for the vast number of people heading for The Valley that day. Looking at the scene from the top of the coach steps, it was a bobbing torrent of flat caps, trilby hats and red and white scarves. I'd never seen such a multitude. We stepped into the throng of people, Brian and I hanging on for dear life to the crates Fred was still carrying. All I could see was feet and legs. I had no idea where Fred was going. Eventually we reached the turnstile and then, for the first time, I was inside a proper football stadium.

We walked up the bank to the top, where Fred held us up in turn to look at the ground. It was magnificent, with its lush green grass and its red and white hoardings. It took my breath away. After giving us a few minutes to stare around in wonder, Fred took us back down the bank. Thinking back, I can recall how much respect Fred had gained among Charlton supporters, as men stood back good-naturedly to let us through. We were allowed to get to a good spot behind the goal. That was when I realised what the crates were for. Charlton were playing Arsenal and there were 70,000 people there. Brian and I each stood on a crate, so our view was perfect. The noise was deafening, and it gave me goose bumps all over, as the same noise still does. It was my first, never-to-be-forgotten, First Division football match.

It became a regular thing for me to go to matches with Fred, and I looked forward to each of them. All through the week before, I would count the days. I became an ardent Charlton supporter. My favourite player was their goalkeeper, Sam Bartram, who had a sports shop just outside the ground. On the way in and out of the ground, I always looked in the shop window hoping to get a glimpse of him. God knows how I thought he could rush from the shop to his football kit, just before kick-off; and then come off the field, change and get back to the shop to serve after the game in time for me to see him as I left the ground!

When I was 10 years old, I was picked to play football for the Arthur Street School team. I was put on the left wing, although I was right-footed. We ended the season having won half the games. I don't remember doing anything remarkable on the pitch during any game, but I did listen carefully to the instructions we were given by the games teacher, Mr Grover, who did the coaching, so it was probably my reliability that kept me in the side. I'd like to think so, anyway; I never believed the story that the school team was always so short of players that anyone with two working legs would get into the team.

I think it was in November that Fred decided that the wives of the men who went regularly to Charlton matches should have a night out. He organised a trip for the ladies. They were to go with the men to a match, where he'd booked the best seats in the ground. After the game, everyone would have a meal, then go on to a show and, on the way home, stop off at an affiliated working men's club for a few drinks. A lot of the men liked the idea, as a way of reducing the weekly earache they were given by wives, so there were two coach loads of people who signed up for the outing.

Everything went well at the match, although the usual colourful comments about the opposition's players and the referee were somewhat restrained. Charlton were playing Chelsea, and it was the first time I ever sat down to watch a football match. I wasn't sure I liked it, but the ladies all thought it was very nice, so Fred was pleased.

After the game, we headed for Hackney and another first for me; a restaurant, which was just round the corner from the Empire. I had my favourite, fish and chips, with loads of salt and vinegar.

After the meal, we all trooped out to find it had started to rain. Fortunately, Fred had gone on ahead, so he was standing at the foyer entrance when we arrived. With much shaking of umbrellas, our party was quickly assembled and escorted through the foyer, directly to our front row seats. A fairly well-known comedian was headlining the show, so, though cold, damp and a little out of breath, everyone was looking forward to a lot of laughs. Beryl, Brian and I were the only kids in the party and we sat together beside Fred and Ida. The show started and the curtains rose.

At what seemed like the same instant, I caught a glimpse of a bare backside under the rising curtain, someone clapped a hand over my eyes and a chorus of outraged gasps and exclamations came from the ladies in the party. I also heard a few expletives and giggles. The show was a nude revue! Fred had left the job of sorting out the entertainment to a booking agent, who thought the party was all men having an evening out after going to the football and had chosen what he thought was the perfect show.

Beryl, Brian and I were hustled out of the theatre, feet hardly touching the ground with our eyes shielded from the stage. Despite the commotion our party caused by leaving, the band kept playing and the show carried on. Within minutes, two coach loads of people were standing outside the theatre in the rain, waiting while someone took a cab to where the coaches had gone to park up. I don't suppose it took very long to get the coaches back to the theatre, but the rain was much heavier than it had been when we arrived, so everyone was thoroughly wet and the coach windows steamed up in seconds when we were all finally back on board. Needless to say, everything was very quiet on the way home, and we didn't stop at the affiliated working men's club.

Chapter 3

Moving On Up

I was 11 when we moved from the shop to a bungalow four or five miles away. I had to leave Arthur Street School anyway, and went to the Torells, which was massive secondary school. When I went for a place in the first-year football team, there must have been more than 200 kids taking part. Needless to say, I didn't get in the first team that season. Without my help, Torells came second in the local schools league, so there were some good players there.

The boy who sat next to me in class, Ronnie Lawes, played left back for the team. One morning, at the beginning of my second year, Ronnie told me that the team was desperately short of a decent goalkeeper, and the team had its first game of the season that afternoon. I was the tallest boy in the class and desperate to play. I saw the sports teacher at lunchtime and told him I was a goalie. He sent me straight home to get my football boots. When I got back to school, I was told to report to the changing rooms. Without ceremony, I was given the goalkeeper's jumper. I was in!

Torells were playing Park School, a team which included seven of my old Arthur Street School team mates. At half-time, we were leading 1-0. The second half was end-to-end stuff, with neither team making any real opportunities. Then, with three minutes to go, one of their players – Victor Young – was brought down in our penalty box. The referee pointed to the penalty spot, and a groan went up from our supporters.

Victor was one of the Arthur Street boys, who had lived in the road next to the one I used to live in. He was a pretty good forward and played for the district and county. When he stepped up to take the penalty, I gave myself little hope of saving the shot. Judging by the gloomy expressions of my team-mates and the few Torells supporters, I could see they all thought the same. I decided not to try anything clever; I would just dive one way. I decided to dive to the left. Victor took a little run up and whacked the ball – to my left. I dived and my fingers touched the ball, just enough to push it around the post. So we won, and I was confirmed as Torells' hero goalkeeper.

We'd played about seven games when, at assembly one morning, the games teacher came on to the stage, wearing his other hat as deputy head. He said he had just received a letter, informing him that three of the football team had been picked for the district team...and I was one of them!

In the previous year, with no football team place, I came second in my class. But at the end of the next year, with all that glory to bask in, football practices to attend, and frequent impromptu matches with new-found soccer pals, I came 14th. Mum decided if I was ever going to have any sort of decent academic qualifications to equip me for a better life, I needed to go to a school that didn't have so many potential distractions.

I always assumed that any life away from being a butcher was a 'better life', but mum's original idea was for me to go to a boarding school. After a lot of arguing on the subject, we arrived at a compromise and I ended up going to Pitman's College, which was a very good day school in Forest Gate.

My day at Pitman's started at 6.30am. when I caught a bus to Grays, which dropped me at the station in time to catch a train to Barking, from where I went by Tube to Upton Park, and then a 30 minute bus ride to Forest Gate – arriving at 8.45am. The return journey took a little less time, but I would never arrive home before 6.00pm, which made it a long day for a 12-year-old – especially when a quick meal would be followed by a couple of hours homework before bed, five days a week.

In my first term at Pitman's, on my 12th birthday, my sister Kely was born. She had a great pair of lungs on her, and mum and dad often looked as tired as I felt for quite some time.

Pitman's played football and cricket, but only took part in inter-school friendlies, so there was no real pressure to achieve high standards. But by my 15th birthday, I was captain of the college cricket team, as well as goalkeeper for the football team.

While I was at Pitman's, I had an exchange holiday. I and a boy called Stanley Holloway went to stay with a family in the South of France – in Saint Mandrier, which is near Toulon. The family had two sons – Alain and Pierre Marliac. We stayed there for two weeks and then they came back to England to stay with us. Alain was my exchange. He ended up very high in the French Embassy - first in China, and then in Russia. His mother and father were teachers, so every morning we had a French lesson with a cup of coffee the size of a soup bowl. After that, we could do what we liked for the rest of the day.

One particular day, the boys took us on a long hike. It was very hot, and we had to walk through vineyards which seemed to go on forever. Then we came to a hill, climbed to the top, and then we were looking down at the Mediterranean. Below us was a path that led down to cement causeways and gun turrets where the Germans had kept their U-Boats during the war. The place was deserted and overgrown. The boys said nobody ever went there. It was quite eerie. We went on to the causeways. As it was very hot, and the water in the causeways was very deep and green, Stanley suggested a swim. The French boys declined, but Stanley dived in and swam about 100 yards. I followed, and I managed about 50 yards when something got a hold of me and pulled me down under the water. I remember trying to struggle free and shouting, with bubbles going up to the water's surface. All at once, I was released, and shot up like a cork to the fresh air. I got out of the water and passed out. When I woke up, I was being stretchered to the village. By the time we arrived back, everybody had heard about it and was waiting. They laid me on a bed. I had large blisters round my stomach and arms where something had got hold of me. It seemed like the whole village inspected me before the ambulance came. I spent a week in hospital. I was later told that they thought it was a giant squid.

It was later, during that summer, when I returned to England that I had a bet with my friends. The bet was I would get a Mohican haircut. When I went to have it done, it caused quite a stir; it was not as common then as it is nowadays. When I arrived at the barber's, the local paper was there with a photographer. Snaps were taken before and after. Not only did the story make our local paper, but it was in two of the national magazines of the time: Reveille and Tit-bits.

A few days after I had the haircut, I went to a local dance at the Co-op Hall. When I arrived, the DJ saw me coming through the door and immediately put on a record, popular at the time, called Western Movies by the American doo-wop group, The Olympics. I had a great night, enjoying the attention my appearance attracted. I also collected my winnings from my friends, which increased my enjoyment no end!

After the dance, I strolled home along a path beside the stream that flowed past our house. I was quite happy, until I looked at myself in a mirror. I stared in horror. It seemed that, on my way home, mosquitoes had attacked my bare head, leaving lumps on lumps. I looked like the Elephant Man!

A couple of days later, when I'd stopped enjoying the way people looked at my Mohican, I had my head shaved completely, so my hair grew back evenly. I suppose I looked a bit odd for that time, but I wasn't at all self-conscious.

I returned to Pitman's College in the autumn, and life carried on much as it had before. One day, when I was playing for the school in a friendly football match, I was approached and asked if

I would like to play for Eton Manor. Apart from those friendly games at Pitman's, I wasn't playing football at all. So of course I jumped at the chance. I enjoyed my games with Eton Manor and performed well enough to earn myself a trial for East London Boys a few months later.

It seemed my time at Pitman's was paying off in a way I hadn't expected, because I found I was able to organise my time and interests in such a way that my football didn't have a detrimental effect on my studies. In fact, I even found time to form a skiffle group. We played our first gig at Stratford Town Hall. Our audience included almost all the Pitman's students, plus a couple of the younger teachers.

At sixteen, I won a scholarship grant for the National College of Food Technology, where I enrolled for a full-time two year course on Meat and the Preparation of Cooked Meats. The course was due to start in September 1958, but mum and dad decided to take the first real holiday they'd had in my lifetime. They were going to see my Uncle Bernard (my father's brother) in Singapore, then go on to tour Australia and New Zealand.

Fred and Ida readily offered to look after me, so I could have stayed at home and gone to College, but the opportunity of seeing those far-off places was just too good to miss. So I went to the college authorities and explained the situation. To my relief, I was given a year's deferment and allowed to retain the scholarship. So off to the Orient I went!

Chapter 4

Run Rabbit Run

Uncle Bernard introduced me to a member of his staff. He played for a local Third Division team in Singapore. When he learned I was a keen footballer, he invited me to play for them in a friendly the following Saturday. Naturally I'd packed my boots, and so accepted straight away.

Nobody sane plays football there in the midday heat, so it was early evening when I turned up at the ground, not really expecting much more than an enthusiastic kick-about with a few passers-by to watch us. To my utter amazement, there were more than 8,000 people at the match, all giving their teams the sort of support you hear at Anfield or St James' Park. Eight thousand voices were backed up by drums, trumpets, rattles, car horns and firecrackers – all encouraging players of eight different nationalities.

I was handed a blue sash and put in goal. It turned out to be the most unusual match I've ever played in. The rules were interpreted in odd ways that would have had Charlton fans either rolling in the aisles or livid with rage. Some players had a peculiar idea of how the game should be played, but their enthusiasm was clear. Many played in bare feet; others wore turbans. Some of the ones in bare feet could still kick the ball the length of the pitch. I played in a couple more matches while we were there, and enjoyed every minute.

After a month in Singapore, we went on to New Zealand. We were going to be there for three months, so I decided to find myself work. I responded to several ads in the local paper and very quickly got a job with the Rabbit Board. This was an organisation created by the New Zealand government in an attempt to control the plague of rabbits that had long been a threat to farmers and native wildlife, having been introduced by early settlers as a food source.

The job was located up in the hills, around eighty miles from Dunedin on the south east coast of South Island. I travelled from Dunedin on a train very much like those you've seen in Westerns, with un-sprung, slatted wooden seats that did terrible things to my backside. The journey seemed endless, but eventually it came to an end in the middle of nowhere. There was no station or houses, just rocks. The guard assured me it was the right place, so I collected my things and climbed down from the train.

The train moved off and quickly vanished behind some massive boulders. There was nothing to do but wait. So I sat on my suitcase for what seemed like an eternity.

Then I heard noises and suddenly a man appeared, riding a horse and leading another.

As the rider approached, I could see that he was pretty old, with a wizened face under a wide-brimmed hat which – I later found out – he wore almost every waking hour. I didn't see him look at me before his horse came to a halt a few feet away. I don't know whether the sigh came from the old man or one of the horses, but I certainly sympathised. December is mid-summer in New Zealand and, even at the nearest part of the country to the Antarctic, temperatures can be above 30°C during the day, and it must have been there or thereabout when I first met the old man, Tom Cruikshank. It was certainly way too hot to be slogging through rough country, even on horseback.

Tom introduced himself, looked hard at my suitcase and bulky haversack, and asked if I could ride. I told him I couldn't and he replied: You'll soon learn. At that, he dropped the end of the rope he'd used to lead the spare horse, turned his own mount around and started moving away. With my haversack perched on

17

my shoulders, gripping my suitcase with my left hand, I scuttled across to grab the loose rope before my horse decided to follow Tom. Somehow, I managed to get aboard while still clinging to my suitcase. My feet didn't reach the stirrups, so my first experience of riding a horse was pretty much a case of hanging on for dear life with my free hand on the reins and my knees gripping the horse's bony back.

With Tom leading the way at a steady pace, we rode for what seemed like hours until we came to a small meadow. There was a stream running through it, and one lonely cow grazing near a small wooden shed. This was to be my home for the next three months. Behind the shed was a hill, with 45-gallon drums, laid on their sides, embedded in it. Dogs were chained to the drums, and it appeared that they lived in the barrel to which they were chained. I assumed the dogs had a role to play in catching the rabbits.

It was very basic in the shed – two beds, a packing case that doubled as storage and table, two tough stools and a Primus stove. I discovered there was no toilet, when Tom explained the purpose of a shovel leaning against the shed just outside the door. He also explained that we would go to bed before dark, partly to save oil for the lanterns, but mostly because we would be getting up very early.

Sure enough, Tom's alarm clock went off at 4.30am. Tom sent me to fill the kettle from the stream while he milked the cow.

Breakfast was soon ready. The tea was hot and strong, and the bowl of cereal Tom slid across the table to me was warm, because that's how the milk was.

After breakfast, my next job was to unchain the dogs that all seemed very happy to see me. As with most dogs, the friendliness due to them knowing that food was in the offing. The piles of raw, skinned rabbit that Tom dished up for them quickly disappeared while I was being given the only lesson I ever had in saddling my horse, Jack. Fortunately, I never forgot how to do it.

Milking Mary, the cow, soon became my regular job – immediately after the jog to the stream for fresh water. Each day, I would follow the same routine while Tom boiled water for tea and a shave. By 5.30 every morning, we were saddled up, the dogs all fed, and ready for work. Because the rabbit 'plague' was so widespread, we never had to travel far to reach a place where Tom decided to work that day.

Each day's target was to kill at least 400 rabbits. Tom always took a gun, but it was never needed; four greyhounds, four lurchers, two black Labradors and two fox terriers took care of everything. Tom must have spent countless hours training them. It was fascinating to watch them work. They all had their own jobs to do. The terriers would disappear into long grass, then the rabbits would appear, running like mad to get away from the fierce little dogs. The lurchers and greyhounds would sprint off, running the rabbits down in seconds. A swift bite around the neck, and a hard shake, resulted in another limp body. Lurcher or greyhound would hurtle off to the next target, while the Labradors picked up the lifeless bodies and brought them back to Tom – often four or five at a time.

Tom would never call it a day until we had reached our quota of four hundred rabbits. Sometimes it would take four hours, other times it could take much longer. To prove how many rabbits had been killed, Tom cut off and kept both ears, threaded on loops of string in batches of a hundred, so eight full loops made a day's target. He often kept the hind quarters of a few rabbits, which we would later have for tea. More rabbits would be kept to feed the dogs. If we finished early, our staple diet of rabbit would change and we would fish in the stream for trout. After a week or two of rabbit stew, trout tasted wonderful.

Some weeks after I arrived there, Tom went off to get some provisions. The store was in a small village about forty miles away, so doing a round trip in a day wasn't possible. He left very early in the morning. After just a few weeks apprenticeship, I was left in charge. Tom had been gone around an hour when, at 5.30am, the dogs and I went to work. Tom had given me instructions on where to hunt while he was away, so I can't claim much credit for the bag of four hundred rabbits by late morning. We were back at the shed for lunchtime. I chained the dogs up, gave them all water and plenty of biscuits to supplement their regular chopped rabbit, then took myself off to wash in the stream. I caught a couple of trout and felt very pleased with myself when I managed to gut them properly and cook them for my supper, just as Tom had shown me. I had another successful session the following day, and my catch provided supper for Tom and me late in the afternoon. When Tom had returned, I really felt as if I belonged.

In 1958, New Zealand still didn't have television so, even if there had been electricity at the shed, there wasn't much available in the way of entertainment. Tom had a battery radio, but that was only used to listen to the daily news and weather forecasts. There was also a two-way radio, but Tom didn't like using it – he said it always brought him more work to do. Tom read a lot. The shelves were bowed with the weight of dozens of books.

I spent a lot of time just riding my horse. When I'd recovered from the aches and pains of my first few days in the saddle, I'd come to enjoy exploring this strange land.

Jack was a ten-year-old gelding who was willing to go anywhere, but at his own pace. This was usually a little faster than walking pace, which suited me fine. It was great, I rode all over the area around the shed, venturing further and further until, one day, the inevitable happened. I'd ridden up into the hills, not really paying too much attention to where I was, just enjoying the warm sunshine, when suddenly everything in every direction looked the same.

For a couple of hours, I tried different routes, but kept coming back to where I started. It was getting dark and I was starting to panic. The idyllic cowboy lifestyle suddenly took a sinister twist. Trying to see further away, I dropped the reins over Jack's neck and stood on his back to see if I could recognise anything, but everything just looked the same. I sat back down in the saddle and stared into space, not knowing what to do. After a minute or two, Jack took a small step forward – and then another. He seemed to sniff the air, and his ears twitched from side to side as he moved. Hoping against hope, I let Jack take over. For about an hour, he carried me through a maze of rocks, none of which I recognised, until finally, we emerged from a gap between two of the larger boulders and there, a few hundred yards away, was the shed.

By the beginning of my sixth week there, I was starting to wish I could stay longer. By then, I knew all the dogs by name and Tom had started to let me do the job on my own. I came to the conclusion he was enjoying the occasional lay-in when I went out early to work. I didn't blame him. He knew I wasn't going to be there much longer, so he was just taking advantage of the situation.

One day as the dogs and I returned from a day's work, Tom was talking to a man from the trotting stables ten miles away. He'd brought a dead horse over as a change of diet for the dogs. He left in his van while I was chaining the dogs up. Our meal was cooking, so Tom and I started to cut up the horse. Tom was impressed with my butchery skills, which took him by surprise. With the two of us cutting and boning, we soon had plenty of meat prepared, so we fed the dogs before we sat down to our own dinner. Just as we enjoyed the occasional trout, the dogs enjoyed the horse meat.

During the night, Tom and I awoke to the sound of the dogs barking. We went out to see what was happening, and could hardly believe the sight in front of us. All the dogs seemed to be foaming at the mouth and straining frantically at their chains. In fact, while we watched, some of the larger dogs actually broke their chains and came racing towards us. They looked so crazed that Torn and I dived back into the shed, slammed the door and locked it.

I don't remember saying anything, and Tom seemed absolutely dazed by what we'd seen. So we simply sat, staring at the door, listening to the dogs barking and howling outside. As the night passed, their barking slowly died down until, sometime after dawn, there was nothing but silence outside. At 7.00am, we slowly unlocked the door and cautiously looked out. To our horror, all the dogs were dead. Tom saddled his horse right away and rode across to the trotting stables. The man who'd brought the dead horse called a local vet, who came out to the shed and took some samples. It turned out that the horse itself had been poisoned, in turn affecting the dogs. I never did find out whether the poisoning had been deliberate, though I did overhear a conversation between the vet and a local policeman who came out to see us. The gist of that conversation was that, for some time, the trotting stable had been having problems, with horses being inexplicably ill at the most awkward times, but nothing was ever proven.

Of course, being the age I was then, I was quickly taken out of the situation. Tom had lost his dogs, and I felt sure I could have helped him in some way. My protests were ignored, though, so back to mum and dad in Dunedin I went. They'd already heard odd bits about what had happened, but when I told them the full story they cut short their planned tour and moved on to Otaga. The move turned out to be fortunate for me, because I was given an opportunity to play cricket for the local semi-professional team, which helped distract me from the memory of the tragic events with Tom. I played four mediocre games for them before we returned to England.

Tom was, of course, devastated. As I well knew, his hard image concealed a softer side. He had trained all the dogs himself and they were the only family he had. He never got over it and, just three months later, I heard that he'd died of pneumonia. I truly believe it was because he simply didn't want to fight the illness, as he could have beaten that had he wanted to live.

Chapter 5

Cars And Girls

I went back to college to my studies. I had been away for about nine months. When I returned home one evening, my father was waiting to see me. By this time, he had three butchers' shops. He explained that one of his managers had died and another was retiring. He asked me if I'd come and work with him and leave college. The enticement was £30 a week and the use of one of the meat vans. I agreed.

The next Monday, my dad tried to wake me at 5am to start work, but I managed to fall back to sleep. This next day, he woke me by rapping his knuckles on my head. He never had to do that again; as soon as he touched the door, I was up!

I worked every Saturday from 6.30am until 5.00pm. At around 4.30pm that Christmas Eve, while I was working in the shop, we had just finished cleaning up and were getting ready for a drink. We had been very busy and we only had one turkey left in the fridge. I was just locking up when a couple came into the shop and asked if we had any turkeys left. I said that we had and went to the fridge and produced the last turkey in the shop. The couple looked at the bird and asked me to weigh it. It weighed $12\frac{1}{2}$ pounds. "Have you anything a little bigger?" they asked. Not wanting to lose a trade, I went back to the fridge and put pork sausage meat and the giblets inside the turkey, adding a little parsley on the top and dusted it with flour. I brought the bird back out on a tray. It now weighed $14\frac{3}{4}$ pounds. The couple went into a huddle. My staff, who were waiting to go out, looked very perplexed. The man turned around and said to me, "We will take both birds." The staff were uncontrollable. I quickly apologised and said that one of the turkeys was for me. They bought the bird, leaving me with a very red face.

Because my football days were on hold, I compensated myself by buying a car every year. When I was 19 years old, I bought a 10 seat Buick with removable seats. It cost me just £35, and did about eight miles to the gallon. My next car was my pride and joy: a new Mini Cooper. My earnings were rising, but I never really had a chance to spend them on anything else as there was nothing open on Sundays. My next car was a gold Sunbeam Alpine with a hardtop. They had only just come out. When I drove it down to Spain, it was the centre of attention everywhere I went.

It was at this time I experienced my first Spanish bullfight. I stayed at a hotel that belonged to a man called Will Helm. He was the main exporter of cork, used for bottles of wine. It was a Friday evening, and there was a lot of excitement in the entrance to the hotel. I later found out it was one of the bullfighters and his entourage. There was one young man with long hair, who was the youngest member of the party. He was about my age and he came and spoke to me. We had a Coke together and he invited me to the bullfight the next day. For anyone unfamiliar with bullfighting, it's normal for there to be three fighters, and they each fight two bulls. It starts with the least experienced, who fights one bull, and then the second and the best fighters each fight one bull. Then it goes through the same process again. Subject to the quality of the kill, the crowds acknowledge it by awarding an ear or, if it was very good, they give it two. In exceptional cases, they can also award the tale. Needless to say, the animals are dead at the time. The first fighter was the young man who had invited me along. He went through all the processes of passing the bull, and then went down on one knee. Everybody in the crowd cheered. The bull scratched at the earth, and then charged towards him. He did a wonderful pass and the animal turned to attack him again. The crowd roared their approval. He finished off the bull with a clean kill, and everybody cheered for him to have an ear, which he readily accepted and paraded round the bull ring. When it came to his second fight, he did exactly the same, but this time he turned his back on the bull. The crowd were in hysterics, as he could only hear the bull coming towards him. He had another good pass and he killed the bull cleanly. The crowd rose to their feet and cheered. He was given two ears and a tail, and he was carried out by the crowd. I was later to find out that he was to become a world champion bullfighter. His name was El Cordobés.

Going back to my cars, when was I was 21 I bought my first E-Type Jag. It was a dark blue hardtop with a 3.8L engine; at that time, the ultimate car. I happened to be coming back from London on Sunday morning with the windows down and the 8-track blaring. I stopped at some traffic lights along the Embankment, and alongside me came a white E-Type with darkened windows. When the lights changed, we both roared off. We went all the way along the Embankment and through the East End. We got to the A13 (the trunk road to the sea) and the white car just left me. I drove to my local pub in Orsett and, to my surprise, the white E-Type was parked out front. There were only two men in the bar; one was Steve McQueen and the other was John Whitmore, the British Touring Car Champion who performed all the racing stunts in *The Italian Job* (These days he's 'Sir John', and lives in California). Steve McQueen had flown over to England to invite John to race his MG.

Next I progressed to a red soft-top 4.2L E-Type. I ordered it from SMACs, a well-known Jaguar garage in Southend. I was taking my other E-Type in part exchange, and closed the butcher's shop early on Saturday to go pick up my new car. When I arrived there, it was outside the showrooms gleaming with chrome spoke wheels and the top-down, pillar box red with black leather upholstery. I was still in my work clothes, with sawdust on my shoes. I didn't care. I could not get into my new car quick enough. It was 18 miles home from the showrooms. I parked the car in the drive. On Friday, I collected my new tailor-made silver mohair suit with a pink shirt and dark pink tie and matching handkerchief for the jacket pocket. After work, I rushed into the house, had a bath and got dressed in my new attire. I was ready. It was about 7.00pm, the sun was still up. I put on my sunglasses and walked to the car. I started the car up, and it purred like a young lion. I put it into reverse and, to my horror, the gear stick came out in my hand. It would not go back. I phoned the garage, but they had all gone home. So I phoned a friend, who was a mechanic. He looked at the car and said it would not go back in; it had to go back to the garage. I was desperate to go out in the car in my new threads, so I pleaded with the mechanic. "There is one thing I can do," he said. "Wait here." He was gone about half an hour. He returned back with a sawn off broom handle. He slotted it in the hole where the gear stick was. It worked perfectly; the car only had 26 miles on the clock. I drove off to the pub to meet my friends. When I came out later, there was quite a crowd gathered round the car looking very curiously at the gear stick.

It was during this period that I started to organise dances and gigs. I'd always had a love for music and at that time I also started to move into the promotion side of the business. I had groups like the Hollies, the Searchers, the Drifters, The Marvelettes, Marmalade, and many more. They performed at the Queen's Hotel, which had a very large function room. This was my first shot at being a promoter.

When I was 28-years-old, I married a girl who was the sister of a friend of mine. Paula and I were married for seven years. During that time, we had a daughter called Fleur and a boy called Chi. At the same time, I bought Burrow Farm. Before I moved into the house, I decided I needed to pave the pathway, because it was all grass and stones. I put a cement drive down with one of the young boys who worked for me on Saturdays. He was called Billy, and was a very good worker. I measured the length and width of the area required and found a ready mixed company, who told me I would need three yards of material.

I drove down to the farm with Billy on a Wednesday afternoon, when the shop was closed. We put shuttering along the area of the proposed path. The cement lorry arrived at 4pm. It reversed to the edge of the path. The driver climbed out and told me I was his last customer and the one before had cancelled his order. He wondered whether I would like the other 10 yards for £20. Having no idea what 10 yards look like, I said yes please. The lorry driver advised us to start laying the cement at the back of the drive, working away to the entrance of the farm. I got Billy to get the barrel out of the shed, with two spades. The lorry's revolving back was making plenty of noise as it twisted round and round. Slowly, the lorry started to pour out the cement, Billy and I stood there with the barrel and spades at the ready. It kept coming, so we stood back a couple of steps. Still it kept coming, so we went back a couple more steps while the cement poured out of the lorry. It was getting so high, we could not see over the cement to the lorry. Eventually it stopped, the lorry left, and Billy and I started shovelling the cement into a barrow. We got to about 15 loads, and went back for another load and, to my horror, the cement had set hard. We could not budge it. Not only that, my car was behind the mound, which was looking more like a small hill. There were no mobile phones in those days, and the house phone had not been connected. So Billy and I had to walk to the local pub and phone for a taxi home. I had to get a company in to break the cement up so I could get my car out. We used the cement for hard-core for the drive. It ended up being very expensive, but I certainly learnt a lesson.

Burrow Farm had a thousand fruit trees on it. It was designed so that you had fruit all the year round, even at Christmas there were red apples. But they did not turn sweet until January or February; there were no leaves on the trees, just the apples. I bought myself an Irish Wolfhound at this time. It was a bitch, but I called her Harry. We used the farm to breed cattle and poultry, which all ended up in the shops. It was while I had the cattle, which used to roam through the orchard, that I noticed one of them limping. This usually meant a stone had caught in a hoof. I tried to catch it, but it just kept moving away from me. So I came up with the bright idea of lassoing it. Eventually I got the rope over the beast's head, and it started to run. So I tied the other end of the rope to one of the trees. When the rope stretched to the limit, the animal started going round in ever decreasing circles. I unfortunately had not got out of the way of the rope so I was lashed to a tree. The young animal ran out of rope and my arms and legs were tied to the tree. We ended up with our noses three inches away from each other. And that's where we stayed for three hours until somebody came looking for me.

Harry, the wolfhound, had come from championship stock and I wanted to see how good she was. But before she could enter Crufts, she had to win a minor show. She eventually did this, and went on to come fourth in the Best Hound category at Crufts.

I now had a bug about wolfhounds, so I bought a cream dog called Marmaduke. Harry was a light brindle. In due course they mated and had one pup, which was also cream. We named him Dean. We also acquired a breeding prefix from the kennel club, which we made Zeus. That is a little like giving a dog its own surname.

I became quite heavily involved with the dogs, building kennels and runs, and ended up with 80 puppies and adults. I used to send them all over the world. There is a lot of history behind wolfhounds, they went back to Roman times, but became almost extinct in the early 1900s. I read everything I could about them: all wolfhounds were either brindle or cream, but in the history books there was mention of black wolfhounds. This set me on a pilgrimage to try and find any bloodlines that could produce a black dog. I eventually traced a strain down to kennels in Devon. I bought one of their dogs, who was a dark brindle. He mated with one of my dark brindle bitches, but the pups came out brindle; there was no black. While I had the kennels, I would be asked to house large homeless dogs for the RSPCA as I had all the facilities. Plus, being a butcher, I had plenty of food. One of the dogs we had by this method was a brindle wolfhound. We called him Sam and he became a member of our family. Sam was very friendly with one of our bitches, called Sophie. She had already had a litter, and she had been a wonderful mum. Incidentally, the dogs were never kennelled - only when in season, and that was for obvious reasons

The farm was quite a distance from other houses – but not the local pub, which was half a mile away. Wolfhounds are very friendly and love kids, but they are very big. Dean weighed 20 stone when he was fully grown, and stood over a seven foot tall on his hind legs. One day, while everybody was out, an insurance man came to the house. The dogs usually stayed in the orchard while we were out. But if anybody came to the house, they would come out and greet you. Apparently, the insurance man didn't like dogs, and he had never seen a wolfhound. It was the middle of winter. As I drove home from work, my headlights caught this man in the drive with a briefcase and dogs sitting all around him. He had been there for six hours.

On another occasion, I had a phone call asking if I could house a lion. They said it was only a cub and I had the room, so I agreed I would take it. I was asked to pick him up at the local railway station. When I went to collect the cub, the man there pointed to a cardboard box. I was horrified to think that the cub was locked in this box, so I quickly started taking the tape off the box. As I did, the cub let out an almighty roar like that of a full grown lion - so I closed the lid again!

By this time, I had just become divorced and had a girlfriend called Jan. We got the cub home and put him in a warm, comfortable kennel with a run. Jan took it food and milk, which it wouldn't touch. She went to stroke it, and it took hold of her arm. It didn't break the skin, but in the morning, Jan's arm had gone completely black. We decided to leave the cub that night. The next day, we went to see Tiny (that's what we called him). He was in the run, still growling and not very happy. One of our bitches, called Smoky, had just weaned her puppies. She was very inquisitive, and stood up and looked into the run. As soon as the cub saw her, he began to purr. I let Smoky into the run; she gave him a lick, and then laid down and let the cub suckle off of her. From that day on, Tiny thought she was his mum.

We could not do anything with Tiny, but we could tell Smoky what to do and the cub would follow. After a couple of weeks, we decided to let him out. He never went anywhere without Smoky. They were inseparable. I used to let the two of them come into the house. Tiny would always jump when he saw himself in the mirror on the wall.

Not surprisingly, nobody wanted Tiny, so we still had him a year later. By this time, he had a mane and weighed three hundred pounds. One evening I came home to the farm to find lots of police cars with their blue lights flashing. I was greeted by the local chief of police, who enquired as to whether I had a lion. "Where is it", the policemen asked. "He is normally on the lawn," I replied and, sure enough, he was on the lawn with Smoky. The police then told us what had happened earlier in the day.

I let one of my friends have a mobile home on the farm. He had a small mongrel dog, which Smoky had befriended. The dog had caught the smell of another dog in season in the village three miles away. He decided to check it out, followed by Smoky, who was followed by Tiny. It was on the way back that the local hedge cutter was trimming the hedge when the mongrel came through a hole in the hedge, followed by Smoky. He'd never seen such a big dog. He said it made him jump. Just as he was getting his tobacco tin out, Tiny brushed past him. Needless to say, this poor chap was more used to seeing lions in a zoo or on the telly than just beneath his feet while merrily going about his business in the English countryside. The policemen said it took them half an hour to get the man out of a tree. It was after that I received a petition from the village asking me to get rid of Tiny, and quite rightly so.

I made extensive enquiries to find a home for Tiny. Eventually, Mary Chipperfield agreed to take him in at Longleat Safari Park.

We hired a large van; Tiny would only go in if Smoky went in first. We made our way through London. It was very hot. We undid the windows, and Smoky stuck her head out one window, and Tiny squeezed his head out of my side. You should have seen people's faces when we went along the Embankment, stopping at traffic lights. Eventually we arrived at Longleat. We had hardly stopped when we were surrounded by a Zebra coloured vehicles, and men with guns. I explained that it was not necessary, and one of the men told me to take Tiny round the back of the big house. As Smoky left the van, sure enough, Tiny followed. At the back of the house, there was a large round cage. It was the same as you would see erected inside a circus. It had a tunnel leading to the main part. We tried to coax Tiny in, but he would have none of it. Smoky was also apprehensive, so I backed into the tunnel calling Smoky, who was followed by Tiny. To my surprise, when I reached the main part of the cage there was a very puzzled lion already there. I hastily made my exit by the metal gate at the back of the cage, followed by Smoky. Tiny was a bit ponderous, so we managed to close the gate before he could get out. I felt very sad leaving him, but unfortunately we had no choice. Even when we were at the end of the drive, we could still hear him calling for Smoky, who did not seem to be concerned at all.

Chapter 6

Black Dog

On another occasion, I was asked to collect a wolfhound from a barge. The old lady owner had died, and nobody knew what to do with the dog. Because it was constantly on the barge, with wooden decks, her claws had grown very long and curly; she had a job to walk. She was a lovely dark brindle called June-oh, who was looking for some real love and attention – which she certainly received from everybody at Burrow Farm. After about four months, we noticed she had become great friends with Sam. When she came into season, I locked all the other dogs away apart from Sam. Eventually, I found June-oh in the orchard giving birth to a litter of ten little puppies. The last one out was black, who we named Tiddles for obvious reasons. Black wolfhounds are rare, and we made it into all of the dog magazines when Tiddles was 10 months old. We took him to a dog show, and he was the centre of attention, winning three trophies, including Best Pup In Show. Tiddles went on to sire a litter of 13 black puppies. Again, this made all the doggie papers, and three of the puppies went to America. I also had a mysterious phone call enquiring about the pups: someone wanted a dog puppy, and could I take one to Southend Airport. I was met at the airport by a very dapper man who told me it was going with him on a private plane to Switzerland. He paid me in cash. I watched as he walked through the barrier and got on to a private plane. It later turned out, it was going to a Swiss Member of Parliament.

Around this time, we received a wolfhound that had been locked up in a barn without any light. He was, as you would expect, very nervy and would jump at the least thing. We knew a local police dog handler who took dog classes for those with problems, and he helped us sort him out. But while we were at one of these meetings, a man came in with a Doberman. He said the dog would not behave on a leash. So the police handler gave him a choke chain to put round the dog's neck and told the man to walk the dog down the hall. The dog started jumping up and down. The policeman told the man to pull the choke chain, which he did. The dog lunged at the man's throat: there was blood everywhere, and they had to call an ambulance to take him to hospital. When the man had gone, the policeman explained that the dog knew the man was frightened. He proceeded to walk the dog down the hall and the dog jumped up and down again. The policeman shouted "Sit!", and pulled the choke chain. But the dog jumped up at the policeman and had him by the throat as well. With more blood everywhere, they had to a call another ambulance. I heard later that they had to have the dog put to sleep.

Tiddles was the last wolfhound I had, and he stayed with me through part of my football days. He also got a first at Crufts.

During my time with the wolfhounds, I moved on in my businesses. Firstly, I had now acquired freezer shops which started to be the in-thing. I also had a factory which produced packed bacon. And I had my first record released, called *Shot Down In Action* (Spark Records, SRL 1120). The record was reviewed on BBC television's *Juke Box Jury*. The only record to get the thumbs-up that week was Minnie Riperton's *Lovin' You*. My record sold about 10,000 copies. I had been singing prior to this, but it was the first record I ever had in the shops. The record company, Bus Stop Records – whose only other acts were Paper Lace and Tony Christie – came up with an idea to promote it. Margaret Thatcher was on the verge of becoming leader of the Conservative party, the only female to have ever held the post. On Thursday 13 February 1975, they put a huge card on the back of a pink lorry: it read "To Margaret, Love Anton". Four men in toppers and tails, each with a red rose in their hands (red roses for a true blue!), walked along by the lorry. Thatcher's Personal Assistant had been contacted, and we were told she would be delighted to receive it outside the Palace of Westminster. Sure enough, she came out of Parliament to see the large card and was given a small handwritten one to take away with her. The next day (St. Valentine's Day), there was a picture of Thatcher with the card on the front of some of the national newspapers. I later received a letter from Thatcher inviting me to lunch, which I never did make. Four years later, she became the first female British Prime Minister; in the meantime, my record failed to trouble the singles chart.

My manager, Peter from College Entertainment, suggested I had some publicity photos taken at a studio in the West End. While I was waiting, I noticed a man looking through what looked like photo albums. He came over and asked me if I was working. I gave him Peter's phone number, and did not think any more about it. The next day, I received a phone call from Peter telling me the man I met wanted me to go and audition for a film he was making. The following day, I went to the Shakespeare Theatre where the auditions were taking place. There must have been 30 of us, and we all looked the same (long hair and beards were in then). I had to read a piece from the script direct into a camera. The next day, Peter phoned to say I was in the last three and had to go for another audition. By the end of the day, I was told I had the part.

The following day I was sent to wardrobe to be measured for my clothes. It was then I was told that the film was called *Courtesan* and I was to play Alexandre Dumas, the man who wrote *The Three Musketeers* saga (which includes the story of *The Man In The Iron Mask*). The following week, all the actors and film crew met at 5.30am in Soho. We were bundled into coaches. The leading lady and director got into a Rolls-Royce. We ended up at a very large country house in Godalming. When we got on the coaches, we were given our scripts. My role in the film was to go round the courts and read my stories. On one of these visits, I met Madame de Montespan, who I introduced to King Louis XIV (the Sun King), and they became lovers. The filming lasted six weeks.

The worst part was sitting around waiting, but I really enjoyed the experience. A month after I had finished filming, Peter offered me a year in repertory touring the country with a play. I turned it down, due to business commitments. Plus the wages were only £30 per week.

Back on the farm, the UK had joined the Common Market and I received a letter from the Ministry of Agriculture, Fisheries and Food, telling me I should get rid of my fruit trees, and that they would pay me five pounds per tree. I had over a thousand trees, so it didn't take much working out. In the middle of the orchard, I had a small pond. And in the garden, by the house, I had a well. I checked and found out that there was water under the farm, so I decided to build a lake. I asked somebody from the Angling Times to tell me what was required. He told me to dig out a four acre hole with two islands, with two deep holes for fish to breed in. First, we dug up the trees. Then big cranes came in to dig out the lake. In the meantime, I had organised with Charrington's Brewery a fishing competition. The lake was nearly fully dug out, but we had still to connect it to the small pond: we left that until last, expecting the water to gush in and fill up the lake. But to my horror, when we finally dug open the pond, the water merely trickled into the lake. I had the fishing competition due in two weeks, and I started to panic. I stupidly put a garden hose into the hole, hoping it would help fill up the hole. I went to bed, full of expectation. In the morning, I went to the hole and peered over edge: the water had gone nowhere, it just soaked into the earth. I had ordered £2,000 worth of fish, but I had to tell them to hold on to them for another couple of days. I was going crazy.

I had a couple of old farmer boys who worked for me, and they came up with a possible solution. We had a stream running around the boundary of the farm, called the Mydyke. They said we could dam the stream, and then pump the water into the lake. I ordered a pump from Sykes, which stood about two feet high. We got it started, and sure enough the water started pumping into the lake. The only problem was, the stream was not very deep and was not running fast enough. After about 10 minutes, the stream had dried up, and the water had made very little impression as it only ran a few feet across the bottom of the lake. The next day, one of the old boys came in with a giant metal key. On one side of the farm was the A128, which the Mydyke ran underneath through a tunnel. One of the old boys lifted a manhole cover on the A road and disappeared down inside with the key. The next minute, water came gushing out into the Mydyke to the extent that I had to order a bigger Sykes pump. By the next morning, water covered the bottom of the lake but we still had a long way to go as part of the lake was 15 to 20 feet deep. We let it keep pumping in, but by the next day, it had still only risen another six inches. The old boys told me to order an even bigger pump. They went back to a manhole and vanished inside: the water came rushing out even faster. I did not dare ask them what they were doing. A 10 foot pump arrived and was soon pumping the water out a lot faster. The next day, the water was three to four feet deep so I asked for the fish to arrive a day after. A farmer friend of mine called Fred phoned me. He said he had a pond, which was full of fish, and would I like them too. Naturally, I said yes, so the people I was buying the fish from went to Fred's and netted his pond. We had about 1,500 fish from Fred, but they were all small from being confined in a small pond. There was every species of fish, and they were released into my lake. The fish I had bought cost me a pound for a pound, but I had also bought some beautiful £20 plus carp, which were released into the ever deepening water.

We kept the pump running until the week of the fishing tournament. The day before the competition, we were still two foot short of water. The old boys told me we should have one more burst of water that night, and I should order a larger pump! That evening, the 15 foot pump arrived. At dusk, the old boys went down to the manhole again. This time the water came out even faster and the big pump really did the trick. I left it running and went to bed. I was awakened by a phone call at 1.00am. It was my friend from the village asking whether I had any water as the village had none. I went out and turned the pump off, as it had now done the job.

The next day, lily pads with lead weights at the roots were dropped into the lake. I noticed one of my beautiful carp on its side with a large hole in its side. I was informed that it had been the victim of a heron. The next day I saw two more of my carp on their sides with holes in them. The old farm boys offered me a 12-bore to rid myself of the problem. They told me it was a protected bird, and they normally ate very early in the morning. So I set my alarm. I was just drinking a cup of tea and there, high in the sky, was a heron. I picked up the gun and tiptoed towards the lake. The earth dug from the lake was left on the side to act as protection from the wind. I hid behind a mound of earth. When I saw the heron drop the other side by the lake, I slowly walked to the top of the pile of earth, saw the heron and raised the gun. But what I had not spotted were these eight people with cameras taking photographs of the heron. I was somewhat surprised and annoyed about them being on my land. They apologised and said they'd been following the heron from its nest and thought it was too early to bang on my door. I for my part explained that the gun was to make a noise and scare the heron off. The fishing competition was a huge success in the end, and we raised £2,500 for charity.

Another thing I became involved in while I was at the shop was helping to find new premises for the Tilbury and Chadwell Boys Club. I was the social secretary, and my job was to raise funds to build the club. With the help of a great committee, we put on all sorts of events. Our local civic hall took a thousand people, sitting down. So I put on a few shows: I had Dick Emery, who incidentally I took home to my mother's to have tea. I had jazz nights with Acker Bilk and others, plus old time music halls. I also put on some up-and-coming bands, The Love Affair, Status Quo and American R&B singer Geno Washington. I also found a smaller venue, called Norman Hall, and put on ladies and gentlemen nights, which were a great success.

After 18 months, we had almost reached our target; we needed just £10,000 more. Essex Boys Club told us that if we could raise £5,000, they would give us the rest. I had a friend in Smithfield, whose name was Lenny Green. He was the brother of Peter Green of Fleetwood Mac. I asked Lenny to speak to Peter about doing a gig for us. I was told they were not allowed to work in the UK for tax reasons, unless it was for charity, so if we gave them £50 each for beer money they would help. We arranged to have the show on a Wednesday. On the afternoon of the gig, at about 3.00pm, I had a phone call from the manager of the Civic. He asked me to go and see him. I arrived to find that the queue had gone four times round the Civic Hall. It was a great success, even though we had to turn hundreds of people away. So a brand new club was built. Sometime later, one of the committee asked me if I would help sponsor his granddaughter, who was a javelin thrower. I readily accepted. My role was to supply her with steak. The young lady in question was Fatima Whitbread, who went on to break the javelin world record with a throw of 77.44m in the qualifying round of the 1986 European Championships in Athletics and became World Champion in 1987.

The Boys Club was predominately a boxing club, and we needed a representative in boxing. So I became an ABA judge, which I did for 10 years and thoroughly enjoyed. During this time, I would judge quite a lot of dinner shows. On one occasion, my girlfriend Jan (who always thought she was missing out on something) asked to come along. When I picked her up, she was wearing a smart white suit, as we were going out somewhere else after the show. She also asked me if she could sit at my table by the side of the ring. The first fight was in the second round when one of the boxers was caught right on the nose: blood went everywhere, including on to Jan's pristine suit. She never came again.

I progressed into the wholesale meat business - mainly pork. I was buying pigs, boning them and supplying sausage factories. This reached 3,000 pigs a week, coming out of Smithfield. It meant the amount of bones we had was enormous. We had 45 gallon bins filled with the bones, and you hardly got any money at all for them, so we did not count them in our costing. The business had been running for about eight months when one of my staff called me to say there was a Chinese man outside who wanted to talk to me. He asked me what I did with all the rib bones from the pigs. At the time, nobody knew anything about spare ribs in England. I was throwing them all in the bin, and the Chinese man offered to buy all the ribs from me. I could not believe my luck: he bought them all and paid cash each week. He would bring anything from £2,000 to £5,000 a week for the ribs. The money from the ribs bought me my first Rolls-Royce. It also allowed me to have a hair transplant. I was not bald but, I had some thinning patches. On the day of my hair transplant, I was told not to eat. I arrived at the clinic to be greeted by two tiny Asian nurses in white coats, and not a lot more; I think that was there to take your mind off what was happening. I put on a gown and lay on the operating table. I felt the first to needles go in. After that, my head went numb and I could hear what I thought was a sizzling in my head. In fact, they were cutting pieces out of the side of my head, taking out hair follicles. It was a bit like a spud gun: they took the follicles out and put them in surgical spirit. Then they cut pieces the same size from my thinning hair. All this time I had a warm sensation down my back, later to realise it was blood. The good follicles were then put in where the thinning hair had been. When they finished, my head was wrapped very tightly in bandage. I went home to bed feeling very sick. Later that evening, I was awoken by the phone. It was a friend, Kevin, and he asked me how I was feeling. While I was talking, I realised I was very hungry. I mentioned this to Kevin, who could always eat. He picked me up, and we went to our local curry house. There was nobody in the restaurant, and I started feeling a little sick. I asked the staff if they could hurry the food up. We sat at the table while all the staff went out into the kitchen. While they were out there, the pub next door emptied out and about 10 people came into the restaurant and sat down. They waited for about three minutes, before one of the men came over to me and asked me when I was going to bring over one of the menus!

Another thing I'd been doing was looking after the West Indian ska and reggae band, The Pyramids (aka Symarip). Prior to my helping them, they had had chart success, including with *Skinhead Moonstomp*. Two things stand out about them for me: the band got the chance to play in Sidney Poitier's film, *A Warm December*. There was a scene in a club where the group was going through a set, and they played a number which can be heard throughout the film. The number (*Nonqonqo*, written by Miriam Makeba) became very popular. The BBC asked us to go and record the number at their studios. At the time the BBC would record popular numbers so they didn't have to pay so much in royalties but also kept the music love and more personal. Once they had a number recorded, they would play it regularly to help it into the charts. I was very excited by this but, as was often the case, one of the bands did not turn up and we lost the opportunity to record the number. The BBC never asked us to again. During my time with The Pyramids, I struck up a close friendship with the lead singer, Roy Ellis. We decided to do a record together, called *Sweet England*. It was the same time as England was in the World Cup. We toured all the radio stations and did a few live gigs. We called ourselves Humbug, being black and white. The record company had the world's largest Humbug sweet made, which we presented to a hospital. We sold a few thousand copies, but it was while we were in the studio recording the record that the engineer told us he was going to take about three to four hours mixing, and we could go out for the time being. We had been in a studio in Tin Pan Alley, so we decided to go to the pictures in Leicester Square. Roy and I decided to go and see the film Mandingo, which is a story about slaves in America. In one scene, the boss catches his wife in bed with one of the good-looking slaves and the disgruntled husband picks up his rifle and leads the slave out of the bedroom to a clearing in the woods. As they are walking along, the slave makes a lunge for the rifle, taking it from the husband and turning it on him. The boss walks slowly towards the slave telling him to put the gun down. The slave does nothing. At this point, Roy stood up in the cinema shouting "Kill him! Kill him!" I of course pulled him down into his seat. When the film finished and the lights went up, everyone turned to find Roy was the only black person in the cinema.

Roy went on to have his own radio station in Switzerland. Also, in 1980, The Pyramids' album, *Skinhead Moonstomp*, was reissued in the wake of the Two Tone craze after a live cover of the title song appeared on *The Special AKA Live!* EP, which topped of the UK singles chart that year. The Pyramids officially split in 1985, but Trojan Records released a 'best of' album in 2004 with a new single, *Back From The Moon*, performed by Roy and former band member, Monty Neysmith. In 2005, the two performed together at Club Ska in England, and a recording of the concert was released. In April 2008, they headlined the Ska Splash Festival in Lincolnshire as Symarip.

One of my customers while I was in the butchery was Bob Wheatley, a very successful man who realised the importance of discos. He had them all over London and the Home Counties, and moved into cabaret, where his flag ship was the Circus Tavern in Purfleet. He would have all the world-famous stars performing there. I would supply the meat and frozen veg for the Circus, which could take eight to 900 diners at a time. One Saturday afternoon, I made a delivery only to be confronted by a very angry looking Bob Wheatley. He told me he had caught the chefs putting food in the boots of their cars, so he'd sacked them. Unfortunately, he could not find any replacements at such short notice for that night. But I told him I was a chef and had been taught at the National Food Technology College. He looked delighted and asked if I could take over the kitchen. Normally, there were four chefs, but now there was only me. 856 people were booked for dinner that night and Paul Melba, an impressionist, was the star turn. He was very popular at the time, and appeared before Her Majesty the Queen at Royal Command Performances. There were 20 to 30 waitresses working. I called them all together and picked eight of the best to help me in the kitchen. It got very busy, and I never left the oven or the grills all night. Every now and then, a waitress would call out certain table numbers and said would

I have a drink with them. I always said yes, to help business at the end of a successful evening. When I finally left the kitchen, I found a table full of flat lagers - about 50 in all. Bob Wheatley asked me to stay on, even after he brought other chefs in. The highlight of working in the kitchen was once cooking for Prince Charles and a dinner party of 40. Another time, Princess Margaret was there. On another occasion, the Circus had Tommy Cooper booked in for a two week residency. Not surprisingly, it was a complete sell out. When Tommy finished his show, which was any time after 1am, he would want fish and chips in newspaper. So it was my job to have it ready for him. He was usually on his own, I would sit with him while he ate. He never seemed to want to go back to his motel, so I ended up taking him back in the early daylight. After a couple of days, Tommy started arriving late for his show so Bob asked me if I would look after him and make sure he got to work on time. The motel was about 20 minutes from the Circus Tavern. Tommy normally went on stage at 11.00pm. I picked Tommy up around 10.15pm. He always insisted I had a drink with him before we left. His dressing table always had an array of different spirits fitting for any pub. He would not leave until we both had a very large measure. On the last Saturday he was appearing, I went to pick him up as usual. We had our drinks. He then asked me if I had a hammer and a saw, because he'd thought of a new joke. I told him I had not got either, so we jumped in the car and headed for the Circus Tavern. I always went through the back lanes, and on the way Tommy spotted a house at the end of a long drive. "Go down there," he said. I stopped outside the house. All of the lights were on, so Tommy got me to go and ask if they had a hammer and saw. It was now 10.30pm, and Tommy would not take no for an answer. I sheepishly knocked on the door. A lady answered, and I only reached the word "...hammer" before she slammed the door in my face. I went back to the car. Tommy then stepped out of the car and went to the door. He started talking through the letterbox. Within a minute, the door opened and a lady and a man appeared, both roaring with laughter. Tommy then walked into their house and closed the door. It took me half an hour to ferry him out of the house, but in his big hands he held a hammer and a saw. We were now 20 minutes late for the show; when we arrived at the Circus, Tommy rushed through the stage door followed by me with a hammer and a saw! As usual, Tommy brought the house down. All the while, I eagerly awaited the new sketch, but he did his whole show without using the hammer and saw. I got him his fish and chips, and this time his wife was there to take him home. He said goodbye to me and asked if I would take the tools back to their owners, which I did.

About a year after Tiny had gone, the fishing lake became a very viable business. It fished very well and soon got a very good reputation. During this time I was approached by a young man called Chris, who had just finished farming college. He could not get a job and asked if there was any work. I took him on as a helper to me. He was happy to do anything and did not mind the hours. After being with me for about six months, I decided to start farming again. I bought Little Mountain Farm in Pendine, Carmarthen. Wales had a lot of dairy farms, so when the cows had calved they were sold very cheaply. I sent Christopher to the cattle auctions, and we soon had a farm full of calves at the right price. I then needed a farm down south to fatten the calves up. I found a farm for sale: Marsh Farm in Pitsea, Essex. It had once belonged to Howard's Dairies. It had an acre under cover, which was used as the milking parlour and was ideal for the calves in winter. The farm was about 150 acres all together, and ideal for putting the calves out in the summer. It cost me £50,000. I had one good summer at both farms, then Chris told me he was leaving to go to Canada with a girl he had met. Nothing I could say would change his mind. I tried to find a replacement, but it was all in vain. So I sold Little Mountain Farm, and kept Marsh Farm. But I was not really working it, and a man approached me about selling it. He said he was an agent, but would not tell me who the buyer was. We agreed on a price of £100,000. After the deal was signed, the agent told me of the importance of the deal: to get to Marsh Farm, you had to go over a level crossing for the main Southend to Fenchurch Street rail lines. After that, 100 yards on the left was another farm, and past the farm was a dirt road. The road was used day and night by lorries taking all types of fluid waste to a dump close to the River Thames. The dump was on top of blue clay, which was not porous and went down some 400 feet. So toxic waste from all over Europe was being dumped there.

One day, one of the lorry drivers stepped out of his vehicle and was overcome by fumes. Sadly, he died and the council decided to close the road to stop the lorries reaching the dump. The only alternate access was through my farm. Unfortunately, I did not know this at the time and I thought £100, 000 was a very good deal. The agent later told me they had a budget of one million pounds to acquire the farm. If you ever go over Pitsea flyover now, 30 years on, you will see the lorries going along the cement road, which was part of my farm.

Chapter 7

Crocodile Rock

By the late 1970s I was getting a bit bored and looking for something else to do. I was still playing football on Sundays for Orsett Green - as the centre forward - and on Thursdays for the Press-Gang, as goalkeeper. Press-Gang comprised of journalists - many of whom went on to become editors of national newspapers – and actors. One of the actors was Phil Davis, who shot to fame in the cult film Quadrophenia and regularly works with writer/director Mike Leigh.

Anyway, I told my accountant I was looking for something else to do and about a month later he phoned and said he had found something for me: a very large health and keep-fit centre with a Spanish styled bar. The bar led out on to Rayleigh High Street, which was very busy. I had the thought of changing the back into a nightclub and the front into a public house. I decided to buy it, but getting the licence and planning permission took some time. Eventually, though, it all came through, and I decided to name the place Croc's - giving me the opportunity of a great logo using a crocodile head. I had a waterfall and pond designed and installed, with live crocodiles enclosed in shatterproof grass. I had the best lighting and sound system installed, and jungle scenes painted on the walls in luminous paint. The bar was called The Trading Post. We put African memorabilia on the walls - like animal head drums, spears and carvings – and I had the staff dress in safari suits (different colours for boys and girls).

The club was licensed for 1500 people. We built a great stage and dressing rooms. Overnight, the whole place became a huge success with the queue stretching all the way down the High Street, and

The Trading Post was always packed. Soon Croc's became one of *the* established nightclubs; it was only 18 miles from London. I was approached by new bands and agencies to use Croc's as a place where they could be reviewed by the record companies and music magazines. The venue was ideal for live bands, but we not only had bands playing: the audience was full of other up-and-coming artists, soon to be household names, like Boy George, Soft Cell, Duran Duran, Spandau Ballet, Steve Strange, Matchbox, A Flock of Seagulls, The Damned, and many more.

One of the things with clubs that have live music is that you have to keep up with the trends of the day, and Croc's became a New Romantic club, and was later hailed as the "longest running alternative nightclub in UK". This meant you saw all walks of life dressing to shock and surprise you. From doctors to dustmen, everyone is equal once they dress up. Boys all had make-up on and very elaborate hairstyles; some of the girls wore string vests, which left nothing to the imagination, and they all used each other's toilets. The strict rule of the club was only New Romantics were allowed in so everybody felt comfortable. Television companies from all over the world would be coming to make films about Croc's, which was very good for business.

One of the local bands that came to see live bands at Croc's was Depeche Mode, from Basildon. I got on very well with them and they were to play at the club on a number of occasions. I received a phone call from them one time, asking if we could get together somewhere. We arranged to meet in The Trading Post, and it was there that the band asked me to manage them. I said I was honoured, but I didn't think I could give them enough time. Two months later, their single *New Life* climbed to number 11 in the UK charts and, three months later, *Just Can't Get Enough* became their first of many singles to enter the UK Top 10. They went on to have worldwide hits, but a couple of years later they were back at Croc's to perform for a documentary about them. A few years ago, a bootleg recording surfaced called *Live at Croc's Night Club June 27, 1981.*

There were many artists who played at Croc's when they were just starting out - singers and DJs. One band who came to Croc's comprised of two boys and one girl. Next to the dressing rooms was a room where we kept the goods that we used in The Trading Post for lunchtimes, including fridges. All three were on stage when I went with one of my bar girls to a fridge to bring some lemons for the drinks. To our horror, we found teeth marks in all of the food - this was in three fridges: it was in cheese, pies, hams, beef and desserts. You could only reach the fridges via the dressing rooms. I spoke to the doorman outside and he assured me nobody apart from the band and my bar girl had been in there. I was furious; I waited for the band to come off stage. I shouted at them, but they just laughed. I told them I would make sure they would never work again. Three weeks later, they were at the top of the charts with *Hold Me Now*. It was the Thompson Twins. A few years later, they performed with none other than Madonna at Live Aid. So much for my threat!

During this period of my life I found I had enough time to start watching my favourite football team. Fred Buttigieg had by now stopped running coaches to Charlton. He was in his 70s, so I bought three Jubilee tickets which gave you your own seat, access to a small bar and lounge, and a half-time cup of tea. Fred, Jan and I went to every home game and we would drive to the ground in my Rolls-Royce. We were never stopped, so we would drive right in to the directors' car park. The Rolls had a pull-out table and a drinks cabinet in the back. So we would go early and have a picnic in the car and watch the players arrive. Drink-driving was not a big issue then: Fred liked a beer and Jan and I would have a bottle of wine. We watched the crowds arrive and saw the Valley come to life; the atmosphere was electric. On one of these Saturdays after the beer, wine and picnic, we went up into the Jubilee Lounge for coffee and a few brandies. By the time we were in our seats in the stand, the players were lining up. As we sat down, Fred said, in a very sincere voice, "This is the first time I've seen four football teams on the field." After that, I made sure Fred only had one brandy with his coffee. After the match, we dropped Fred home and would go straight to work at Croc's. It was a really great time in my life.

Chapter 8

The Merry Millers

One of the things I missed most about working late was not being able to see *Match of the Day* and Jimmy Hill. But, to my delight, the video happened along so I was able to set it and watch football at whatever time I wanted - sometimes four or five o'clock in the morning. Strangely enough, as most people who work late will know, you cannot go straight to sleep after you return home. So the video was great invention for me.

It was during one of *these Match of the Day* programmes that Jimmy Hill introduced Rotherham United and said that they were coming up for sale. My ears pricked-up: you did not hear of a football club coming up for sale often, and that night I could not sleep. Next morning, Sunday, I got Rotherham's phone number...but I should have realised nobody would answer. So bright and early on Monday I watched the clock reach 9.00am I phoned Rotherham again, and this time a woman answered and put me through to the secretary - a Mr Jim Bennison. He told me he would speak to the owner and phone me back. It seemed like a lifetime, but eventually around midday, I took the call I was waiting for: Bennison gave me the telephone number of the owner. When I rang, the phone was answered by a man speaking in a very heavy Yorkshire accent, who introduced himself as Mr Eric Purshouse. I explained the reason for my call and that I was genuine about my interest.

We decided the way forward was to meet and look at the books, and also the football ground. Once I put the phone down, I rang my accountant and lawyer, who were both available Friday. So I phoned Southend Airport and hired a helicopter. We left

Southend at about 10.00am on the Friday. The pilot had his instructions on where to land in Rotherham, and we were met by Purshouse and his son. They whisked us away to the ground, and my lawyer and accountant went straight to Bennison's office. While I was given a guided tour of the ground, changing rooms, the indoor training facilities, and then taken to a part of Sheffield where Rotherham had their training ground, I was completely in my element. I was then taken back to the club's ground and my lawyer and accountant discussed their findings with me in the boardroom. On the face of it, they could not find any skeletons. But the club was running very tight because of the low gates. I was not put off by this and so I shook hands with Purshouse on a deal of £67,500 for a 70% holding in Rotherham. The helicopter took us back to Southend, via seventh heaven!

On landing, my first job was to find the £67,500. I had recently sold Burrow Farm, so the money from that and the sale of one of my Rolls-Royces would just about cover it. While the transaction was going through, I was invited to watch Rotherham play Sheffield Wednesday. To my horror, at half-time in the boardroom, Purshouse announced that he had changed his mind about selling the club. I asked to see him privately, and we went into the loo. I was absolutely raving: "You could have told me that over the phone," I said as I put my hands around his throat. I returned to Grays and phoned my lawyer on Monday morning. "I'm not sure he can change his mind," said my brief.

Unbeknownst to me, Purshouse had hired a private detective to check me out. And by the next Friday, he had changed his mind again and decided to let me buy the club after all. None of this came to light until much later. I went up to Rotherham to sign the contracts, and there were television cameras in the room. It made the news, and night that I stayed at the Brentwood Hotel, a lovely Grade II listed building on the outskirts of Rotherham town centre. Rotherham weren't playing that weekend, but I wanted to go to the club to meet everybody as soon as possible. The next morning, I was chased by the media. The newspapers, radio and

TV all wanted interviews. While I was having breakfast, a local reporter from the Star asked me if I was aware that some of the staff had resigned, including the manager and his assistant: all that was left was the physio, Barry Claxton, to run the team.

I had a meeting with Bennison and the other director, Cliff N. Right, who had been a Wing Commander in the RAF and later an auctioneer, but now retired in his 70s. The pair suggested I advertise in the national newspapers for a manager, but at the same time they both seemed very apprehensive about me. While the advert was being placed, I invited the pair and their wives to have a couple of days away at the Cambridgeshire Hotel so that we could get to know each other better. It was while we were there, with the alcohol flowing and everybody in a more relaxed mood, that I asked why all the staff had left. They told me that Purshouse's check on me had found that one of the most notorious men in the East End of London lived at Burrow Farm and it apparently scared him to the extent that he called a meeting of the staff and told everybody that their lives might be in danger, and advised them to leave. In fact, I had just sold the farm to Billy Blundell, but at least it cleared up the mystery and, after that, everybody seemed far more relaxed.

Once I had bought the club, I decided I needed a new image. I always thought of chairmen with big cigars, so I went out and bought myself a box of Churchill cigars, and learnt to puff on them without taking the smoke down. At about the same time, I was walking down London's Bond Street and saw this big fur coat in a shop window. I went in and asked if they had one in my size. They said it was the only one they had, that it had been made for a photo shoot for one of the fashion magazines, and I could buy it if it fitted which, happily, it did. Cigars, fur coat, and a Rolls-Royce: I felt I had the right image. My first game in charge was with Claxton standing in as manager against Colchester. It was snowing but we got a 1-1 draw. By the following Tuesday, the response from the advert for new manager had resulted in 28 sensible replies – and plenty of crank ones! It was just a week before Christmas, so we scheduled the interviews for the first week in January. I had a phone call at home from Bennison asking if he could give my phone number to John Sadler, a reporter from The Sun newspaper. I said it was okay, and a few minutes later Sadler phoned me. He said he had someone who might be interested in the manager's job, and could this person phone me. I was very intrigued. Ten minutes later, the phone rang and it was Brian Clough. He told me he was ready for a change from Nottingham Forest and, if the money was right, he would be interested. And he'd bring Peter Taylor with him. We agreed to meet on Boxing Day at a hotel just off the M1 after our teams had both played matches (we were playing at Hull, and Forest were at home). Clough and I had agreed to meet in the car park; him in a dark blue Mercedes, me in my silver Rolls. I arrived at 8.00pm which was the time we had agreed. I was expecting the car park to be full, but there was just a dark blue Mercedes. The Mercedes flashed its lights and I drove over and stopped at the side. Clough and Taylor sat in the back of the Rolls-Royce. We started to talk, but Clough said he couldn't see my eyes, and we should go into the hotel bar for a drink. Jan had booked us a room at the hotel, so she went straight upstairs while Clough, Taylor and I went to the bar. Clough said he would come to Rotherham for £150,000 plus another £100,000 per year. I agreed immediately. We shook hands on it, and had another couple of drinks. We agreed we would make a joint statement on Tuesday. I was very excited. On Monday morning, my phone rang. It was Clough. He told me his contract with Nottingham Forest stated that he could not leave for another month or two but Taylor could come straight away. In the end I had reservations about taking Cloughie, so I moved on.

So I went ahead with my interviews for a manager at the Stifford Lodge hotel in Grays, about one mile from my home. There were some very well respected managers and players who had applied who I had only previously watched on television or read about. I was really in awe of them. The person I was most impressed with was the man whose hands were sweating, who didn't ask about wages, and only talked about the Rotherham team, who he had been to watch. His name was John 'Ian' Porterfield, the man who scored the winning goal for Sunderland at Wembley in the 1973 FA Cup Final, giving them a shock victory over Leeds United, and currently the last man to have replaced Sir Alex Ferguson as a football manager (at Aberdeen, in 1986). He became my first manager. The last team Ian had played for was Sheffield Wednesday, so he only lived six miles from Rotherham, which meant there was no moving involved. We had a press call to introduce him. Because of the flamboyant image I had created, the press were speculating on who this well-known figure might be. It was a bit of a surprise when we introduced Ian, but he got down to his task straightaway, and it certainly took the pressure off me from a media point of view. In 1979, it was quite unusual for anybody to buy a football club, so I was in demand for all types of interviews on radio and television. I was on the Russell Harty show twice. On one of these, I appeared with the actress, Dame Anna Neagle, and the chairman of fine art auctioneers Christie's, who was about to retire. We met in the foyer of the BBC. I had my fur coat on, and by the time we were in the lift the man from Christie's told me where the different pelts of my coat had come from - mainly from China and Canada. I shudder at the thought of wearing it today, but my life had changed completely. I still had Croc's and the meat wholesaler, but football was taking up more and more of my time. In 1980, I was invited as a guest to attend the Football League Cup (then the Milk Cup) Final at Wembley between the holders, and then European champions, Nottingham Forest, and Wolverhampton Wanderers, captained by Emlyn Hughes. I had a pre-match meal with all the football dignitaries, then sat and watched the match in the best seats in the house. It was a completely new world to me.

Being a Chairman or a Director of a football club allowed you to attend most matches in the League: I would phone Bennison to see if there was a mid-week game in London that I could see, and he would have tickets left at reception of the club. My love was football, and it still is. I would watch any football match, from kids to the First Division or Premiership. My weekend would start if Rotherham were at home by driving up from Essex on Friday, and going straight to the ground for a meeting with Bennison, who would bring me up to date with what had happened in the week. I'd then sign cheques and go and have a chat with Ian to find out how the players were and what the team would be for Saturday. I would then have a walk around the ground; training had finished, so there would only be the players in the physio room with Claxton. On match day mornings, I would go to watch the Rotherham youth team, then back for lunch with the first team, then watch my team play. It was great. By the time Ian took up his post, it was the end of January and a little too late to try for promotion. But we ended up in a respectable mid-table position. That season was a complete whirlwind for me: I had the opportunity to watch football three or four times a week, and my knowledge of places in England became a lot better, although I would travel from Essex to places - like Torquay, Hull and Grimsby – and back in a day. I felt like I was on a permanent holiday, with home games taking me four hours to get there.

Reflecting back on that first season, straight away Ian was starting to build the team he wanted. His first signing was Phil Henson – a very experienced player formerly with Manchester City, Sheffield Wednesday and Stockport. He also had a spell in Holland with Sparta Rotterdam. He was later to be part of our Division Three Champions. Ian's second signing was Graham Brown, a goalkeeper from York City, and a bargain buy. His displays in the latter part of the season were very competent, and he soon became a favourite with the fans. Vic Halom was signed from Oldham towards the end of the season, and his specific responsibilities were player/coach. But he played the rest of the season as a striker, and I saw him score one of the best goals I have ever seen against Charlton: it was breath-taking. That was as far as the transfers went that season.

That first summer as a chairman, I was very busy in and around Rotherham and Sheffield: opening fetes; presenting trophies, at all sorts of sporting events; speaking at dinners; talking on football forums on the radio; and generally promoting Rotherham United. Somebody who assisted me with local knowledge and pointed me in the right direction was a young man called Derek Dalton. He was Rotherham's greatest fan and in 1983 became Braun/Shoot Fan Of The Year, which was a national competition.

Unfortunately, Derek contracted polio at the age of two and spent most of his time in an iron lung. But he always managed to get to Rotherham matches, home and away. He had a converted mini-bus so he could take his wheelchair in and be pushed into all the grounds. Many times when I went up to Rotherham on Friday, I would go around to his house and sit with him while he was charging himself up in his iron lung ready for Saturday's match. I was always made most welcome by his mother and father. Derek's room was full of football memorabilia. One day I went to an FA dinner and sat opposite the legendary Pele, who I arranged to sign a picture for Derek. This naturally took pride of place in Derek's collection.

After home games, Derek always came around to where the boardroom was and I had a glass of scotch with a straw ready for him, as he could not hold a glass. This was to warm him up after sitting out in the cold and not being able to move.

As our friendship grew, Derek would phone me: he had a machine that could be controlled by blowing in it – from turning the TV on to changing stations, and phoning numbers. Occasionally it would not be possible to get somebody to drive him to the away games, and he would ask me. I would end up driving his mini-bus, foregoing my role of travelling on the team bus. It stopped me from having a drink, which didn't hurt! I think our friendship reached new heights when he asked me to put a bottle under his blanket so he could go to the loo with my help.

That summer, my phone never stopped ringing – even while I was on holiday. Ian would wake me very early each morning. I don't think he had a holiday, as he was so keen to sign new players and get his team fit and prepared for the 1980-81 season. He signed:

- Rodney Fern from Chesterfield, where he had been leading goal scorer for three seasons. Before that, he played for Leicester City and was part of their FA Cup Final team in 1969; they lost 1-0 to Manchester City, but managed to beat Liverpool at Anfield on the way.
- Midfielder Jimmy Mullen from Sheffield Wednesday, who went on to be the club's captain.
- Ken Tiler, a defender from Brighton, who was also once at Chesterfield.
- Billy McKean from Peterborough United, who had also played at Brighton, Chesterfield and Mansfield.
- Ronnie Moore – for £100,000 – from Cardiff City, previously with Tranmere Rovers.
- John Seasman from Millwall.
- Tony Towner, a record signing for Rotherham at £165,000.

The amount of money spent by Rotherham on transfers was unheard of for a Third Division team; at the next chairman's meeting I went to, they were all asking me if I was mad – spending that sort of money for an untried manager.

By the time August came around, I could hardly contain myself with the excitement for the new season. I was a bit of a dabster for presentation, so I had the team kitted out with blazers, grey flannels and club tie; they started to look like a unit. Our first match was in the League Cup against Bradford. We lost 3-1 at home, with Gerry Forest scoring our goal. The away leg we drew 0-0, so were out of the cup – not a good start. The first league game was against Fulham at home. We drew that, with Ronnie Moore making his home debut and scoring. Gerry Forest scored the other. Next it was Blackpool (0-0), then away to Portsmouth where we lost 3-1, Mike Gooding scoring our only goal. The last game in August was against Huddersfield at home – we drew 0-0. So in our first four games, we had only picked up three points and we were fourth from bottom.

During this time, I had been travelling up and down the motorway on my own. But this changed when one day I went round to my mother's and father's house.

Incidentally, my father did not like football, but my mother and her family loved it. My father's friend, Bert Coker (who used to come and watch me play on Sundays), was there. He'd had a stroke, but was almost back to normal. I asked him if he would like to come with me to football, and he jumped at the chance. He ended up coming to most of the matches with me. He was great company: he had been an RAF pilot in the war, and had millions of stories to tell, which I had plenty of time to listen to on our journey to the games. One of the stories he told me was on his fifth escape from a Prisoner Of War camp. He managed to get to the docks, where coal boats from Sweden sailed. He waited until nightfall, and managed to board one of the Swedish boats. The crew hid him in a cupboard in the hold. They gave him food and water and closed the door. A little later, he felt the boat moving. The trip was about 36 hours. Eventually, the boat came to a stop. He felt the boat hit the quay as it tied up and engines off. Bert opened the cupboard door and ran up on to deck, shouting and shaking hands with the crew...only to find the ship had had engine trouble and returned to Germany. Soldiers were on deck and returned him to the P.O.W. Camp, where he stayed until four months later when the war ended.

Rotherham's first game in September was against Barnsley - a local derby. We had nearly 11,000 paying customers who saw us win 2-0, Ronnie Moore and Richard Finney getting the goals. Finney had joined Rotherham straight from school. Next, Swindon away, where we lost 2-1, Tony Towner scoring our goal. Then, Reading at home, where we again won 2-0, Ronnie Moore this time scoring both goals. It was after that game that I went to the players' lounge. All of the team were there with their families. The atmosphere was absolutely amazing: it was like a family party. The whole team had gelled.

I remember driving home thinking we were now going to be a very hard side to beat; I had goose bumps just thinking about it.

Rotherham's next game was away to Sheffield United in front of a crowd of 20,000. Rotherham were always underdogs to the Sheffield clubs. I had spent the Friday night up in Rotherham ready for the big game, which was being televised by Yorkshire Television. In the morning, I went to watch our youth side with my youth team staff. As with most teams, they were very dedicated. Mine were always pleased to see me and it gave me a chance to meet some of the players' parents. Can you imagine, if you like football, going straight from a youth team match to the hotel, where the first team were having a light lunch? They then went into a private room, where Ian gave them a team talk and I had a coffee in the lounge. After about 20 minutes, the players got on to the team coach and headed for Sheffield. I decided to drive myself, as I had to head back to Essex straight after the game.

When I arrived at Bramall Lane, the directors' car park was being resurfaced and I was sent to the other side of the ground. I parked my car and the man at the gate asked if I wanted to walk round the outside back to the boardroom, or did I want to walk round the inside, by the side of the pitch? The latter appealed much more to me. As I walked out on to the pitch, it was just like Charlton on my first game with Fred when I was nine: the crowd; the noise; the lush green grass. Suddenly, at the far end of the ground, I could hear my name being chanted. It got louder and louder. I headed towards the Rotherham supporters – running the gauntlet past the Sheffield fans. I stood in front of our supporters. The noise level was rising significantly. I just stood there with a lump in my throat. I applauded them and headed back to the directors' box.

We beat Sheffield United 2-1, Richard Finney and Mark Rhodes scoring. Mark was another from our youth side. After the game, Yorkshire Television asked me for an interview, which I gladly accepted. Martin Tyler was the interviewer and he asked me what I thought our chances were for the season. I replied that we would win the league and people should get their bets on early. Martin cut the interview and explained to me what I had just said, "I don't think you should say that," he said. "It's OK," I replied.

We started the interview again. He asked me the same question, and I gave the same answer. The interview went out that night. As I left, I could see the television crew shaking their heads.

Our final game in September was against Walsall, at home. We won that 2-1, with Ronnie Moore and John Seasman scoring. We had now moved up six more places in the league. The first game in October was against Exeter, which we won 3-1 (Ronnie Moore, John Seasman, and an own goal). Next we were away to Chesterfield, who were top at the time. They beat us 2-0. After that, it was Burnley away; we drew 1-1, Tony Towner scoring from the spot. Then Gillingham at home: a 2-0 win, Gerry Forest scoring and another own goal. The Chester at home (0-0); Colchester away (0-0); Oxford away (1-1). We played seven games that month, but only moved up two places.

It was about this time that Newport County – also in the Third Division – were making the headlines: they had won the Welsh Cup, which automatically put them into the European Cup Winners' Cup. They had John Aldridge, who was a prolific goal scorer and went on to be one of the all-time top scorers (while at Somerton Park, he averaged a goal every $2^1/_4$ games. He of course rose to prominence in the late 80s with Liverpool, where he was unfortunate enough to become the first player to have a penalty kick saved in a Wembley FA Cup Final – the one where Wimbledon surprised everyone by beating the team of the decade). In the first round of the Cup Winners' Cup in 1980, Newport played Crusaders FC of Northern Ireland at home and beat them 4-0 (the second leg away was 0-0). The second round was against Haugar Haugesund of Norway. It was 0-0 away, but they won 6-0 at home, which took them into the Quarter Finals; they were to play FC Carl Zeiss Jena of East Germany. Richard Ford, the chairman of Newport, and his wife Jan were friends of ours and invited me and my Jan (plus Ken, a director of Reading, and his girlfriend Helen) to the away leg. We flew from London to Frankfurt with the team, accompanied by an abundance of the British press. When we landed, the press were put on a separate coach. We drove to West Berlin and, once we went through Checkpoint Charlie and into the Eastern Sector, two men with long black leather trench coats boarded our coach. By the time we left East Berlin, it was dark and snowing and everything looked very bleak and grey – the only lights were the street lights, which looked a bit like the ones in the Michael Caine Harry Palmer films. We seemed to drive forever, but eventually we reached our hotel. It stood on a slight hill, surrounded by some ugly looking flats and a few shabby shops. It was very cold, so we quickly hurried into the hotel foyer. We were given our keys and told dinner would be served in 15 minutes. When we went in for dinner, we were ushered into a private room. We were given fillet steaks with fresh vegetables, followed by a lovely dessert. We later found out that the hotel's main restaurant served no such luxuries. As we finished our meals, the door suddenly burst open and the room became full of scantily glad girls and boys, all dancing. Our host apologised, saying there was a carnival taking place that evening. As it was two days until the game, the manager decided that as the team had been travelling all day, it would be okay to stay up for a little while longer!

Next morning, we were awakened early and, with the team, taken on a coach trip. First we went to the Carl Zeiss factory, world renowned for its optical business, where they made us all sunglasses. Then we went to the town of Jena, where we were allowed to walk in the shopping area. Jan and I wandered down a side street, where people came from nowhere asking us for jeans. Suddenly one of the trench coat men appeared and ushered us back to the coach.

By now, Len Ashurst, the Newport manager, was getting a little fractious because he wanted to start the team's training session. Eventually he had his wish, and the rest of us went back to the hotel. Earlier when we had looked out of our bedroom window, we could see the shops opposite all closed and empty. Now, one of them had a long queue outside of it, so Jan and I hurried down to see what they were selling. To our surprise, they only had small flowers in pots: nothing else. They sold out very quickly, leaving a lot of people very disappointed when they closed the shop.

That night, when the boys came back from training, we all met in the private room for dinner. We had just finished eating when the door burst open again. It was the same people but they had swapped costumes. The host again announced the carnival – telling us it went on for two days. It was the eve of the game, so this time the team had to go to bed. The rest of us took it in turns to stand outside the lifts and turn girls around and send them back downstairs. But the girls went outside, shouting up at the windows trying to disrupt the players' sleep. Eventually they left.

Next morning, the team did a little light training. It was very cold and snowing. The boys went back to bed in the afternoon; the rest of us were busy packing, as we were taking all of our belongings on to the coach to the game and heading straight for Frankfurt to get our plane after the match. The coach picked us up at 17.30, and again there was a fluttering of snow. It was very dark, but as we got near the ground, you could see the lights. The ground was already full to capacity; it had been since 15.00. When the team reached their changing rooms, it was like an oven. It must have been more than 100 degrees; you could hardly breathe. All of the windows had been sealed, but we managed to allow for some cold air to come into the room. Our party, all wearing yellow and black scarves, headed for our seats. To our surprise, we were all separated: Jan and I sat in one part of the stadium, accompanied by a Russian soldier each side of us. I turned around to see all of our friends in the same predicament.

The game started, and the home team scored first. Newport equalised before half time. During the interval, the soldiers told us to stay in our seats. The second half started and the home team scored again. By the time it came to the 90th minute, the referee was looking at his watch as Newport were on the attack. Tommy Tynan received the ball and scored. It was 2-2. I jumped up with delight, only to have a rifle butt rammed into my ribs and told to sit down. There was nobody to greet us after the match. No tea, no sandwiches. But we did not care. We sat on the coach and waited for the team. They boarded the coach to rapturous applause. On the way back, we lost our guides at the checkpoint and arrived back in London in the early hours.

Unfortunately, Newport lost 1-0 at home and Carl Zeiss Jena reached the final – only to lose to FC Dinamo Tbilisi in Düsseldorf.

Meanwhile, back in Rotherham, the Merry Millers played seven games. First, Millwall at home, where we won 3-0; Ronnie scored two and Phil Henson the other. We then drew 0-0 with Chesterfield, who were second in the league at the time. Next it was Charlton away; they were top of the division and we lost 2-0. But against Blackpool at home we won 4-0 (Ronnie scored a hat-trick and Mick Gooding the other). Fulham away was 1-1, Rodney Ferm scoring for us. When we went to Craven Cottage, the then chairman was Ernie Clay, a very dear friend of mine – a man who did not mince his words. He had been a tank commander in the war, and his tank had been hit. Although he escaped, the experience had left him a little deaf. As a result, he occasionally shouted. He was a very big man, and he once told me he used to be a bouncer, which I could quite believe. Malcolm Macdonald was Fulham's commercial manager. Supermac (as he had become known after putting five goals passed Cyprus while playing for England in 1975) signed for Arsenal in 1976, for a fee of £333,333.33. He played two full seasons for the Gunners, but suffered a knee injury in a League Cup match against (of all teams!) Rotherham at the start of the 1978-79 season, from which he was never able to fully recover. Having been born in Fulham and starting his professional career with the club, he applied to become their manager when the post became available. Ernie said he must be mad, but Supermac was given the job. His old post was advertised nationally as follows: "*Our marketing manager has committed business suicide by taking the manager's job; we therefore need a new one!*"

On the 22nd November, we played Boston away in the FA Cup first round, winning 4-0. Ronnie scored two, and Ashley Taylor and Peter Corr the others (the pair both came up through the ranks). The last game in November was against Newport, where we won 1-0 – Ronnie again. We were now in 10th place.

When I went up to Rotherham on a Friday, I would get Jim Bennison to see if our Saturday sponsor was a hotelier. If so, I would get him to book my overnight stay at that particular hotel – just to give a little business back. One such Friday took me to a hotel on the moors. After going straight to the club and then on to a dinner where I was the guest of honour, I finally went to this hotel. It was snowing and very late. The porter let me in, and I ordered a large brandy. I was drawn by the big fire in the lounge, where I could hear two people talking with American accents. They sat in armchairs by the fire, and I was invited to join them. They had been to see a heavyweight bout in Sheffield. One of the men introduced himself: it was Jake LaMotta, the Raging Bull. We talked for hours; he told me about his daughter, boxing in general, and also about some of his fights. When the porter drew the curtains, it was daylight.

December did not start very well for us: our first game was away against Plymouth Argyle, and we lost it 3-1 with Rodney Fern scoring our goal. We then played Barnsley at home in the second round of the FA Cup in front of 15,000 people and lost 1-0. Then things perked up when we beat Brentford 4-1 at home (Tony Towner 2, Ronnie 1, Rodney Fern 1). On Boxing Day, we travelled to Hull, where we won 2-1 (Mick Gooding and Phil Henson). The last game in December was at home to Carlisle; we won 3-0 (Ronnie 2, Rodney 1) and were now up to fourth.

I had been looking at home attendances over the years and regular as clockwork, the Saturday before Christmas we always had the lowest attendance of the year. I think it because either dad had to help with the Xmas shopping or they had to look after the kids while mum went. I decided to put a circus on when we played

Brentford. The circus was called Gandley Circus, plus we had Father Christmas and his Little Miler Elves. The circus had Cossacks, riders, cowboys & Indians, a fire-eater, clowns, a Western roper, knife thrower, trapeze act, speed juggler, and a dog show. The show went on from 1.45-3.15 – it even made the kick-off 15 minutes late. Our attendance was 6,000, which beat some of the earlier ones, so I deemed it a success.

After Christmas, some of the papers were talking about Rotherham as possible promotion candidates. But it was still January, and that month we had five games: first Gillingham away (0-0); then Oxford United at home (again, 0-0); next Newport County away, where we won 1-0 (Rodney Fern scoring); we played away to Huddersfield Town in front of 17,000 and lost 1-0; last game in January was at home to Portsmouth and we won 3-0 (Tony Towner 1, John Seasman 2). That month, the rest of the results went well for us and now we were third.

In February, we only played three games: Swindon Town at home (we won 1-0, thanks to a Mick Gooding goal); Sheffield United at home (we won 2-1, Ronnie and Tony Towner scoring); and Reading away (1-1, with Rodney Fern scoring for us). We were now second. It was during February that a friend of mine – Peter, who had a shoe factory in Italy, which is where he spent most of his time – asked if he could come to Rotherham with me to see them play Sheffield United. I had already organised a plane from Southend, as I had to be back at Croc's that evening. There was just Peter and myself flying there. We landed at East Midlands Airport at about 1200. A car was waiting for us and drove us to the hotel at Rotherham for lunch. We had a bottle of wine with lunch and a brandy in the boardroom before the game. We were quite jubilant after the match, having won 2-1, so we had a couple more brandies before driving to East Midlands Airport. When we arrived, the pilot was waiting for us. We walked across the tarmac on to the plane. The plane taxied out towards the main runway. It was dark and we had to wait for a large jet to land. Our plane then turned on to the runway. The engine revved, but suddenly the lights on the plane all went out. We had to go back to the reception area while the pilot tried to fix the plane. Peter and I naturally made our way to the bar to warm up. An hour and four more brandies later, the pilot came into the bar to find us. He explained that it could not be fixed until Monday. Peter and I were fairly insistent about needing to go home (nothing to do with the brandy). The pilot said in that case, he would need two strong torches as, at that time of night, the runway at Southend Airport would not be lit up. We eventually acquired the necessary torches and headed for Southend. As we made our approach into the darkness, the pilot told us to put our torches into each of the side flaps in the windows to act like headlights. We landed safely. I think the airport was all closed up. In the cold light of the next morning, I realised how foolish we had been.

In March, Rotherham played four games: Exeter away (we lost 2-1, Ronnie scoring our goal); Chester next, away (we won 1-0, Rodney scoring our goal. We now had 48 points and were still in second place; Charlton were top on 50 points); then we played Colchester at home and won 2-0 (Ronnie scoring both goals); next Burnley at home and we won 1-0 (again, Ronnie scoring). For the first time that season we were top of the table. The media coverage was quite intense, but exciting. Now, we were the team to beat!

Our first game in April was against Millwall away: we won 1-0, thanks to a Rodney Fern goal. We then played Charlton at home – a real needle match, as they were top at the time. We ended up winning 3-0 (Jimmy Mullen, Seasman, Fern all scored). The next match was something I'll never forget; even writing this now brings a tingling sensation all over. We were playing Carlisle and won 1-0 (thanks, once more, to Rodney Fern). I was in the Carlisle boardroom after the match when I heard this huge cheer coming from the changing rooms. There was a knock on the boardroom door, and a member of staff came in and walked over to me. He shook my hand and said, "Congratulations, chairman – you have just been promoted." All the other games that day had gone our way and we could not now be caught. It was a wonderful surprise.

I ordered champagne for the boys in the changing room, and went down to congratulate them with the bubbly flying all over the place. Outside, the Rotherham fans were chanting. Ian and his backroom boys – John McSevency and Barry Claxton came with me to greet them. The noise was deafening. I found Derek, who was delighted, to say the least. I had given him a glass of champagne, which he drank with relish. We all drove back to Rotherham on the coach; it was quite late when we arrived home, but the entire town seemed to be there waiting for us. The rest of that night was a complete blur!

There were still four games left and, although we were promoted, we had not yet won the Third Division title. On Monday, we played Hull City at home and drew 1-1 (Seasman scoring our goal). The following Saturday we played Brentford away and lost 2-1 (Ronnie scoring for us). Then on Tuesday, in front of 25,945 people, we played Barnsley away – a game they had to win to also clinch promotion. Barnsley, who were our neighbours, won 1-0 that evening and the party really got going as the Barnsley board were friends. There was now only one game left in the season. Rotherham had 59 points; Barnsley and Charlton both had 57. In those days, there were only two points for a win, so even if we lost our final game and Barnsley or Charlton won, there was still quite a margin of goals between us. It was in our hands.

The last game of the season was on 2nd May against Plymouth. They were lying fourth with 52 points. All my family came to the game: my mother and father; my children, Fleur and Chi; and, of course, Jan. Yorkshire TV was there for the ninth time that season.

After the first 45 minutes it was 1-1, with the ever-dependable Ronnie Moore scoring our goal. In the second half, with ten minutes to go, Rodney Fern received the ball with only the goalkeeper to beat. As the keeper came out, Rodney lobbed the ball over his head to make it 2-1. When the final whistle went, we were champions on 61 points. Barnsley beat Newport and

Charlton beat Gillingham, so they each had 59 points. Again, the festivities started straight away, with the Barnsley directors coming over after their game. In the evening, we had a party in our huge gym for all the supporters, with two bands and DJs. Plus we gave everyone a special celebration medal. A great night, but it was just the start.

At this point, I would like to mention three men, the type you will find at most football clubs, who keep the club going behind the scenes. I hope they won't mind me saying that they were senior members. They were: Albert Wilson, our groundsman who achieved miracles with our pitch; and our voluntary helpers, Walter Pratt and Charlie Smelt.

Unless you have been involved with a success like this, you can never appreciate how it affects so many people's lives. British Steel and the Coal Board both invited me to tour their local factory and mines. In their letters, they said that the output production was higher than any other of their factories or mines, and that this was due to the Rotherham workers coming back to work elated with our results. Jan came with me on both tours.

I happened to be at a meeting of Yorkshire Football Chairmen in York and mentioned that I was going down the mines. The chairman of Sheffield Wednesday said he had never had an opportunity to do this, so I arranged an invite for him to come with us. When we arrived, we had to change into miners' overalls. We were then taken right to the coal face. Those boys certainly earned their money and it was a real honour to have been invited. It was the same at British Steel: Jan and I were taken up a gantry overlooking the very hot bubbling steel. Our guide dropped a piece of wood towards the heat, but it burst into flames before it touched the bottom. We were told that a few of the workers had committed suicide from there. The company then took an ingot from that batch of steel and presented it to their family. Both companies gave us a wonderful welcome and it made us appreciate our supporters even more.

Everywhere you went in Rotherham, you could see congratulatory signs and flags – and pictures of the team in shop windows. I was invited to most of the celebrations, which I tried to attend. When I returned to Essex that week, I was amazed by the number of people who had been following Rotherham. I had congratulations coming from everywhere.

It was June by the time everything started to settle down. All the players and staff were taking a well-earned rest, but I had returned to Rotherham to organise prices for the coming season and pick the new home and away strips. Next I had decided to move to Yorkshire, as I felt I needed to be on hand for the club – plus I had forgotten to mention I had married Jan in February and she was pregnant. We set up home in Worsbrough, just outside Barnsley. Also living in the area were Arthur Scargill, Charlie Williams, Jack Charlton and Mick McCarthy, who still played for Barnsley at that time. Strangely enough, I had not had my usual abundance of calls from Ian. In fact, I had not had one. I put this down to the amount of work he had done during the season and he was just having a rest.

I was still having drinks being sent over to me whenever I went into a bar or restaurant in Rotherham. On one occasion, my secretary from Croc's, Jackie, came up for the weekend. Her car had broken down, so she came up in her young brother's beat-up jalopy - I think it was a Ford Capri. Jan and I decided to take Jackie out for a meal. Jackie insisted on going in her brother's car so that I could have a drink without worrying about driving. It was a Saturday night, and we drove from Rotherham to Worsbrough, which was about 15 minutes away. All of the restaurants were very busy. I had been recommended to a very popular steakhouse. When the three of us went in, it was packed. I managed to squeeze through to the bar and ordered a drink, which the manager insisted on paying for. People were queuing for a table. The manager enquired as to whether I would be dining. I replied that I would. The next moment, a table was being lifted over people's heads and placed just inside the restaurant. We were invited to sit at the table. Everybody had to walk around us, either to get in or out of the restaurant. Immediately, drinks were being sent over to us from Rotherham well-wishers. The manager insisted on picking our menu for us, plus the wine. Needless to say, every time I went to put food in my mouth, a Rotherham supporter would come up to talk to me. It was all very flattering. When we had eventually finished our meal, I asked for the bill but the manager insisted that it was on the house. We thanked him and made for the door. The manager walked with us. We said goodbye at the door, but still the manager walked with us out to the car park, which was full. The manager looked at some of the expensive cars. As we walked towards them, he kept rushing to a car to open the door. I kept saying "Not this one," as we proceeded to the next expensive car. Again, I had to tell him it was not ours. Eventually we reached the Capri. His face changed; he looked puzzled. Jackie unlocked the driver's door, and the manager held it open for her. The three of us climbed in the car. The manager still had his mouth open, not sure what to do or say. He then started cleaning the windscreen with the sleeve of his jacket. As we drove out of the car park laughing, he was still standing waving with his mouth open.

The rise in status from Third to Second Division meant the ground had to have a safety certificate. Many alterations were made, including new barriers – and part of the Tivoli End ripped up. On the Millmoor Lane side, the seats were open to the elements, so I had a stand built to cover them. It was all very hectic that summer.

Chapter 9

Crazy Horse

It was during June that I received a phone call from a reporter asking me if I was aware that Ian Porterfield was moving to Sheffield United. It came as a great surprise. I tried phoning Ian, but he was never in! So I phoned Reg Brealey, the chairman of Sheffield United, who confirmed that he would like Ian as his manager. I am afraid I was quite hurt and annoyed at the same time. There is no loyalty in football and contracts do not seem to be worth the paper they are written on.

Eventually, Ian confirmed he was going to Sheffield United. At that point, I knew if his loyalty was not with Rotherham, I did not want him. Reg took Ian from me when I wanted to keep him. I had put £300,000 into the team in a bid to win promotion. I was shocked when Reg poached him because it came out of the blue, and I sued him for compensation and won.

I now had to find a new manager for Rotherham.

While all this was going on, I had bought three greyhounds. I named them 'Rotherham United', 'Millmoor Boy' and 'Tivoli'. Rotherham went on to be a very successful dog.

Originally I raced them down south, with Rotherham making the front of the racing paper. When I moved to Yorkshire, I put the dogs in a kennel locally. The nearest race track was Owlerton in Sheffield. Rotherham United was entered in a race there. The procedure is for a new dog to the track to two trials before to get an average time, the first races usually having the slowest times. Down south, Rotherham United had been used to an outside hare and six dogs racing. In Sheffield, it was five dogs with an inside hare. Rotherham United's trial did not go very well, as he tried to run to the outside. He suffered knocks on both occasions, so his time was not a real indication of what he was capable of. He was booked in for the first race the following week. In the meantime, Rotherham United's trainer trialled him at home with an inside hare. He soon got the message.

The race the following week caused quite a stir in the local papers: Rotherham United racing at Sheffield! Jan and I took Derek and his mum and dad, plus a few of his friends. The odds for Rotherham United were high – 15/1 – as he had the slowest time. The trainer assured me that Rotherham United would go a lot faster after his work-outs. There was a lot of laughter at his time and friendly banter from the Sheffield crowd. But sure enough, Rotherham United came out of the traps like lightning and won by 14 lengths. The crowd were in uproar. There was a steward's inquiry, but the result was upheld. A very nice evening was had by all. Rotherham United went on to represent Yorkshire, together with Kevin Keegan's dog, in an inter-county competition.

While on the subject of greyhounds, I must tell you a story that happened while I was working in the butchers. An old boy used to come in one of my shops. He said he kept greyhounds. He invited Jan and me to see one of his dogs in action. It was at a flapping track – that's one that is not regulated by the National Greyhound Racing Club, you and the dog just go along and are entered. Jan and I went in his car with the dog sitting with Jan in the back. When we arrived, the man told us to wait in the car park and take the dog for a walk. We were still outside when the first race started. The dog heard the bell ring and the running of the hare; he was uncontrollable, jumping wildly up and down, pulling on his lead and barking. Eventually, he old boy came out and asked Jan to parade the dog as he was in the next race. The dog became very excited as was led around by Jan. He was put in his trap. When the race started, I don't think his paws touched the sand for about 12 feet. He was like a rocket, leading by 10 yards at the first bend. But at the second bend, which was very tight, he went straight into the barrier and crumpled in a heap. The man ran out and picked him up. The bookmakers were shouting at him and people were booing. We put the dog in the car and went straight home. The dog was okay.

Later I learnt that the man worked for a very well-known trainer, who had gone away for a couple of days and left the man in charge. That particular dog was in the final of the Greyhound Derby and should never have been out of the kennels. Plus the track was a lot smaller and tighter, which the dog was not used to. We never saw the man again.

Anyway, back to Millmoor. I started looking for a manager in earnest, as it was getting close to the time when the players would need to start training again. At that time, secretaries of football clubs were the lifeblood of the game; they seemed to have a secret pact and knew everything that was going on. They had their own meetings, plus they were always in touch with each other enquiring about where away teams should stay the night before a game, or where the police would meet the coach coming to the ground. It sometimes became very personal, as most secretaries had been in their positions for many years and where all on first name terms.

On one occasion, because of the financial situation of most clubs, an emergency meeting of the chairmen was called to try and improve the situation. I was on holiday at the time, so had to fly back into Birmingham for the Solihull meeting.

I was greeted by my secretary, Jim, who informed me that one of the chairman, who was an accountant, had written a very thick dossier on 'How To Make Your Club Viable', which was why the meeting had been called. Jim also confided in me that the chairman in question's secretary had informed him that they were losing £10,000 a month. All the FA Committee were there, with the former Labour MP, Jack Dunnett, as chairman, and Jimmy Hill in attendance. Needless to say, everybody was trying to help.

But after the opening address and explanation of why we were there, I stood up and put a question through the Chair asking if it was true that the dossier had been written by a chairman whose club was losing £10,000 a month. Everybody at the top table started to fidget, but nobody answered the question. So I asked it again. This time, the chairman in question stood up, so I asked him the question direct. He replied that I was correct. As there seemed little point in reading through the dossier, I and a few other chairmen retired from the meeting and I flew back to my vacation.

When I returned from my holiday, I went to see Jim Benson to find out how things were going. He asked me about the manager's job, as the media where driving him mad with names flying about all over the place. Jim asked me if I had ever thought about Emlyn Hughes as a manager, as he had heard he was mentioning management to the Wolves secretary, where he was still playing. What a great acquisition he would be: ex-England captain; ex-Liverpool captain; European Cup and League medals galore; and currently enjoying his first stint as a team captain on BBC's A Question Of Sport. I asked Jim to make some discrete enquiries. It resulted in me meeting Emlyn with Jim in London. Can you imagine? I had only ever seen him playing some great matches on TV, plus when I was a guest of the FA at the Milk Cup final. Emlyn was really natural and very excited about the position. We discussed everything – from money, moving house, and a company car. After a couple of hours, we shook hands on Emlyn becoming the next Rotherham manager. We decided to keep everything quiet until the press conference, which was scheduled for two days later. The night before, Emlyn stayed at a small hotel outside Sheffield. I had dinner with him, and afterwards I phoned Derek and told him I was bringing someone round to meet him. Can you imagine Derek's face? He was full of approval and sworn to secrecy. Again, Emlyn was great with him. The following morning, I drove to the ground. The media were already there. They were ushered into the sponsor's lounge and given tea and biscuits. I had arranged for Emlyn to turn up a little later. We went to Jim's room, and Emlyn put on his Rotherham tie and jumper. There was a back door into the sponsor's lounge. Emlyn stood outside while I went in and gave a quick introduction of our new manager – not mentioning his name. Then Emlyn walked in. It was a complete surprise as nobody had mentioned his name in connection with Rotherham before. Then there were spontaneous cheers and claps of approval: the media were like putty in his hands.

Mind you, I very nearly went down in history as the man who killed him off, along with another legend, Bobby Moore.

Rotherham had won promotion and our first game of the new season was going to be against Fulham. We found out that Fulham were playing a pre-season friendly in Ireland and I thought it would be a good idea to take Emlyn to watch the game, so we could see what we might be up against.

I was also in regular contact with Bobby at Southend, and when I mentioned we were going over for the game he asked if we could pick him up on the way. So I chartered a twin-engine plane from East Midlands, stopped off at Southend airport to pick up Bobby, and then we went over to the match.

We had a good night and flew straight home, but on the way we got caught in a really bad storm with lots of rain, thunder and lightning. I don't know whether the door of the plane had not been secured properly, or whether the storm was just that bad, but all of a sudden the door flew off and dropped into the Irish Sea below us. The plane was rocking and we all thought our number was up. The pilot said we had about 20 minutes flying time until he could get us to land at Southend, so we told him to just do his best and carry on. Obviously we made it back safely, but I couldn't help wondering what people would have thought of me if I'd been responsible for wiping out a couple of legends.

We had a Football League meeting around June. Each league sat at their own table, but as we had not yet played a game in the higher league, I was on the Third Division table with all my friends. It was during that evening that I was invited to have a drink with Sir John Smith, 'the dapper chairman' of Liverpool. He was a very nice and well-educated man. He asked me whether I would be interested in joining The Sports Council. I thanked him and told him I was honoured, but I did not feel I could do it justice what with all my other commitments. It was also during this time that one of the directors of Sheffield United, who was on the International Committee, told me it would be very useful to swot up on my French because the committee was looking at me to join. I never heard another thing about that, but it was nice that Rotherham United and myself were now so highly regarded.

One of the other perks of being a chairman was you were given two tickets for the FA Cup final – in addition to the club's allocation. That year, I took the Third Division cup (which, incidentally, I had to insure as it was leaving the ground) and drove to Essex. I knew where to find Fred – at the Tyrells Hall Club in Tilbury. I took the cup in, which he paraded round as if he had won it. When he returned to the table, I produced his long overdue FA Cup final ticket. Fred could not believe it; this was something he had always dreamed about. I rounded off the day by picking him up in the Rolls-Royce, giving him his Rotherham director's tie to put on, lunch before the game at Wembley (rubbing shoulders with all the football elite) and then enjoying the match from the best seats in the house. It was like taking a child to a toy shop. Fred said afterwards that it was one of the most memorable days of his life and I must confess, seeing him so happy, it was one of mine too (even though the match itself finished 1-1 after extra time).

Once Emlyn had completed all of the formalities, he started the job in earnest. He told me he was quite happy with his squad at the moment, so not to expect requests for players.

I had decided to take an office in the club for the rest of the summer as there was so much going on. There was no Premiership then, so the First Division was the top league. The club was suddenly attracting visitors and well-wishers nearly every day. It was great for me because most of them were past and present footballers. Mike Summerbee turned up one day while I was with Emlyn. Mike was one of England's and Manchester City's great wingers, who was now selling hand-made shirts. From that day on, he would measure me up and make my shirts. He became a regular visitor.

Brian Tiler, the former captain of Aston Villa who took them to the League Cup Final in 1971, would call in regularly for a coffee. He started his footballing career with Rotherham (playing over 200 games for them) and was now in insurance – but trying to get back into football in some capacity. He would bring Don Megson (the father of Gary) along. Don was the former captain of Sheffield Wednesday, making over 440 appearances for the club. He had recently returned from managing Portland Timbers of the North American Soccer League. He also helped take his team to the FA Cup final, so you can imagine I just sat there spellbound listening to Emlyn, Brian and Don talking about matches gone by.

Emlyn told me he had taken on a scout and asked me to meet him. To my delight and surprise, it was Harry Gregg, the former Northern Ireland and Manchester United player, who was voted best goalkeeper of the 1958 World Cup; Harry was sometimes referred to as 'The Hero of Munich', because he helped to pull Bobby Charlton and Matt Busby from the plane during the air disaster that year. Another great man, who called a spade a spade. Harry took Emlyn and myself to Halifax to see a 16-year-old goalkeeper, who we later signed for £12,000. His name was Bobby Mimms, who eventually went on to play for Everton and Spurs, and also Blackburn Rovers at the start of 'the Jack Walker revolution'. When he was first with us, I would often pick him up outside his digs as he was waiting for his bus. A very nice lad.

While football was in recess for the summer, I would often drive down to Croc's, which was still a thriving business. On one of these occasions, I was invited to a showbiz party in London's Portland Street. My driver took me to the party with instructions to pick me up at 12. At the party, there was an immaculately dressed African gentleman who looked like a fish out of water. When it was 12, I walked outside and it was raining. The man was trying to hail a taxi. I offered him a lift, which he gladly accepted. He had us take him to the Sierra Leone Embassy. As he stepped out of the car, he asked me if I had a business card. I gave him my card, and he closed the door.

While I was still in Essex, I received a phone call from the African gentleman inviting me to lunch at The Ritz the following day. I accepted and met him in the bar at 1.00pm. He introduced himself as Eric Adoso. After lunch –over coffee – he asked me if I knew anything about diamonds. I said I did not. "Could you find someone who does?" he enquired, "It might be interesting." I agreed to try when I got back to Yorkshire. I phoned my accountant, who gave me the number of a jeweller in Hatton Garden. When I phoned him, he was expecting the call. I explained about Eric, and he warned me to be very careful as this might be a con. I asked how I would know if it was not. "See if he has any blue-white stones," came the reply. I phoned Eric and asked him what the jeweller had suggested. "Can you meet me at Gatwick Airport next Monday? I will be coming back from Sierra Leone." He gave me the flight number and I agreed to meet him. That Monday, he came out very quickly, explaining that he had Diplomatic Immunity. We got in the back of the car and headed for London. Eric pulled out a piece of tissue paper from his pocket. Inside was what I can only describe as pieces of broken glass from a car window screen. He told me they were uncut diamonds. I dropped Eric off at the Embassy and stayed in London that night. The next morning, I phoned the jeweller and took two of the stones round to him. After inspecting them, he confirmed they were both blue-white stones. He now insisted that it must be a con.

I phoned Eric and said we should meet. I explained about the jeweller, and Eric proceeded to tell me what he was trying to achieve. He said a high ranking member of the Sierra Leone Government thought there was going to be a military coup and he wanted to get his wealth out of the country and live in England. Eric asked me to go to Sierra Leone, but I again explained that I knew nothing about diamonds. Eric said, "It does not matter. We will select them for you, so long as you have a buyer." I phoned my jeweller, who was happy to oblige, so long as he only had to pay for them once he had had a chance to check them out. So I cautiously agreed.

My first job was to obtain a visa for Sierra Leone. There was a queue outside the Embassy when I went to apply, but I was told to go to the front and ask for Eric. He came out and ushered me into a side room. He took my passport, and returned five minutes later with the necessary stamp on it. "You will need to have your tropical jabs," Eric informed me, and directed me to the hospital which was just down the road. So I went straight there, paid the fee, and had the required injections.

I went back to Essex to play in a showbiz charity football match the following Sunday. So I stayed at my flat in Grays. My sleep that night was quite uncomfortable. I awoke the next morning, and my testicles were aching. To my horror, they were like two oranges. By lunchtime, they were like coconuts and I could hardly walk with the pain. I phoned my doctor, who told me it was a reaction to the injections – one of which was for elephantiasis, which had caused this. He prescribed me a very large truss to wear, which would take the weight out of the coconuts. But even with that, I was still walking like Gabby Hayes (Roy Rogers' sidekick with the beard), and I was supposed to be playing in the football match in two days' time. Fortunately, when it came to the day of the game, they were now the size of tangerines and I definitely wanted to play. I was in goal, and used a smaller truss.

Pre-match, the lads took a few shots at me and I felt quite comfortable. My defence were all ex-pro footballers, so I did not have to do much until the second half when our centre-half passed the ball back to me. As I bent down to pick the ball up, my truss pinged off leaving me screaming in agony. The ball trickled past me into the goal.

The following Tuesday, I met Eric and we flew to Sierra Leone. When we arrived, we were taken straight through customs and into a black Mercedes. It was evening and everything looked orange and dusty. Once on to the mainland, we drove through high-walled gates and went into a big house. I was introduced to a gentleman – not sure who he was. Then we went back into the car and I was taken to the Bituman Hotel with a beautiful room and balcony overlooking the sea. Eric had stayed behind at the house, so his driver and an associate carried my case into the room. They said they would pick me up in the morning, and then left. I had a long, hot shower. When I came out, my case had been unpacked and my clothes put away. On the balcony was a rather large lobster salad with a bottle of white wine in an ice bucket. That evening I slept very well.

The next morning, I was waiting in the hotel foyer when the car came to pick me up. Eric was in the car. We drove out into the country to what looked like a small fortress. There were guards outside. They all had turbans on. I went into the inner sanctuary, where there were two men – also in turbans. They produced a bag of what looked like broken windscreen pieces and spread them on a black cloth. They told me to pick 10. They told me that they were a present for me. They then produced another bag of broken windscreen and told me that this was what I was to give to the jeweller. I took my 10 pieces, and Eric took the other bag.

I spent another day being shown the sights, and then flew back to London. Again we walked straight through customs into our C.O. Plated car.

I met up with the jeweller the next day. He was amazed at the size and amount in the bag. I felt my role was over. I never heard from Eric or the jeweller again.

I returned from my African adventure to find the team were back in training. Emlyn had taken on as chief scout, Arthur Turner, and Barry Claton, our physio, as his assistant. Our first league match in Division Two was to be against Norwich City, who had just dropped out of the top flight. We were now having even more visitors to Millmoor – mostly football player friends of Emlyn's, plus media people all wanting to interview him. As he was still doing A Question Of Sport on television, this was all good for promoting Rotherham. Our season tickets were selling very well, plus Emlyn had arranged a very good shirt sponsorship deal with Patrick Football Boots. By the time of the first game, the whole team was buzzing.

On the day of the match, I arrived at the ground early to soak up the atmosphere. The TV cameras were there: they interviewed Emlyn, and then me, at about 2.00pm. Just before Emlyn went down to the dressing room, we were in his office having coffee when the phone rang. It was his old manager at Liverpool, the legendary Bill Shankly. He spoke to Emlyn, and then he asked to speak to me. First, he told me all about Emlyn and how to get the best out of him. And then he went into his love of football and all that it stood for – this was the man who once famously said, "Some people believe football is a matter of life and death...I can assure you it is much, much more important than that." By the time he had finished talking, I felt I could have gone out and played. It was something I will never forget. Emlyn told me later that Bill kept a daily diary and put everything in it – even weather details. Needless to say, Emlyn followed suit. Sadly, Mr Shankly passed away the very next month.

The Norwich game ended with us winning 4-2, which was a great start to the season. As the season progressed, though, we lost more than we won and by the time we had played 15 games, we were seventh from bottom.

I had a phone call from London Weekend Television asking if they could follow me with cameras for a 'weekend in the life of Anton

Johnson' feature. I was very flattered. Before our next home game, they started following me around Smithfield Market at 3.30am on Friday, and came down to Croc's where I stayed until 8.00pm and then headed for Rotherham. I was driven by Peter, one of my staff.

The next morning, the cameras were waiting when I came down for breakfast at the hotel. My commercial manager joined me, and we went over the commercial finances of the club. After that, I was taken to the club by Peter, followed by the LWT TV van. They filmed me talking to Jim Bennison and Emlyn. I then went back to the hotel for lunch. It was just as I was returning to the ground for the game that the interviewer from LWT asked if I could drive the Rolls myself, with my fur coat on and smoking one of my very large cigars. They were going to play my new record, Hey Baby, over the footage. The interviewer sat by my side with a microphone asking questions while I drove. I reached a roundabout and, unfortunately, I had forgotten to put the window down; as I turned, I rammed the very large cigar right down my throat. I nearly choked! Then, when we arrived in the boardroom, the interviewer asked me to light the cigar again. I did so while I was talking to the directors. The cigar proceeded to unravel like a huge flower, until I could no longer see over it. Needless to say, they cut that part of the weekend. However, extracts of that film were used later when I was the subject of a *World In Action* programme.

One day, while I was at the club, I received a phone call from my mother. She was very emotional and crying.

When I had lived at home, we had a headmaster and headmistress living at one side of us. They had two beautiful blonde-haired, blue-eyed daughters who were a lot younger than me, and I had seen them grow from screaming little girls into pretty teenagers. Their mother's sister had married a rich Arab and went to live in Saudi with him. When one of the girls was 19, she was invited out to see her auntie. The girl readily agreed and flew out to Saudi on her own – supposedly to be met by her auntie. Somehow, they missed each other and the girl went missing for over a week. Eventually she was found wandering the streets. Her mother and father had flown out to look for her. The girl looked as if she was in a trance when they found her, she could not even talk to her parents. They brought her back home and she did not talk to her sister either – she just went straight to her room. The next morning, when her mother took her up a cup of tea, she had hanged herself. She had left a letter which told how she had been bundled into a taxi while waiting for her auntie. She was taken out into the desert, where there were a lot of Arab men who did all sorts of diabolical things to her. She was kept there until the men had had their fill, then they dropped her back into the town. In her letter, she apologised to her family but said she could not live with herself.

That was what my mother had phoned to tell me.

By the time Christmas had come, we were sixth from the bottom. We had played Liverpool at Anfield in the Third Round of the Milk Cup in November and lost 1-0, with Ronnie hitting the post. In the league, we had lost to Wolves (2-0), Newcastle (5-1), Leeds (1-0), Derby (3-0) and Blackburn (3-0). We had only beaten Chelsea at home (1-0), so it was not the best of starts. That December, the weather was Arctic and no games were played for about a month. Snow was everywhere on New Year's Day, when I received a phone call from Emlyn. He asked, as we had not played for a while, whether we could join Nottingham Forest and hire a plane and play a couple of games in the Channel Islands – one in Jersey, and one in Guernsey. I readily agreed.

The day before we were due to go, Brian Clough phoned me and said he was not coming to Jersey, so would I mind looking after the Forest lads. I was delighted to oblige. One of the Forest team at that time was Martin O'Neill. We arrived to warm sunny weather. It was a great three days.

When we arrived back to East Midlands Airport, Emlyn asked for a meeting. He told me he needed two new players to improve the side. He already knew who he wanted: one was Joe McBride, a left-winger for Everton who was also a Scottish Under-21 International; the other was Gerry Gow, then of Manchester City and formerly with Bristol Rovers, who was an absolute powerhouse in midfield. By the time we bought them, it was the end of January and we had not won a game since Chelsea on 27 November.

Our first game with the new boys was on 2 February, when we beat Derby County 2-1. Four days later, we travelled to Ninian Park, Cardiff, and pulled off our first away win of the season (2-1). But we were still hovering dangerously above the relegation zone. On 9 February, we beat Grimsby Town 2-1. Four days later we played Cambridge and won 1-0. The following Tuesday we played Shrewsbury and won 1-0. On 23 February, we beat Wrexham at home 2-0 and then Crystal Palace at home 2-0. On 6 March, we played Oldham away and won 3-0 and now when you looked at the Second Division table, we had moved up to third behind Watford and Luton. In just 32 days, our league record was: played nine, won nine; goals for, eighteen, against, three; points, 27. We had climbed 14 places in just over a month. Emlyn's new boys had really paid off and our achievement was appreciated throughout the Football League. Not only had we captured the popular imagination, but had provided conclusive proof of the excitement created by the newly introduced three-points-for-a-win system.

During the 1982-83 season, more and more football clubs seemed to be getting into financial difficulty. One such was Bradford, and I was asked to assist in the restructuring of the board and the club's finances by one of the major accountancy firms who had been called in. I am glad to say there were some local people who came forward after being lifelong supporters and saved the club. It took a few meetings, but it was all worth the effort that everybody put into it.

Another club was Wolverhampton Wanderers. Again, a major accountancy firm had taken over. There were two or three consortium enquiries about it. The problem Wolves had was it owed £250,000 in VAT. It was never my intention to take over Wolves, just to help. I found out that one of the few assets the club had – apart from the players (which, incidentally, you could not put on a balance sheet) – was the freehold of the Supporters' Club, which sat opposite the entrance to the ground. I approached the chairman of Wolverhampton Council, who was an ardent supporter. I explained the situation and that the club had been given three months to find the money.

I am not sure whether the people of Wolverhampton – particularly the Wolves supporters – knew what happened next.

The chairman called an emergency council meeting. He told me to bring the secretary of the club to the council offices for when the meeting had finished. The chairman came out of the meeting, clutching a cheque for £250,000. The council had bought the freehold of the Supporters' Club and given it back to them for a peppercorn rent. Wolverhampton council and its chairman certainly saved the day.

Also during 1982-83, I had a meeting with some local businessmen who had asked to see me. The basis of the discussions was they wanted me to name my price to sell Rotherham. It had never come into my head prior to this. They explained that it was their town and their football club. In fairness, they had all been sponsors in one way or another. I said I would think about it. While this was going on, Brian Tiler came to see me. He told me that the chairman of AFC Bournemouth – Harold Walker, a local solicitor – had been speaking to him and asked if I could do anything with the club. I met Mr Walker, who was a lovely man, but very frustrated. Even though Bournemouth won promotion, he said he did not think the club would last until the end of the season. The local council had thrown out their scheme for a market at Dean Court, and also declined to help in giving real help over lottery sites at the beach and town centre. Harold said that they had experienced frustrations with the powers that be over the years (unlike Wolverhampton). By the time I met him in early 1983, Bournemouth were also struggling in the league.

Tiler said he could resolve the Bournemouth problems if I bought the club. I had another meeting with Harold in a hotel in London and asked him if he just wanted financial help. He said, "No, I want to retire from football." He wanted out, and said I could buy his shares for £150,000.

By this time, the pressure for me to sell Rotherham was growing. I had another meeting with the local businessmen. As I was contemplating buying Bournemouth, I was assured that Rotherham would be in good hands and they were prepared to pay me in cash if required. I called a meeting of my office staff to explain the situation, but to my surprise they were already well aware of the situation and some had even negotiated new salaries – even though I had not struck a deal yet.

By mid-January, Rotherham were mid-table on 32 points. I felt that if I was going to sell, now was the right time. As I was trying to help these clubs, I was getting lots of media coverage with one of the national newspapers referring to me as the 'King Of Clubs'. I had a phone call from Michael McGarry, the chairman of Derby County. He asked to meet me because of all this coverage. I asked if we could meet where we would not be noticed, so we arranged to meet in a hotel in Nottingham. I asked Michael not to tell anyone, because people thought I was trying to buy football clubs. He told me he would bring along his secretary, which should have rung some alarm bells. I arrived at the hotel to find that a small conference room had been booked. Michael and his secretary had already arrived. They explained to me that the players' wages had not been paid for two weeks, and they had exhausted all possible means of raising money. Michael was at his wits end. I said, "The first thing we must do is pay the wages; I'll see what I can do." The next thing I knew, I was handed the keys for Derby and Michael and his secretary left the room. As I collected my thoughts, I phoned Jim Bennison. He told me I could not pay the wages myself, but that one football club could loan another money. I asked him to see how we stood at the bank, and that I'd phone him in the morning.

As I left the conference room, to my surprise the media were waiting for me in the foyer – cameras flashing and reporters asking questions. I did not answer them, driving away in silence to the understandable frustration of the press pack.

I stayed in Derby that night. When I came down for breakfast, the morning papers all had photos of me from the night before and were saying I had bought Derby County.

After breakfast, I drove to Derby's ground. Again, the press were waiting outside. I went straight into the secretary's office without speaking. He was already there. I phoned Bennison, who said we had sufficient funds to pay Derby's wages. I let Jim speak to the Derby secretary. They had the money sent the same day by one of the money couriers; everybody was paid that same day.

Over the next few days, I made the Derby boardroom my office. The phone never stopped ringing. I had the young lady in the office making sure no press had access. There were plenty of would-be investors and buyers, which I asked the secretary to vet.

One of the people who showed interest was my friend Mike Watterson. Mike was the man who brought the World Snooker Championships to Sheffield's Crucible Theatre and into thousands of living rooms. He managed most of the Canadian players and was thought very highly of. He came to the club with his advisers. They went through the books, met McGarry and worked out a deal. The only thing I did after that was organise for the ram that advertised the all wool carpets to go on to the pitch with Watterson to be introduced to the fans prior to the first home game. Rotherham had its money paid back by Derby shortly thereafter.

A few months later, Mike and I sued some national newspapers successfully for alleging that he was a puppet for me in the purchase of Derby, which was untrue.

On another occasion, a chairman who had befriended me after our first chairmen's meeting became my mentor in showing me the rights and wrongs of the job. He called to ask if I could meet him. He lived in London, and we agreed to get together at his house the following evening. At that time, I had a chauffeur called Harry. Harry took me to the very upmarket area where he lived. I was greeted at the door, and invited into his study-come-library. We chatted a little, then he said he had someone who wanted to speak to me. He rang the number and spoke to someone, saying "Anton's here, I'll pass you over." I took the phone and a loud bellowing voice said, "Hello, this is Robert Maxwell. I wonder if you have time to come to see me." I said I had, so he told me to come to Maxwell House in Wapping for a coffee. For those who don't know, Maxwell was a Czechoslovakian-born British media proprietor and former MP for Buckingham, who rose from poverty to build an extensive publishing empire that included the Daily Mirror. As I was about to leave, he too was putting on his coat. I asked if I could drop him somewhere. He accepted my offer. He was having dinner with the Thatchers, so we dropped him off at Downing Street.

When I arrived at Maxwell House, I was ushered into a lift. I then had to change and change to another lift, which took me to the penthouse. There, I was greeted at the door by some young Asian ladies who apologised and said Mr Maxwell had been delayed but would not be long. I was offered a drink. Fifteen minutes later, the door burst open and a very large, imposing Robert Maxwell shook my hand. I told him how impressed I was with the penthouse, and he showed me around. The tour included the largest Jacuzzi I have ever seen: it took up a whole 30' x 30' room. We then went into a room which had a panoramic view of London at night. We sat down and were served drinks by the Asian ladies. Bob (he told me to call him that) enquired about my football involvements, as he thought I had bought the other clubs.

He told me he had bought a club (Oxford United), but really wanted Manchester United. He asked me whether I thought it was for sale. (I later phoned United's chairman, Martin Edwards, who told me to ask Bob to phone him. In 1984, Bob did attempt to buy United, but he refused to pay the price that Edwards put on the club.)

Later on in the evening, after Bob and I had drunk a little more and became very talkative, he brought out a brown envelope. In it were photos of look-a-like Bob Maxwells. He asked me to choose one. I do not know the reason for this but, sometime later, Bob's body was found floating in the Atlantic Ocean. It had just been revealed the Mirror pension fund had been plundered. Within days, he was buried on the Mount of Olives in Jerusalem. While the official verdict was 'accidental drowning', some have suggested suicide, murder and a whole host of other theories. I had picked out a pretty good lookalike. I realised soon after that I may have sent a man to his death. I have good friends in Israel who say they saw Bob there after his alleged death.

Another time, Doug Ellis came to one of Rotherham's home games and asked for a private chat. He had been to a couple of my games so I knew him vaguely. Doug was very distraught and told me he had been ousted as chairman of Aston Villa. I asked if he wanted to be a director of Rotherham, but he said no, he wanted Villa back. A few days later, he contacted me with the name and phone number of someone on the Isle of Man, a scrap metal dealer who apparently owned shares in Villa. Doug asked me to see if I could do anything to help. I obliged by making a few phone calls to the Isle of Man. I spoke to the person a few times and made him aware of the financial liability involved in owning the club, and he backed off. Weeks later I had a call from Doug telling me he was again chairman of Villa, and thanking me – for what, I'm not quite sure – and saying if there's ever anything he could do for me, not to hesitate to contact him.

After closing time, the local Italian restaurants in Essex took it in turns to finish off the evening by hosting meals for one another.

Over the years, from working late in my night clubs, I was accepted as one of the gang and would frequent late night meals with them. On one of these occasions, I was approached by the Italians: they wanted to see Juventus play Villa in the European Cup, but all the tickets were sold out. So I phoned Doug, who told me to come up. I met the Italians at a hotel in Birmingham, and we all went to the ground together. While they waited outside, I went in and returned with tickets for a box - which Doug had left for them. The boys could not believe the great seats they had. I said I would meet them in their box after the game, and went to the boardroom and joined Doug. When the game was over (Juventus beating Villa 2-1), I had managed to talk one of the Italian directors into taking two of the Juventus team up to the boys' box. You should have seen their faces. Even after all these years (and despite the fact that Juventus went on to be beaten by Hamburg in the final), they still talk about it.

Around this time, I was asked by another football friend if I could take a look at 'for sale' Wigan. The main man at Wigan then was Ken Bates – assisted by Bobby Charlton (now Sir) – who was selling his shares so that he could buy Chelsea. I flew into Manchester Airport and was greeted by Bobby (one of my all-time heroes). I spent a little time at Wigan, and met Ken in London, but nothing materialised (though of course Ken did famously buy Chelsea - and all their debts - for £1, and spent the next 21 years with the club). I mention all this now only because, at the time, the media did all the speculating.

Back at Rotherham, everybody was waiting for me to sell. Even Bennison had been offered a deal to retire. I went to see Derek Dalton in his iron lung. Strangely enough, although you think you are very important as chairman, in fact supporters are only truly interested in results. So Derek was quite happy with the situation as he thought Rotherham would improve. I spoke to Emlyn who, like most managers, was only interested in the team and felt chairmen were a necessity, and that's all. So everything was amicable: I decided to sell my Rotherham shares. Bennison contacted the FA to let them know.

As the deal was going through, I contacted Harold Walker at Bournemouth and agreed the purchase of his shares. The Rotherham deal was taking a little longer than expected, so I was advised to buy Bournemouth in a company – rather than my own – name. I was also advised that I should not become involved in the day-to-day running of the club until the Rotherham deal was finalised.

I decided to give Brian Tiler the role of chief executive. He was delighted with the opportunity to return to football and he started work straight away. Bournemouth were hovering near the bottom of the Third Division, and one of his first actions was to give Don Megson the manager's job. I would occasionally go down to Bournemouth as a supporter to watch matches while the Rotherham deal was going through. I would go down the day before a game and stay at the Royal Bath Hotel. As at Rotherham, I would go down to the ground the next morning. Two people who really impressed me were John Kirk, the physio, who did a great impression of Tommy Cooper (and I should know!) and one of the coaches, who I could really relate to: nice and chatty, but who only wanted to talk football. There were only a few other people I spoke to who were like that: Bill Shankly; Sir Bobby Robson; and Malcolm Allison. I knew of the coach from his footballing days at West Ham: it was Harry Redknapp. We got on very well and he would take me to see his young sons play on Saturday mornings. I kept a very low profile at Bournemouth games, although the locals would act as if they knew what's what.

I received a phone call from a chairman who must remain nameless. He told me he had backed the consortium who bought Rotherham, but there was a lot of in-house fighting about who should be chairman. He asked if I would stay on as chairman – in name only. For a while, I agreed.

It lasted longer than I thought. I would go to some of the games, but did not become involved in the day-to-day running of the club. Jim Bennison had now left, so I was not privy to what was happening at the club. I normally went to the games Rotherham played down south. One particular match was against QPR. I had been invited to stay with the team on Friday night at the Whites Hotel in Bayswater. That evening, I received a phone call from Terry Venables. He was the manager of QPR and very successful; he led them to promotion to the First Division that season, and had just guided them to the FA Cup final (where they lost in a replay against his former club, Tottenham). I had met Terry on three previous occasions: twice in the Milk Cup – we won 2-1 at home, and drew 0-0 away – and drawn with Rangers at home 1-1 in the league. We had got on very well. His dad, a very nice man, had a pub, which Terry occasionally helped him with.

I was at a match when QPR beat Arsenal 4-3 and Terry invited me to a club. We stopped at his house on the way home and before we went in he told me that he'd just told his wife he was leaving her, and we were going in to collect his belongings. Thanks Tel.

On this Friday evening, Terry picked me up at Whites and took me to Tramps nightclub. We were sitting at a table when we were joined by George Best and his girlfriend and former Miss World, Mary Stävin. The conversation naturally involved George's football career. He was playing in the USA at the time, but wanted to return to England. He was past his best, but he was still a crowd-puller (when he signed for Hibernian in 1979, gates increased dramatically; the attendance quadrupled for his first match). Bournemouth were now out of trouble as far as the league was concerned, but were lacking a bit in sponsorship and gate receipts. After Terry dropped me off back at the hotel, I phoned Brian Tiler about my conversation with George.

Brian then spoke to George, and I sent £74,000 to the San Jose Earthquakes for George's release. The following week, he played for Bournemouth. The average gate before then was 3,000-4000; the first week George played, we had 9,500 paying spectators, plus all the extra sponsorship deals. George played five times for Bournemouth, but he paid for himself. Plus, he brought a little colour to the Cherries. I kept in touch with George, and often met up with him in London when he was looking after his son, Calum. Whenever he was babysitting, he never had an alcoholic drink: he idolised his son. He told me how disappointed he was with the hierarchy at Manchester United for not keeping a tighter rein on him.

Tiler – with the help of Don Megson, and ably assisted by Redknapp – kept Bournemouth in the Third Division that season. Everybody was delighted – especially Harold Walker, who said it was as good as winning promotion. In the meantime, Rotherham were losing a lot of games and, after the 4-0 defeat to QPR on 19 March, Emlyn was asked to resign. He refused and was therefore sacked. George Kerr took his place. George had had success with Grimsby, leading them to promotion to the Second Division. When he arrived at Rotherham, they were third from bottom and he had 10 games to help them avoid relegation. At this time, I was still chairman in name. The final game of the season was away to Leeds United and we had to win to stay up. I went to the game, but the score was 2-2. Rotherham hit the post and bar. It was a very sad day for me and all of Rotherham; it was the polar opposite of the previous season. As far as I was concerned, a lot of the problem lay in the fact that Rotherham had sold Paul Stancliffe (a great solid centre half) for an undisclosed figure to Sheffield United, who he then helped to clinch promotion to Division Two.

During Emlyn's time with Rotherham, I remember he had wanted to sign the former Northern Ireland and Manchester United striker Sammy McIlroy from the Tampa Bay Rowdies. So we flew to Miami. But after meeting Sammy, Emlyn changed his mind. Still, we went to watch the Rowdies play and Emlyn was called on to the pitch, introduced as the ex-England and Liverpool captain to a mostly European crowd who cheered their approval. That evening we had dinner with Gerd Müller, the man whose winning goal against England in the quarter-finals of the 1970 World Cup in Mexico brought about a change of government! Gerd owned a restaurant and bar in Miami. On another occasion, I was with Emlyn in his office when he was into his second series of *A Question Of Sport* and they'd just had Princess Anne on the show[1]. The phone rang, Emlyn answered, laughed and put the receiver down. "Somebody's having a joke. It sounded like Brian Tiler. He said the Queen has invited me to dinner." Five minutes later, the phone rang again. It was the Queen's private secretary, and he really had been invited to dinner. He told me later that one of the other guests was the first woman Governor of a UK prison, and they ate steak and kidney pie! The last time I saw Emlyn was in London at a cricket match. Supermac was also there. We had a couple of beers and all said our goodbyes, not realising that sadly Emlyn was to pass away a year later – leaving behind a beautiful wife, Barbara, and two great kids.

---

[1] In an earlier show, Hughes had erroneously identified a photograph of a heavily-muddied jockey as John A. Reid, only to be told it was Princess Anne. When she came to the programme, she made it plain she was not offended by this and was put on Emlyn's team – who then caused a national debate when he defied protocol and put his arm around her.

Chapter 10

Final Whistle

As 1983-84 season began, Bournemouth and Rotherham were both in the Third Division.

During the summer, Southend United were put up for sale. The chairman had died and his sons did not want anything to do with it. It was my local club and, after I became involved in football, I had always thought what potential it had. Although in hindsight it was wrong, I asked one of my family members to enquire about Southend. There was quite a lot of things going on at the club; I think a number of people were jostling for positions there. I do not think anyone was fully aware of what was happening. Certainly no one knew of my interest at that time.

Before doing anything else, I contacted Rotherham. The unfortunate thing there was I was still owed money by the purchaser and I was under contract with them to assist the club until they had resolved their problems. This meant that I had to stay as chairman, in name. So as the season started, I was still listed in the Rotherham programme as chairman.

I was having lunch one day with Ernie Clay at Fulham. It was just a social visit, as there was no football being played. We would meet occasionally. He was a bit of a father figure to me, and knew everything that was going on in the game. Earlier in the day I had a phone call from Brian Tiler, who asked to see me. He arrived at Fulham just as Ernie and I had finished lunch. Ernie gave us the use of his boardroom, and said he would send in some coffee.

Brian was a very capable chief executive for Bournemouth. He put the board together and ran the club as a business. I really had nothing to do with it. But on this occasion he told me he was sacking Don Megson and was going to advertise for a new manager. He actually already had someone in mind for the job, but asked for my opinion. I told him as far as I was concerned, I would look no further than Harry Redknapp; I felt he was ideal, and – having been the youth team coach under the previous manager, David Webb – he knew the players inside out. Brian asked, "You're quite certain about that?" I replied "Yes."

The next day, the papers all had the story of Harry being made manager. I was delighted for him. There are many people in every walk of life who are very talented but never have their opportunity; I was glad to play a part in giving Harry his chance. I knew he would make it - he was so keen.

I decided to buy shares in Southend. In the interim, the board had sacked the manager, and by this time people were aware of my intentions. I was invited by the Southend board to sit in at the interviews for a new manager. They picked Peter Morris – a very nice man who told me later that he thought there were too many chiefs and not enough Indians at Southend.

Eventually the contract was signed and I had shares in the club. Again, because of my situation, I did not get involved too much; I was busy sorting out my problems.

Southend, Bournemouth and Rotherham were all in the Third Division. Rotherham promised to release me from obligations as soon as possible, but that did not happen before they had played both Bournemouth and Southend. When I went to these games, I would just sit in a neutral director's seat, feeling a little uncomfortable but enjoying it all the same. It was while all this was going on that I received a phone call from Rodney Marsh in the United States. He told me Bobby Moore was helping him coach, but really wanted to return to England – could I help?

He put Bobby on the phone, who said he did not mind what he did. So I ended up giving him the commercial manager's job at Southend. Harry Redknapp, Brian Tiler and I met Bobby in Bournemouth when he arrived back in England. Harry and Bobby had of course played together at West Ham. The four of us sat down in the foyer of a hotel, and I was spellbound just listening to their stories. Brian knew I enjoyed meeting football people and one time arranged for us to meet Tommy Docherty. 'The Doc' has the ability to make you laugh before you even sit down; he has such a dry sense of humour, and regaled us with countless football stories. It's no surprise to me that for the past 20 years, he's made a living as an after-dinner speaker and media pundit. In 1967, after leaving Chelsea, he became the manager of Rotherham. One particular story he told us was his way of dealing with a wayward youth team player: when he really annoyed him, he waited until he was sat on the loo before calling them in to his 'office'. He said he never had any more trouble from the player after that!

Bobby soon became a huge success at Southend and had the sponsors eating out of his hand. He was very obliging and a complete gentleman; one of the nicest people I have ever met, in fact.

Eventually, I was released as chairman of Rotherham and was able to relax a little more. Peter Morris had been captain of Ipswich when Bobby Robson was manager, so he and Bobby had lots to talk about, which I often sat in on. One morning I was having coffee with them in the boardroom when the phone rang. It was the manager of Orsett Green, the Sunday League team that I played for. He said they were two players short for Sunday morning, could I find anybody? I said I would try, but I would need signing-on forms. The manager agreed to drop the forms off at the reception at Southend, and told me where to take the forms if I managed to find someone to play. After I put the phone down, Bobby turned to Peter and asked, "Are you doing anything on Sunday?" "No," Peter replied. "You have got your two players," Bobby said.

I said nothing to anybody about this, and I met the pair of them on the Sunday at the Orsett Cock pub in the car park. The game was an 11.00am kick-off. We arranged to meet at 10:15. The two climbed into my car, and we drove to the ground, which was five minutes away. We were the last ones to arrive. Bobby and Peter just walked into the changing rooms with their bags. Bobby said: "Alright, chaps? Where are our kits?" You should have seen the rest of the team's faces. Even more so, those of the opposition!

After the game, we all went to the local pub. Bobby and Peter were great. They signed autographs and spent an hour with both teams. Quite recently, I bumped into a couple of the team and they still talk about it.

In January 1984, Bournemouth were drawn against holders Manchester United in the FA Cup. The game was to be played at Dean Court, and there was an air of excitement at Bournemouth. I went down on Friday and met with Harry and Brian, who were quite relaxed about the situation.

On Saturday, the ground was full to capacity, and the television cameras were all there. I was in the boardroom just before the game when the secretary came in and said George Best wanted to speak to me. George was working for the BBC that day. I invited him in, but he asked me to go out to the car park. He took me to the back of a Mercedes, opened the boot, and inside was a huge cutlery set, in what looked like gold. The inscription read, 'To George Best'. George asked me if I would buy it so he could have a bet on the horses. I said instead I would loan him some money. When I did, he insisted on me taking the cutlery, which I told him I would leave in the secretary's office. He never did come back for it, so we auctioned it off for charity. Years later, I met George in a club in Soho, where the barman told me he'd drunk a bottle of brandy before I'd arrived. George introduced me to his wife, Alex, and we had a photo taken together for old time's sake. The next week, he was rushed to hospital. I never saw him again. George was one of the all-time greats, if not the greatest.

Back to the game, and Harry had really got Bournemouth buzzing. I had only ever gone into changing rooms once before, and that was when Rotherham won promotion.

But on this occasion, I went down to the Bournemouth changing rooms at half-time. The team were playing so well, I said if we won I would take everybody on holiday. We beat Manchester United 2-0. Afterwards, Ron Atkinson kept his team in their changing room for an hour (the final minute of the match was delayed after fighting broke out on the terraces; the United fans were none too happy), and then made them get straight on their coach. The Bournemouth team had their holiday in Portugal. We were in a villa complex. I took my father, and we shared a villa with Harry, Brian, John Kirk and the coach Harry had brought with him from Weymouth. We had a great time. Everybody was singing their favourite songs at the villa. Harry gave a rendition of his father's all-time favourite, *In My Father's Eyes*. Harry's son, Jamie, said recently in one of the daily newspapers that, had it not been for the win over Manchester United, his father might not have been given his opportunity. So well done, Harry; I still believe he would make a great England manager.

It was not long after we returned from Portugal that Brian phoned and said – as had happened before – that the local people wanted to buy Bournemouth. It came as a bit of a relief, the thought of only being involved with Southend, so I left Brian to arrange for the sale to be sorted out. During my involvement with Brian, we would often travel all over the country to watch football matches – and even abroad. I had been with Harry and Brian on many occasions to watch games. After I left Bournemouth, I did not see so much of the pair of them. But had I still been involved with the club I would almost certainly have been with them in Italy on that dreadful day when Brian was killed and Harry ended up on a life-support machine[2]. I remember seeing a picture of Harry being

---

[2] In June 1990, Tiler was killed and Redknapp badly injured when a car smashed head-on into a minibus they were travelling in; the pair were in Italy watching that summer's World Cup finals.

stretchered off the plane with tubes hanging from his body. But just look at him now – well done, 'H'!

Meanwhile, Southend had not been doing so well, and one evening Bobby and I went to see Oxford play. We often went to midweek games together. It was really amazing how people reacted to seeing him. Bobby was always dressed immaculately, and had time for everybody and their requests for autographs. It was on the way back from Oxford that Bobby told me the board were considering sacking Peter Morris, and if this was the case he would like to put his name forward. He got his wish and became manager.

At this time, I was receiving plenty of flak from all angles. One of the situations involved the supporters' Xmas Club (where people paid money in each week and drew it out at Christmas). I was approached in December by members of the board of Southend saying funds for the Xmas Club were short. I asked how much, and they said £37,000. I found out that the money had been used by the club and not repaid (Keith, the Southend secretary, told me it had been used for wages when the club was running a bit short). I did no more than give back the money out of my own pocket; otherwise there would have been some very unhappy people. And that was the last I saw of the money.

The club was really in disarray because I had not stamped my authority on them straight away. People had retreated into their own little corners and were not helping each other. Peter Morris was right: too many chiefs and not enough Indians. Bobby came to see me and told me people were not pulling together, and he was finding it very hard to get on with his job, which was reflected in the results.

I had a brainstorm: unbeknown to Bobby, I phoned Malcolm Allison who I knew was a friend of his. I explained the situation and asked if I could pay him to come and help his friend. Malcolm said he would be delighted. I asked him not to say anything, as

I had not mentioned it to Bobby. I then just happened to say to Bobby that I thought Big Mal might help. Bobby agreed it would be a great idea; I think he felt a little like a fish out of water on his own.

I was still receiving plenty of adverse publicity in the press at this time. I had sold Bournemouth and left Rotherham, but the papers were saying I was the Mafia and taking over football. Nobody had bothered to enquire – it was all speculation – but it made good reading.

On another occasion, I was out driving when I noticed a car had been following me. I drove into a road which I knew to be a cul-de-sac. I let the other car go by, and then pulled across the road so the other car could not get out. I walked to the car. There was a driver and a passenger with a film camera. They did not deny anything. They said they were working for World In Action and, sure enough, a programme came out six months later painting a very black picture of me. Unfortunately, once it had been broadcast it was too late to defend myself. Nobody had come and asked for my side of the story. All of the people interviewed were either those I had sacked, or directors who lost their positions, so I was not flavour of the month with them. The programme said I was involved with the running of eight clubs; theoretically, they were right, but I was only trying to assist five of them. Because of all the attention, I was summoned to FA headquarters. Again, all the media were there. I went into a 'behind closed doors' meeting. I explained what had been going on in full. After the meeting had finished, the FA held a press conference and said they were happy with my explanation.

By now I was becoming a little disillusioned with football: everybody seemed to be stabbing me in the back. People who had been so-called friends and others I had helped in many ways, including some of those who had worked for me, had all turned. The internet was just coming into its own then, and devoted supporters of the clubs I had been involved with took the opportunity of having a real go at me on different fan sites. I do not blame them; they did not know all the facts.

I was still going to football matches with Bobby and now Malcolm - mostly midweek games in London. After one of these, we met our girls and I took them all to our local fish restaurant in Grays, Mumfords. One day, Bobby repaid me by inviting me out to lunch – he told me he wanted me to meet someone. It was Sir Alf Ramsey. I cannot remember what I ate that day, I was totally mesmerised. Quite often, Bobby would tell me to make sure I was at the ground on certain days, and sure enough I was never disappointed: I think I eventually met most of the World Cup-winning team there.

One morning, while Bobby and I were in the boardroom, the phone rang and Bobby answered. He went into a deep, serious conversation. He told me after it that was Indira Gandhi, the prime minister of India, who had invited him to open a new stadium there. Not long after that, Mrs Gandhi was assassinated by two of her bodyguards.

While all my problems were going on at Southend, nothing prepared me for what happened next. My mum and dad were friends of Sir Fred Pontin, who generously allowed them the use of his penthouse at his hotel in Torremolinos every winter. The hotel used to be called the Pontinental, but was changed to Bel Playa. My parents would go from January to March. This particular year, my mum phoned to say my dad had suffered a stroke. I immediately flew to Malaga. I arrived at Bel Playa to be told that my mum was at the hospital. I went straight there, and when I saw my dad I was completely shocked by his appearance. He did not know who I was. My mum was naturally distraught and looked very tired. She told me the specialist who was supposed to see my dad had not turned up. It was now 8.00pm, and my mum had been there since 7.00am. I went down to the hospital's reception, and they told me the specialist had gone home. After lots of arguing and shouting, they eventually let me speak to the doctor on the phone. He apologised and said he had not been told about my dad, but would return early the next day.

I took my mum back to the hotel. She told me that my dad had fallen out of bed twice at the hospital. Once she was in her room, I went straight back to my dad. Sure enough, he was lying on the floor. He also had large wads of cotton wool in his ears. I later learned he had complained about the noise next to his room; it was the lift, so they had tried the cotton wool, although there were plenty of other empty beds. I put my dad back in bed, and just looked at him and held his hand. Twice he turned over and would have fallen out of the small bed had I not been there. Eventually, the lights started going out. The man in charge of the private hospital told me I had to leave. I said I wanted to stay, but he said I must go. I refused, and said I just wanted to sit with my dad. I offered to pay for a nurse to sit with him to ensure he did not fall out of bed. He still said no, and that I had to go. Again I refused. Fifteen minutes later, I saw a blue light flashing through the window, then in walked two policemen. I was taken to the police station, where I explained to the desk sergeant about my dad. He offered me a cigarette and said, "Don't worry; your father will be all right." They let me go, so I hailed a taxi and was back at the hospital in 15 minutes, to find my dad on the floor. The lights were all out, so I put him back in bed and sat holding his hand. A few minutes later, the blue lights were flashing again. This time they put me in a cell. The sergeant said he had told the hospital to keep a check on my dad, and if I went back again I would be in serious trouble. They let me out after an hour and drove me back to Bel Playa. The hotel was used by many pro-football teams for a short break in the winter. It was also one of Ron Atkinson and his wife's haunts. I went to the bar. A young man came and sat with me. He knew who I was and he'd heard all about my dad. He spoke with real sincerity and, if anything, a little spirituality; he certainly hit the spot. It was very comforting, and we spoke until it was dawn. The young man was Iain Dowie, someone I have true respect for.

The next day, I phoned Jan and asked her to arrange for an air ambulance with dad's doctor. It arrived around 5.00pm with a doctor and a nurse. Dad was taken to the airport, stretchered on to the plane with mum on board. We flew to Southend Airport, where an ambulance was waiting. He was rushed to hospital. His doctor told me, apart from the stroke, he had been severely dehydrated and had needed over three pints of fluid. I am glad to say that dad lived another 20 years after that, with all his faculties.

Southend problems put paid to another ambition of mine: during that season, I had become close friends with Terry Venables, and he had invited me to some of their First Division games with QPR. The most memorable was watching them beat Arsenal away. I had also got to know the QPR chairman, Jim Gregory. Jim was thinking of selling Loftus Road for a property development and was prepared to sell me the club. My dream was to take them to play at Southend where I could put football on every week: First Division one week, Third the next, with a reduced season ticket for both. I had spoken to Terry about it, and I also spoke to the FA, who said that so long as both teams had their own chairman and directors who were independent from each other, they could not see a problem. My problem was the people at Southend, so it never went any further. Jim was left to stay in charge of QPR and look for a different buyer, and Terry went on to manage Barcelona before becoming a chairman several years later at Portsmouth, where Jim was then in charge.

My love for football was purely that: there was never any intention to try to make it into a business. I never took chief executive wages, which would have been allowed. It was pure and simple: I just loved football – from going to top games and watching kids on Saturday morning, and still playing twice a week myself.

When I was at Southend, the youth team would play home games at Roots Hall under floodlights. There were never many people there, mainly families. But there were two regulars getting their drinks of Oxo or coffee at half time: me and Jimmy Greaves, whose son played for Southend's youth team along with my nephew, Matt Johnson. Some nights it would be freezing, with the wind coming in off the sea. But we were both there watching.

Things at Southend did not get any easier for me. There were too many commercial opportunities, which some of the hard-nose, no-names wanted to take advantage of, but I was in the way. One evening, I was stopped in the club's car park and told I could earn £$^1/_2$M if I relinquished the reins at Southend. You can imagine what I said. Unfortunately, it did not end there: one day, Bobby phoned and asked me to meet him at a pub. He told me he wanted to see me because he did not trust what was happening at the club. He said people were going around at the club asking if they could find any dirt on me, and told me to watch my back. This really took me by surprise. And poor Bobby was not having the best of times; the games were going against him, and he had mentioned in confidence about his health.

The inevitable happened. On 22 October, just after 6.00am, there was the knock on the door. The police came in, went through every room and drawer, filling up cardboard boxes and taking them to their cars. I was bundled into the back of a Black Maria and driven to Southend Police Station where, by some coincidence, press photographers were waiting. I was locked in a cell for 36 hours – at one point, questioned in the middle of the night by two beer-smelling detectives. The next morning I was questioned again. They wanted to take my photo and fingerprints, but my lawyer said "No," as everyone knew who I was anyway.

As you can imagine, the press had a field day. The charges the police brought against me were: stealing a television from one of the supporters' rooms; stealing £600 over 16 weeks from the boardroom raffle, which meant I stole £40 a week after my initial payment of over £300, 000 into the club. I was released on bail pending further enquiries. While all this was hanging over my head, we had another visit; this time from the Yorkshire Police.

Same procedure, only there was no paperwork left in the house because Essex Police had it all. Again, I was locked up in the middle of the night. Two detectives came to my cell, also smelling of beer. One of them had a piece of paper in his hands. "If you sign this, we will let you go home," he said. I looked at the paper. It said I had been misappropriating funds from the Rotherham lottery! I replied that I had not done any such thing and would not sign it. "If you don't sign it, we will take you to Leeds' nick and make sure you are put in a cell with either a psychopath or a gay," they warned. I still refused. Just as they closed the door, I shouted to them to come back. As they came back in the cell, "Could you make that a gay," I said. They door slammed loudly, and they left.

The next morning, they came back into my cell. They told me they had Jan upstairs and I could see her before they took me to Leeds. Jan was five months pregnant at that time. She was sitting in a small office. "We will leave you alone for five minutes," one of the detectives said. I explained to Jan what they had said. "What are you going to do? You're not going to sign it, are you?" she asked. "No. I will have to go to Leeds," I said.

The detectives returned. "Come with us now." I was taken back down to the cells to collect my belongings. The detectives took me to the back of the police station, where a van was waiting. "Last chance – sign now," they said. "But I have done nothing," I replied. "Okay. You can go home," they said, and allowed me to go. Jan was still on her way to the car park. As you can imagine, it was quite extraordinary, but again it had been a field day for the press: a real assassination job. As I reflect back on it, I think the whole thing was a set-up. They certainly did a great job of ruining my credibility and reputation.

The recent phone hacking scandal amuses me because I know my phone was bugged when I owned Southend. My phone should have been cut off because I stopped paying the bill – but the service continued for three years! I think it was all part of the plot by the Football League and the police to discredit me.

Two months later, I received a letter from the Yorkshire Police saying no further action was being taken and they were closing their files. But they had done their job, whoever instigated the investigation. People still remember the first articles when you are arrested, and by the time the follow-up information clearing your name is printed, it makes two or three paragraphs in the newspapers. And even then, it would still be a case of 'there's no smoke without fire'. You just cannot win.

In my local, where I used to be the centre of attention, I had now become a leper; people turned their backs on me and left me plenty of space at the bar. It did not stop me going in there: I had done nothing wrong. One evening, a chap came into the bar with some friends. He came over and shook my hand, and insisted on buying me a drink. He then proceeded to tell everybody that I had saved his wedding.

Some months earlier, I had been in my accountant's office and one of the girls there was crying. It was Friday and she had just been told that no wedding cars were available for Saturday due to a double-booking. She was inconsolable. At that time, I had two Rolls-Royces; Jan used one, and I had the other. I offered them both to her. She thought I was joking, but was happy when I brought the two cars round to her that night. I had arranged for my two doormen to dress appropriately, to decorate the cars, and then chauffeur the bride and bridesmaids. It certainly made the young lady's day, and the bridegroom had not forgotten. The boys stayed in the bar with me for the rest of the evening. It gave me quite a lift after all I had been through.

On another occasion prior to my arrest, I had been approached by the local newspaper, the Evening Echo. A young man, who stood no more than 28 inches tall, had been doing the Duke of Edinburgh's Award. It was his ambition, when he reached gold, to go to Buckingham Palace in a Rolls-Royce. I duly obliged by taking my two cars round so he could choose one. I knocked on the door and his mother came to the door. She invited me in, and we went through to the living room where I was greeted by the young man in a special high chair. He was assisted to the front door, where he picked the silver car. I am glad to say I helped to make his wish come true.

I was eventually charged with the two supposed thefts from Southend, and was given the opportunity of going to the local magistrates' court or the crown court in Chelmsford. I decided on the latter, as I felt the other could have been a hung court.

We were two weeks into the case, which was heard by a jury. The prosecution called Jan to the witness box. She was very heavily pregnant at the time, and the stress had taken its toll. She had to be rushed to hospital, so the trial was suspended. The trial returned to Chelmsford after Jake was born. Jan was again in the witness box, and Jake was in his carrycot in an adjoining room – looked after by the court usher, a very nice lady. Jan was feeding him herself, so at one point we had to adjourn for this. The trial went on for about three weeks. Every lunch time, I was locked in a cell. One day when Jan was giving evidence, we arrived early and had a coffee in the cafeteria. One of the prosecution team approached us and said we should not be sitting together. We had just come from home and had been in the car together for over an hour!

The trial eventually came to an end and I was put down in the cells while the jury retired. There is never any certainty about a verdict, however innocent you are, and it made me wonder about people in earlier days who were accused of murder and, if found guilty, were hanged. My jury took one hour and 30 minutes to reach their verdict. I was found not guilty on both counts. After all the days and weeks with this cloud over my head, I felt quite emotional. Before leaving court, I went to the loo. Two of the jury were in there; they shook my hand and said they were never in any doubt about my innocence. The judge in his summing up had also expressed an opinion about it being a farce. There were people in Southend who had a lot to answer for. I know who most of them were – some were supposedly my friends, but things change when greed kicks in.

I was now considering my position. My love of football was understandably waning. All the time I was involved with the game, it was costing me money. I now had four children – Fleur, Chi, Ames and Jake – who needed supporting. I was approached to sell my shares in Southend to a development company, to which I readily agreed. But when it came to the sale, I was told I would get my money only when flats had been built. I felt these people were not using their own money, so it went no further. Over the next few weeks, I was still being hounded by the press and also had people coming up with all sorts of other schemes to buy the club – still no money upfront, though. The local paper had plenty of fans' letters having a go at me. You cannot blame them, because most of them were convinced that what they had read in the papers was true. When I went to home games, supporters would be hurling abuse at me. I thought to myself, I do not need this – life is too short. You put your own money into a club, but have to accept that supporters are fickle. Any chairman would tell you that. If the team are losing, it's 'sack the manager' or 'get your cheque book out'. Unfortunately for managers and chairmen, it is all about results and not long term planning.

There were also some very hostile professional businessmen who were doing everything in their power to get rid of me. They attacked me about shares and numerous other legal issues, which meant I had to go to lawyers to defend myself. In the meantime, I turned my back on the club to let them all get on with it.

Another director, who was a friend of mine, resigned. He said it was disgusting what they were trying to do with me and he would have nothing more to do with it. I fought these greedy people – and believe me, they had no morals. I found out later that they were the ones who had called the police to have me arrested. After two years of fighting, I had spent £500,000 on legal fees. I was told the greedy ones were using club money to help their case against me in the finish. I just walked away from the whole thing, losing my investment, shares, and the £37,000 I had given to the Xmas Club. But it was such a relief: I didn't have to deal anymore with these people, who deserved each other. I would still meet Bobby Moore, who had been a real friend throughout my problems.

On reflection, I was lucky enough to meet some of the greats in football, which I will always cherish. There were also some unexpected meetings – such as Elton John in the small boardroom at Watford. Elton and I were having a drink after a game – Watford had beaten Rotherham 1-0. Anybody who knows Elton is aware that he is football mad. He asked if Emlyn would be coming into the boardroom as he really wanted to meet him. He kept looking at the door, waiting for Emlyn to arrive. Sure enough, Emlyn did burst into the room. He just casually said, "Hello Elton," and came straight over to me to complain loudly about the referee not allowing us a penalty!

Another musician who became a friend while I was helping Derby was Roy Wood, the multi-instrumentalist and founding member of The Move, ELO and Wizzard. I used to play snooker with him, and at that time he told me he was not busy. I tried to talk him into playing some gigs, and he said he would think about it. He told me to phone him later. After a couple of weeks, I tried him again, but he said "No." He told me he was too nervous.

There were many other personalities who would come to the games, including a certain MP who would have two armed bodyguards with him; you never knew what sort of ne'er do well you might bump into at football – and I should know!

But the enjoyment I have had far outweighs the problems, and I do not regret a thing. There is a saying:

"There is my version. There is your version. And then there is the truth!"

And here is another truth. People have often asked me if I ever encountered any match fixing, and although I ran an honest ship I was once offered the chance to try to alter the course of football nature while I was at Rotherham.

We were joint bottom of the table and I had recently sacked Emlyn Hughes, and our chances of survival were looking bleak. I was walking to my car one afternoon when another car pulled up and a burly Irishman jumped out and came over to me. He said: "If you want to make sure your team stays up, I can arrange it, but it will cost you £50,000." He then handed me a piece of paper with a phone number on it and told me to call that number. I managed to find out that, somehow, an opposing centre half and centre forward could be paid to have an "off" day. However, I wasn't prepared to become involved in anything like that, so I let it pass and did not call the number.

We needed to win our last game of the season, against Leeds, but unfortunately we drew and were relegated. I was left wondering what might have happened if I had made the call – and the "investment". But as I said, I would not do anything dodgy. Of course the fans were not pleased, and I was lucky to get out in one piece after that final game, as I went to the toilet and found myself surrounded by four angry fans. I didn't mention the visit from the Irishman in case they took their anger out on me.

Chapter 11

Extra Time

After the dust had settled, I realised there was more to life than just football. I was completely consumed by the game and had a general disregard for everything else. It was now time to get my life back on track.

The first thing I had to do was move from Southend, as reporters were still shouting through my letterbox because I would not answer the front door. I had to jump over the fence in the back garden to get away from them.

Through a lawyer friend, I was told about a snooker club that was having financial problems and could be acquired quite cheaply. It was in Ollerton in Nottinghamshire. After paying all my legal fees, money was a bit tight, but with a little help I managed to find the deposit.

The place was called *Cue Corner* – a large, two-storey converted Co-op store. Downstairs, there was a bar and what they called 'a concert hall', plus six snooker tables to the rear. Upstairs, there was another bar and 10 more tables. The place had a very nice entrance, plus a huge car park.

I went looking for accommodation while the family stayed in Southend. Ollerton was predominantly a mining village and most of the locals worked in the coal industry – what was left of it. I arrived just after the miners' strike, and the scars were everywhere. It was a picket line in Ollerton that saw the first fatality of the strike - Yorkshire miner David Jones was crushed to death shortly after the walkouts had begun. Some houses were daubed with the word 'Scab', cars were damaged and whole families ignored each other. Women were still arguing with each other in the streets, and some men were crossing the road to avoid each other. On the face of it, it was not perhaps the right time to open a new business there.

The village had two pubs and another social club. It was the tradition on Saturday for the ladies put on their finery and be paraded through the village by their husbands, also dressed to kill. They would stop in each pub for a drink, and finish up at the social club for a dance.

Ollerton also holds the distinction of being close to the first UK Center Parcs site, which helped a lot of the families in the village to obtain work.

I eventually found a row of three cottages, on the edge of the former RAF Gamston airfield, and I managed to do a deal with the farmer and took all three. Two were later used by some of my staff. You could see the A1 from the bedroom windows, but it was far enough away not to hear any noise from the traffic. The nearest town from the cottages was Retford.

Once the family were settled, I could start promoting *Cue Corner*. First, I needed my own professional player for the club. Not too far away lived the Canadian Bill Werbeniuk, who had reached the quarter-finals of the World Snooker Championship four times. In 1983, he was ranked eighth in the world. Now, he was past his best but still a name. I managed to get him to *Cue Corner* on a regular basis, and he would always bring a few snooker faces with him.

My first encounter with the club's committee was interesting. It seemed very much like 'the tail wagging the dog' - like most committees, they craved authority. So I went to a toy shop and presented them all with Sherriff's badges. After that, they seemed to loosen up.

At first, *Cue Corner* was not very busy, but slowly our customers increased. Sunday was usually a waste of time. Apart from two or three snooker tables being used, the place was invariably empty. One Sunday, I phoned a local agent and requested two scantily clad ladies who could work behind the bar. The response was instant: the next Sunday, we had an extra 20 men in. By the second week, we had them waiting at the door. By the third week, we had eight people serving behind the bar and Sundays were no longer a problem. I then went about increasing Saturday business. Most Saturdays weren't too bad, but many couples were still going to the social club. Of course, I had the concert hall, which was not being used to its full potential, and I started putting on Saturday night shows with celebrities such as comedian Mike Reid and the Barron Knights. We soon had people coming from far afield, so Saturdays were now nice and busy.

Cue Corner was a members' club, which meant guests had to be signed in. I had to make sure this was done properly, because I had ruffled a few feathers at the social club. One of the benefits of having a club licence is that you can have big pay-outs on the one-armed bandits and, because we had so many customers over the weekend, I was able to invest in another - which amazingly paid for all the staff wages and overheads. I had a problem with some of the people who played the machines, they were gambling addicts.

Sadly, I would have wives pleading with me not to let their husbands play on them, because they would go straight from work to the club and blow all their wages. It was very hard for me, but I had to insist to these fellas their wives had told me of their concerns and they couldn't play the machines. I don't think it actually stopped them. They just didn't come to *Cue Corner* to gamble any more.

My next challenge was to make Fridays more lucrative, so I decided to hold a 'disco-nite'. There were a lot of 18-plus kids in town and the nearest venue for them was in Nottingham, which was some distance away. I hired a well-known DJ from a club there to be our resident disc spinner. It only took a few weeks, and Fridays were full and buzzing. The rest of the week we had snooker, pool and darts tournaments, which kept us ticking over nicely. We were doing very well and I was happy with the business.

One Saturday morning, a black Mercedes pulled into the car park and three burly men stepped out. They asked to see me in private. We went to my office, where they asked if I could use any extra cash. Basically, they wanted me to take £100,000 a month and launder it for them. I thanked them very kindly, but said I didn't need any extra money. They left mumbling and grumbling, leaving a phone number just in case I changed my mind. I tore the phone number up as soon as the black Mercedes had driven out of sight.

Quite a few of the miners came from Newcastle and Sunderland, and Saturdays could get very boisterous. You may imagine I'm going to recount the endless fights between blokes. But most of the scraps involved ladies. I have seen as many as 20 punching lumps out of each other on the *Cue Corner* lawn, all stripped to the waist, with the men standing watching and cheering with a beer in their hands.

One of the saddest things that occurred while I was there happened to a couple who had five year old boy twins. One of the boys was sitting with the upstairs bedroom window open, watching a feather floating down. He leaned out to catch it and fell to his death. Six months later, his brother was riding a kids' motorbike in the family's orchard, hit a tree and was killed. The twins were the couple's only children. They moved away after the tragedies.

Something I haven't mentioned is that, apart from wine, my only other tipple is Special Brew. I can hear the gasps now, with visions of me sitting on a park bench with a ruddy complexion. I know the drink is normally associated with tramps or boozers down on their luck. But it wasn't at all like that with me. In my younger days, I would go drinking with friends who poured pint after pint down their necks and would forever be skipping to the loo. I found if I had a can of Special Brew[3], I could sip it slowly and it would still have the same effect as five or six pints of lager, but I didn't have to keep going to the gents. See, there is method in my madness.

When I was involved with football, I always made sure they had a case of Special Brew in the boardroom. In those days, not many people knew what or how potent it was. When I progressed to *Cue Corner*, I always kept a case for my own personal use (but only for when I wasn't working), but I never sold them behind the bar. I know how dangerous it can be if you are not used to it.

One of our members at *Cue Corner* was a young man called Brian. He was a 26-year-old miner, 6' 4", weighing 20 stone. He came in every weekend with his girlfriend, mum and dad, and other relatives and friends – about 30 people all together. All very nice and customers you could have a laugh with. Brian was the champion yard-of-ale drinker in all of Nottinghamshire. When he came up from the face of the mine, he would have five pints of Mansfield Bitter before he started his serious drinking.

For those unfamiliar with drinking and pub etiquette north of Watford, a pint of beer must never have a head on it. And half pints must never be served in a stemmed glass.

On Saturday evenings, when Brian was out with his entourage, he would always call out from his table and challenge me to a drinking contest. On Valentine's night, I was walking around *Cue Corner* giving the ladies flowers. When I reached Brian's table, sure enough, he challenged me again. I was expecting it, and said I'd accept the challenge so long as we drank Special Brew. "What's Special Brew?" he asked. So I sent one of my staff to fetch a bottle. Brian drank it down in one gulp: "Not bad," he said.

---

[3] At 9% alcohol, Special Brew is part of a group of strong lagers termed 'super-strength'.

We agreed that next Saturday, when the upstairs bar was closed, we would hold the competition. Saturday came, and I could see that Brian was a little wary as he was only drinking half-pints of Mansfield – which I had been sending over to him in a stemmed glass with a cherry and little umbrella on top. Prior to going upstairs, I had given my manager a bottle of vodka, which I told him to empty into Brian's glass during the course of the competition.

It came to 11.00pm, and everybody was in good spirits as we went upstairs. I had put on a little spread and told them everything was on the house for the rest of the night. We sat at a great big table, Brian with his back to the bar. My manager and one of the barmaids served the drinks. Brian and I started with two bottles of Special Brew each. No sooner had I raised the first one to my lips, when Brian finished his second. He called for two more. As I finished my first two, Brian had drunk half his second quota and decided to have something to eat. He came back to the table and downed his fourth bottle. I was now struggling with my second batch, and seemed to be talking without moving my lips. Brian's next drink was on its way, and I looked over, somewhat perplexed, to my manager at the bar, who showed me the vodka bottle – upside down, not a drop left in it. I finished my second round, as Brian was getting stuck into his third. He drank about half a glass, and told everyone he was surprised at how strong Special Brew was. He stood up to go to the toilet, took one step and fell to the floor. His friends picked him up and put him back in his chair. He sat and looked at me, struggling to finish my third round. I eventually did, but now sounded as if I was talking in a different language. Brian raised my arm and his friend shook my hand. The rest of the night was a haze, but Brian never challenged me again.

I had been at *Cue Corner* nine months when one evening who should come in but Derek, his mum, dad, and a friend who drove them down from Rotherham in his van.

Derek brought me up to date on the Merry Millers, including details of a petition with the fans asking me to go back. I thanked him but told him I had moved on with my life. I asked him to pass on my regards to all of the supporters. After that, Derek and his family would come down to *Cue Corner* once a month. Some evenings, his dad played the organ while I sang. We would entertain for a couple of hours, which we both really enjoyed.

There was one person who came into the club quite a lot. He was tall and thin, very well spoken, and wore expensive shoes and clothes. One evening he and I were talking and he told me he worked for Brabham[4]. His name was Paul, and he did the financing for the company. He told me he was trying to find someone to sponsor Jack Brabham's son, Gary, in British Formula Three. Paul asked if I could help, saying in return they could bring the Formula Three car down and place it in the foyer of *Cue Corner* for a week and have Jack Brabham down for photos to put in the local paper. I thought it would be a great idea, and agreed to help. Sure enough, the car turned up and created a great buzz. One Friday, true to Paul's word, Jack Brabham came to *Cue Corner*. We had some photos taken, and then I took Jack and Paul to dinner.

It was not until we sat down in the restaurant that I realised how loudly Jack spoke – he was almost shouting. He told me it was from the roar of the engines when he was in the paddock trying to talk to his mechanics. I was invited to the British Grand Prix at Brands Hatch, which I thoroughly enjoyed, although the cars went by so fast it was a job to tell who was winning.

By now I had taken *Cue Corner* as far as I could and was looking around for something else to do. But while I was looking, the local Miners' Welfare Society booked the concert hall for a gentlemen's evening. It seemed to be a great success, as the staff and me were so busy we never left the bar all night. I was delighted...that is,

---

[4] Actually Motor Racing Developments Ltd., but more commonly known as Brabham after the company's co-founder, Jack Brabham – the only man to win the Formula One world championship driving one of his own cars.

until the following Sunday when one of the newspapers carried the headline "Johnson Goes Into Porn". It told the full story of the gentlemen's evening – which was quite descriptive for a family newspaper. I was not aware of anything like that going on. All I could hear was shouting, but our bar was knee deep in burly miners. Needless to say, I did not allow anymore gentlemen's evenings while I owned *Cue Corner*.

I started looking for other business interests in the vicinity. Just five-six miles down the road, in Mansfield Woodhouse, was a golf club with a restaurant and bar. I ended up buying this, which kept me quite busy, I also took over a leisure complex in Harrogate. I had all three premises running for about a year and a half, but I was still being hounded by the media looking for a story. I was invited to do some work with Yorkshire Television, who I had previously worked with on a couple of quiz shows when I owned Rotherham. I was also offered further work with Radio Hallam. But I turned them both down. It was very flattering to be deemed newsworthy, but at the same time more and more Rotherham supporters were trying to talk me into going back and I was still being chased by the gnomes at Southend because the shares were still in my name. I reached a point where I thought enough is enough – I had to move further away.

I sat down with Jan and we made the decision to take Ames, Jake and ourselves to the United States. While I was organising the move, I sold the three businesses – I actually lost money on them, but none of this was about money – I just had to move away.

LOVELY BUBBLY: Celebrating buying Rotherham United

KID FRIENDLY: A visit to a children's hospital
with Jimmy Mac and Shades Valence of the BBC

CRAZY HORSE?: Emlyn Hughes signed a copy of his book for me and let me know I was the best chairman he'd ever had!

HUGHES THAT BOY: Emlyn signs as my manager

PUPPY LOVE: June-oh's first litter of 10. This was the only litter of black Irish Wolfhounds ever bred.

BEST DAYS OF MY LIFE: Standing in the presence
of a legend. With George and his wife Alex.

ONE FOR THE FUTURE: A fresh-faced Harry when
he first worked for me at Bournemouth.

KIDS' STUFF: Here's me and Jan with
our newest grandchildren

THAT'S MY GIRLS: My two eldest
grand-daughters Lanni and Fenn.

TYKE THAT: Being interviewed by Yorkshire TV's Martin Tyler after a Rotherham win over Sheffield United at Bramhall Lane.

CROSSROADS: Here I am with the man who played Darth Vader, at a Green Cross Code launch

A WALK IN THE PARK: Me with Roy Ellis,
of The Pyramids fame.

IT'S A FAMILY AFFAIR. The Johnson clan.

SUPER SHILTS: Congratulating Peter Shilton
on his Player of the Year award

KRAY DAYS: Just some of my Reggie Kray memorabilia

GOING FOR A SPIN: Three of my records,
including Shot Down in Action from 1975. We used
Margaret Thatcher as part of the promotion for the single.

HELLO PET: I had a thing about wolfhounds and here I am
with Tiddles, one of a litter 10 pups June-oh gave birth to,
with a rare black coat. He went on to win dog show trophies.

ROAR BLIMEY: Tiny the lion cub with his "mum" Smoky.
The pair were inseparable after the dog,
incredibly, let him suckle on her the first
time they met. She must have been bonkers.

Chapter 12

Welcome To
The United States

The year was 1987. I went to London and booked a Pan-Am one-way flight to Miami for the four of us. You could not book one-way now unless you live there. We sold all our furniture and said goodbye to family and friends. We had no forwarding address, so we told them we'd write once we were settled – remember this was in the days before Facebook and mobile phones. Now it's virtually impossible to escape.

The whole thing was an adventure. Once we were on the plane, nobody would know where we were. All the tension seemed to flow out of me. When we landed in Miami, we took a cab to a motel. Next morning, I looked through Yellow Pages and hired a car. We drove to Fort Lauderdale and booked into another motel. It was so relaxing. There were no ringing phones or flashing cameras. Nobody took a second glance at me. It was wonderful.

We eventually settled in Jupiter, which is on the East Coast of Florida. Jupiter is best known for its favourite son, Burt Reynolds. Nearly everything in town has something to do with Burt.

In that first month, I went fishing, taught the kids how to swim, and added some pounds to my waistband. I had a friend in Boston, Massachusetts. Jan and I were his kids' godparents. I phoned to see how he was doing, he was pleased to hear from me, and very surprised that we were in the US. After that, we phoned each other almost every other day. Then one day, my friend Jay phoned and asked me what I was up to. I told him I was sitting by the pool, with a cool beer in my hand, watching the kids swimming. "Do you fancy coming to Boston? I need some help," my friend asked. We were close pals, so I didn't hesitate: "Of course," I replied. "Good," said Jay, "I have booked you on a flight tomorrow to Logan Airport. I'll meet you there." Jay was a very successful businessman and owned a company that employed more than 200 staff.

It was December and in Florida it was 80 degrees F. In the north it was considerably colder. As we were approaching Logan Airport, all we could see was snow. Jay was there to meet us, with some warm coats. We drove out of the airport, through the tunnel and on to the motorway. After 45 minutes, we came to a small town called Upton. Jay took us to a house just outside of town. There were woods everywhere. It was the 23rd December, and my friend had thought of everything, from the Christmas tree, turkey, decorations, Christmas pudding and festive drinks. He told us he'd see us the day after Christmas. "By the way, there's a Jeep in the garage," he said as he handed me the keys. He left as the snow began to fall again, real Christmas weather. We had only been in the house half an hour when there was a knock at the door. It was one of our neighbours bringing us some homemade cookies as a welcoming gift. Within the next hour, all the rest of the neighbours had also visited us bearing various gifts. The house was warm and cosy, with oil central heating and a large fireplace loaded with logs ready to burn.

Christmas Day came and went very quickly, the following day (which is not an official holiday in the US, though the term "Boxing Day" is used by some Americans – particularly those who live near the border with Canada) Jay picked me up. As we were driving along, he explained that he was involved in a business venture with a builder, who he had given one million dollars, but was receiving no return on his investment. He had set-up a joint account with the builder, and could only see money going out – none going in. He took me to the headquarters of the workman. It was a very impressive six storey office block.

Jay said he did not want anybody to know I was anything to do with him, and that he wanted me to try to fix a job there so I could try and to find out what was happening to his money. I explained to him that I didn't have a work permit, but Jay said not to worry about that, "They take on anybody. I'll wait down the road." So I went into the reception and asked about a job. Half an hour later, I was given the janitor job for the whole office block. Although I found out later that the builder owned the whole block, he rented some of the offices out to lawyers and accountants.

I found Jay and told him I was starting work the next day. He took me home and said he would give me a call at the weekend as he was flying out to Chicago for a conference.

I arrived for work in the Jeep at 6.30am. My job was looking after and cleaning the toilets and offices. The office staff came in at 9.00am, which gave me a couple of hours to get started. As I progressed with the job, I found it was better to tidy everything up in the evening, because you did not have to keep looking at the clock, plus I could take a couple of hours off during the day if Jan wanted to get out (there was still plenty of snow about).

Jay phoned me at the weekend as promised, and I told I was just getting my feet under the table before snooping in earnest.

One of my jobs was emptying the waste bins from the offices and putting the trash in a dumpster in a yard at the back of the offices. One evening I was emptying the rubbish into trash bags, and one of the bags had coffee spilled over it. I took it to the dumpster outside, where the temperature was 30 degrees below zero. It was nice and warm inside, and I only had a shirt on as I did not intend to be outside for long. Unfortunately, the spilled coffee was all over my hands and as I leaned over the dumpster, my hands froze on to the metal. I couldn't move. It was dark and was starting to snow. I could see my hands starting to turn blue. Everybody had gone home and no one was about. It was not looking good.

Thank goodness the janitor from the office block next door came out and realised what had happened and came to my rescue. Apparently it is quite a regular occurrence there, and the janitor had a spray which released my hands. Yet again, I was grateful to be rescued. In New Zealand it was a horse that helped me out of a sticky situation in the outback, this time it was a maintenance man. Either could have ended in a very lonely death. One in the middle of nowhere, the other in the middle of a city surrounded by millions of people yet still alone.

The builder I was supposedly working for had crews of men which had their own building jobs. Each crew comprised the foreman and his assistant, plus two plumbers, electricians, tilers, carpenters, labourers, painters and drywallers. Each crew was allocated a job – it could be anything from building a house to a condominium, or even a room extension – anything in the building trade. They would be given a budget for the job and it had to be completed for that price or less. If it was, the crew were paid a bonus.

One day while I was cleaning the ladies and gents toilets, one of the foremen came in and said he had been told by the boss that he wanted them retiled. I was becoming a little bored with my job, so I offered my services. "But who will do the cleaning?" asked the foreman. "I will," I replied. And I was given the task. I did the job – floor and walls all tiled – in a week, plus I still did my cleaning. I am glad to say everybody was most impressed, including me.

By this time, I had been able to access the office accounts department. It had taken some time to work it out, but the builder had another account with the same name at another bank. It was registered as a company, but solely in the builder's name. It was into this account that the builder was putting the money from the jobs. Naughty.

I had started calling into a little bar on my way home, a mile from where we were staying. I would just nip in for one beer, and had struck up a friendship with a man who had a glass eye. To draw attention to the bar tender, he would hit the eye with a quarter coin, making quite a noise. If he was there before me, that's how he 'bought' me a beer. We soon became very close. Eventually he told me he was a retired FBI agent. He retired because of his eye, which he lost 'on duty'. When I felt I had his confidence – even to the point of telling him that I had no work permit – I explained Jay's building situation. He told me that the builder could face seven years for that, if I had the evidence. It gave me food for thought.

Jay would regularly phone me, and I would tell him I was working on it and he needed to be patient. One day, one of the foremen became ill and, because of my tiling job, I was asked to step in and take charge of his crew. I was given the job of renovating an old shack that was on the side of a hill just outside of town. It had a wonderful view looking down on to a lake. It had been an old cowboy's living quarters, with an old fashioned stove and one end used for storage. I was given six weeks and an $80,000 budget. The design was left to me. You didn't have to worry about building inspectors out in the country. We made a bedroom upstairs with a veranda overlooking the lake, and a nice deck on the side with a Jacuzzi surrounded by a white wicker fence. The job was finished in four and half weeks, at a cost of just $68,000. The property was sold within four weeks, so everybody was happy. The crew insisted I had a drink with them as they had all received a nice bonus. They presented me with a big old fashioned key set in a slice of a log. The key was found by one of the crew while we were working on the house. One of the carpenters had made it. I was really flattered.

It was nearly six months since I had started the job as a janitor, and I now had the evidence Jay needed. I went to his office and explained what the builder was doing.

"I would just like my money back," Jay said. I asked him, if I arranged this, could I have his 50% share in the company. Jay said he would be only too pleased with this proposal.

The next day – a Friday - I waited until 5.00pm, when I knew the builder was still in his office, and went in to see him. Although I had been there six months, he had only spoken to me twice – the last time to say "Good job," on my renovation work. I asked his secretary if I could see him. "I'll ask," she said and went in to see him. She came out saying "Sorry, he's too busy." "I'll wait," I said. "He won't be very happy if you're still here when he comes out," said the secretary. I waited for half an hour, and then just walked into his office. "Get out!" he shouted. I told him I was a friend of Jay's, who'd sent me to find out where his money had gone. I told him I had evidence, but still he shouted for me to get out of his office. I told him I'd give him the weekend to think about things. Needless to say, that was the last day I worked as a janitor at the office. When I arrived home, Jan was waiting at the door. "The builder has phoned; he wants you to go back to the office."

I went back to a man huffing and puffing. After five minutes of talking rubbish, I interrupted and told him I wanted Jay's million dollars and his 50% of the company.

Again, he started shouting, so I walked out. You have to remember there were no mobile phones then. So I reached home to be greeted by Jan again saying the builder had called. I phoned him back and he told me he would like until Monday to think it over.

Monday morning, I received a call at 7.30am. It was the builder: "Be in my office at 11.00am," he said. When I arrived, there was the builder plus his lawyer who pulled out a lot of paperwork which basically said that I could have 50% of the company plus Jay's million dollars if the builder's skulduggery was never mentioned again. I duly signed the paperwork and left with a share certificate for 50% of the company plus Jay's million.

I went straight to Jay's office. He was over the moon. He phoned his lawyer to make sure I received my 50% of the company, and I went down to the bank where the company kept its accounts. I met the manager, who had already been informed of the takeover. Again, there was more paperwork to sign, but by the end of the day I owned half of Buddies Builders.

I had taken on staff and contracts, so I was soon up to my neck in work and problems. But it was profitable fun.

In the meantime, my 18-year-old daughter, Fleur, and my 16-year-old son, Chi, came to stay and everything was great. Fleur worked in the office, and Chi helped the contractors – plus he was allowed to drive.

All this time, I had done nothing about obtaining a work permit – it had completely slipped my mind. Jan had become pregnant again, Ames was at school, and Jake was at nursery...life was going along quite nicely, with no hassle from the media or the gnomes.

Jan gave birth to Wish at Milford Hospital on 8 July 1988. For just a short stay – less than one day – we came out with a daughter and a $10,000 medical bill. I should have been insured.

The business was running smoothly, with more than a hundred staff. But we were under pressure from our mums and dads back in England to take Wish home. So we arranged for Fleur and Chi to stay in Boston, and we booked a two-week holiday. The grandparents were delighted to see Wish, Ames and Jake. Everything was going well, we were happy and I was looking forward to getting back to my new life in the States. When we landed at Logan airport, that's when trouble came knocking on my door again. As we went through immigration, the officers were talking to Ames, who was just five. She was full of enthusiasm about going back to school and kept telling them, which must have rung alarm bells as we were carted off to an office. After an hour of questioning, we were given the option of re-boarding a plane or going to court at a later date. With Fleur and Chi waiting outside, I chose the latter option.

The next day, I went to the best immigration lawyers in Boston who told me two things: that they could delay the case for at least six months and that they felt I would be able to stay because I employed so many US staff.

It transpired that they were right about the six-month delay, but wrong about being able to remain in the country.

Fortunately, I had time to put my house in order. When we eventually went to court, they asked for two things: mine and Jan's passports. They wrote in pen across our indefinite visas "VOID". So much for my $1,000 an hour lawyer, who told us not to worry as they would still get us back to the USA. They never did, even after many meetings in London with them. If only I had sorted out a proper working visa, who knows whether we'd still be there to this day?

Eventually, Jan and all the family came back to England and I had to sell the business for a tenth of its value given that everyone knew I had to leave the US. In spite of this, I have to say the whole experience was great, and I became a family man again. Strangely, I didn't find the work as demanding as football had been.

There were lots of great memories – like going out with the sledges in the winter, chopping up wood for the fire, finding a stream in the woods behind our house, which nobody seemed to know about, where I could fish and always be guaranteed a couple of trout, going for the weekend to Cape Cod, home of the Kennedy Compound (JFK's 'summer White House') and having woodchucks (the animal from the films Caddyshack and Groundhog Day) eat all the vegetables I had grown, except my tomatoes. But one the most unusual things I saw, was when I drove into the country and noticed fields of red. They were cranberry fields. I found out some fascinating things about cranberries. What they did was put a bank around each field, flooded them and, as the berries became ripe, they floated on top of the water so they did not bruise. Then they were netted. There was red as far as the eye could see – an unbelievable sight, much like the multi-coloured maple leafs that litter the ground in Boston during Fall.

Chapter 13

America, stars and bars

My son Chi was now nearly 17 and expressed an interest in butchery. I said I would work with him until I thought he was qualified (which meant I couldn't do anything else, meantime). I was a member of the Butchers' Guild and in the past had done quite a bit of lecturing on the subject. We eventually found a butcher's shop for sale in Penge, South London. It was a Victorian premises with five bedrooms – enough for all the family. It was next door to Penge police station. While we were living there, we received a bill, which had been sent to that address every year for more than 100 years, from the police charging us for light and air as one window looked into the courtyard of the station. On a regular basis, our neighbours would also ask me to be a witness when they were charging someone. Often this would be around seven in the morning when they were about to change shifts. As we started work at six, I would walk over in my white coat, sit and listen while the charges were read out, sign the witness sheet and go back to the shop.

The shop became busy and Chi ended up with six butchers working for him. We then bought another shop in Penge market. As we had been there more than two years, I felt I had taught Chi most of what I knew and I was needed less and less in the shops.

Jan had given birth to Ryan, so I now had six children, three boys and three girls. In the last six months, I had become friendly with Ames and Jake's headmaster, Brian. He introduced me to his friend, Andrew. The pair were working on local radio and, as our friendship grew, I too became involved. They covered Le Mans, Cowes Week, some golf tournaments, and Andrew organised promotions for Camel cigarettes. Meanwhile, I had given Chi the two businesses and, after a time, he decided he wanted to go to college to learn butchery – something the Johnsons had done for four generations. So he sold the shops and became a full-time student for two years.

I had now moved back to my roots in Orsett and bought The Orsett Cock public house – a real landmark in Essex, and the place where I'd met Peter Morris and Bobby Moore some years earlier. There I joined up with a lot of old acquaintances from my pre-Rotherham days. As you can imagine, I had plenty of stories to tell, and no shortage of interested people to ask questions about this colourful local character – all of which was very good for business. It was 1994, and the Orsett Cock was very busy.

One of the first people to seek me out was a friend I played football with on Sundays who had taken part in the game with Peter and Bobby. His name was Roger Fleet. He was about six years younger than me and had been in the magazine business, but had just sold his company to WH Smith and was now at a loose end.

I had installed a big screen in the function room at the rear of the Orsett Cock and, on Mondays, Roger and I would sit and watch football matches with other customers. It was while we were together that we decided to start up a magazine that we would give away at football matches, with money coming in from the revenue generated by advertising.

We approached some well-known ex-footballers to write articles, and Roger thought we should try to buy out an established magazine. He found the ideal vehicle: the world's first ever monthly football magazine, Charles Buchan's Football Monthly, which was launched in September 1951.

Roger and I had a meeting with the two owners who were elderly gentlemen. Sales of the magazine had dropped from 100,000 to 25,000, which they said was due to the competition. Roger pointed out that these magazines had to be paid for, unlike our proposed freebie. The owners liked our idea, and wanted to stay on as directors, which we both readily agreed to as their experience would be invaluable. It was nearly Christmas, so we all agreed that we would sign contracts as soon as possible in the New Year.

On New Year's Eve, Roger – who had lost his wife two years previously, and had two teenage daughters – came to our party at the Orsett Cock. At the end of the night, we said our farewells until we met again to finalise the deal.

I had booked to fly to New Zealand, and Roger was going to his holiday home in Majorca, right next door to Gerry Marsden of Gerry & The Pacemakers. I took Jan and Ryan – who was now three – while the rest of the kids stayed with their nans and granddads. We had been there two weeks, and had just decided to buy a house on the beach at Brighton on South Island, when I received a phone call telling me that Roger had been found dead in bed. I was just coming to terms with the shock of that when, two days later, Jan had a call to say that her mother had been rushed to hospital. We decided to book a flight home immediately, but while doing so (and I have to acknowledge Qantas' magnificent help here), Jan received another call to say that her mother, Joan, had passed away. Jan and I hardly said a word to each other on the 30-hour flight home. What was there to say? But I cannot remember Ryan being any trouble.

We arrived back in Orsett, and went round to see Jan's dad. I don't have to explain how everybody was feeling. Then we picked the other kids up from school.

In the evening, when the kids were in bed and Jan had gone to see her sister, I went down to the bar of the Orsett Cock. The place was packed, and we had eight bar staff working and a DJ playing. Unusually for me, but understandable in the circumstances, I decided to prop up the bar and gather my thoughts. At about

9.00pm, four old ladies came in. They spoke to one of the barmaids, bought four orange juices and went into the function room. They looked completely out of place, with the music blaring out. I called the barmaid over and asked what they had said. "They wanted to know if there was another room, so I showed them the function room," said Sandy.

A little later, an old man came in. He had a full beard and looked about 80. Again, he spoke to a barmaid, bought half a pint of lager and went into the function room. I was becoming intrigued, so I went round to the function room to find the old man sitting with the four ladies. The music was deafening, but they did not seem fazed by it. I noticed that they were sitting at the table Roger and I used on Monday nights.

I decided to go over to make sure they were okay. Just as I reached the table, the old man said "We have been sent here, but please do not worry – he's only concerned about his two daughters. You have lost somebody recently." At first, I thought he was talking about Joan, but in fact it was Roger.

The hairs on the back of my neck stood up, and I had goose bumps on my goose bumps. The old man told me how the four ladies had become psychics over the last 15 years, but his first experience came just after he had been in the trenches in the war. A bomb had exploded by him, killing his best friend. A few years later, he had been on holiday in France. He was in a cafe when he felt something touch his leg. When he bent down, there was a lighter on the floor. He picked it up, and it was his friend's from the war. From that day, he could see things – and he came to me because of Roger's concern for his daughters. After he had finished explaining this, the five of them got up, said "good night," and left. I had never seen them before, and I've never seen them since. As soon as they left, I went upstairs and phoned a mutual friend of Roger's and mine. His name was Jeff, who also played football for the Sunday League team. He had been Roger's trustee and arranged his funeral, which had already taken place.

Jeff told me that the youngest daughter lived with Roger's mum and had mixed with the wrong company, but had resolved that problem. However, he was unsure about the eldest daughter, Laura, as she was at university in Preston.

I waited until Jan returned, and explained what had happened. We decided that I needed to go up to Preston in the morning. I phoned Roger's mum, and was given the address for Laura. I reached Preston at 4.00pm the next day, and managed to find Laura. We both became very emotional, talking about Roger. After the tears, I took her to dinner and tried to find out if, apart from the obvious, there were any problems at Uni. She could not think of any, so I booked into a local hotel and the next morning made an appointment to see the head tutor of Laura's department.

When we met, he was unaware of Laura's tragedy and told me that her work had not been good enough and they were considering failing her and asking her to leave.

However, given her circumstances, he agreed they would give her another year to straighten herself out – which she did, and passed all her exams. She ended up working for one of the big television companies.

While running the Orsett Cock, I was given the opportunity of acquiring other pubs by a company called Entrepreneur. If they lost a manager, they would ask if I could take over the pubs until such time as they found a permanent replacement. Sometimes we would have them for a year or more. At one time I had 10 pubs, two night clubs, and a sports complex in Blackheath with six football pitches, squash courts, cricket pitch, a huge house, bars and a function room – in all, covering about 10 acres of land. So Jan and I were kept very busy and had to employ a full-time accountant to help us out. It was around this time that we decided to leave the Orsett Cock and buy a house. Just before we moved, Ryan had started coming into our room in the middle of the night, and I would end up sleeping in his bed. Ryan was about four, and after six months in our new house, we ended up moving back into the pub as the manager had left and we felt it best to go back. Just before we did, we happened to be driving past the Cock and I told Ryan we'd be moving back in. "Will that lady keep pushing me out of bed?" he asked. While we had been at the pub, many of the staff told me they thought they had seen and heard strange things. I must admit I had felt a presence in parts of the pub, particularly in the cellar, which had a storage room. To me, it always smelt of an old auntie with BO. I would often go to the room and scrub it out with bleach and disinfectant, but by the next day the odour would be back. Occasionally I would catch the smell in other parts of the pub too. Eventually, I called a medium, who I knew quite well. Her name was Mandy Masters. She was born without arms due to the thalidomide drug scandal, but had gone on to great things in the media. Mandy asked me to take her down to the cellar. "Leave me here," she said. About an hour later, Mandy reappeared in the bar. "Yes, you have a white-haired old lady in a grey dress, who was an old maid, wandering about. She will not cause any trouble, but she missed not having any children." On one of the bar walls we had a picture of the pub when it was a coaching house, with the staff standing out the front. "That's her," said Mandy, pointing at an old lady in the picture. "She calls herself Liz." I took the picture off the wall and looked at the back; there was an inscription which read: "Hope you like this picture, Elizabeth. Your old friend, Walter." Spooky.

Chapter 14

Gentlemen Reg

During my time at Southend United, I was approached by a man who had written a story about football, but could not find a publisher. He asked me if I could help. I read the book, which was okay but I felt it lacked a lot of in-depth knowledge about the game. I explained this to the author, who asked if I could persuade Bobby Moore to take a look at it. Bobby agreed with me about the book's content. "Do you think you could do anything with it?" I asked Bobby. "I could try," he replied. I had an idea that if Bobby rewrote some of the book and injected some real inside knowledge, we could put his name on the cover and maybe come up with a winner. The author readily agreed, and I arranged for a ghost-writer to help Bobby. They spent a few weeks collating their input, and the finished article was very good indeed. The author was naturally delighted and I easily secured a publishing contract with Bobby's name as co-writer. But when it came to the actual contract, the author became greedy, Bobby withdrew his name and the book was never published.

Sometime later, after the great and legendary Bobby Moore had died, I was at the Orsett Cock and a man kept phoning and asking to have a meeting with me. Eventually I agreed to meet him and he told me he was from a company anxious to buy the rights to the manuscript that Bobby had co-written. "It's worth a million pounds if we can have the rights," said the man. I had to tell him it was Bobby's wishes to scrap the book, and he left very dejected.

The last memorable thing that happened during my eight year stint at the Cock was meeting up with an old DJ friend, Chris

Rowlands. Chris was now working for a company that took tourists around some of London's scary/historical/educational attractions, like the London Dungeon. One of the stops was the famous Blind Beggar pub[5] in Whitechapel, East London, once frequented by notorious gangster Reggie Kray. Chris told me they had the opportunity of acquiring the boozer and some memorabilia from Reggie who, although in prison, was ready to help. The pub was not being run very well and when Reggie heard I was in the business, he asked me to take it over.

Chris took me to the Blind Beggar, and I had a look around. But I decided I could not give the pub enough attention. "Think about it," said Chris, "I'll give you a call next week." Two days later, at about 8.00pm, I received a phone call. It was Reggie, phoning from Wayland prison. He asked me about the Blind Beggar, and I explained how busy I was. "Will you come and visit me?" he asked. I agreed I would. "My wife will phone you and make the arrangements," said Reg. Sure enough, half an hour later, I had a phone call from a lady called Roberta, who introduced herself as Reggie's wife. Over the next week, I was receiving calls from Reg and Roberta, and we eventually set a date for a visit. I had to go to Roberta's house in Norfolk first, which was five miles from the prison. I picked up my pass and went down to Wayland. I think it was harder getting in than trying to get out. As you can imagine, security was very tight. I met Reg in the visitor's hall. He greeted me like a long-lost brother, giving me the familiar hug of a powerful man. He commented on my suit, saying how much he liked it. We sat talking for an hour, with Reg trying to change my mind about the Blind Beggar. As I was leaving, the warden came up to our table with a large sack of mail. "He has one of these every month," the warden said. Reg and I did the customary hug and said our goodbyes. "I will phone you," said Reg. Sure enough, Reg would

---

[5] The Blind Beggar, in Whitechapel, is notable as the place where Ronnie Kray shot and murdered George Cornell in front of witnesses, and also as the location of William Booth's first sermon, which led to the creation of the Salvation Army.

regularly phone me most nights. Often the kids would answer, and Reg would talk to them for ages. It reached the point where if one of the kids answered the phone, they would call out "Uncle Reg is on the phone." He told me he really liked to hear them calling him Uncle Reg.

By the time of my third visit to Reg, we were into a routine: the first thing I did when I arrived Wayland was sort out coffees and sweets from the vending machines, because Reg wasn't allowed any cash. By now, I'd also persuaded Reg that I couldn't take on the Blind Beggar, but we made a compromise. It was the year 2000, and Reg wanted me to help Roberta launch a Champagne with his name on it.

Jan and Roberta formed a company called Ronnie and Reggie with a logo of two Rs joined back to back. I contacted one of my friends in the wine business. He went to France to organise the bottling, while Roberta designed a label featuring the famous boxing stance of Reggie's with the words "The Best Drink Behind Bars". Reg and Roberta were in charge of the orders, which amounted to a few thousand cases, and Jan and I looked after the deliveries. There were many well-known and professional people ordering the champagne. All in all, it was a very worthwhile enterprise, and Reg was over the moon with it - mind you, I couldn't see many people refusing to buy any if they were offered it.

I kept in touch with Reg, who was always thinking of other ways to make money, despite his incarceration. His mind was very active and it must have driven him crazy being locked up for more than 30 years. He was always giving me memorabilia – from his brother Ronnie's funeral, to a boxing match programme with Reggie on the bill. I lost touch with him when he became ill, but I have to say he was always 'the gentlemen' and had so much time for my kids. He was also greatly respected by staff and inmates at the prison. RIP Reggie Kray.

Chapter 15

One for the road

I had a couple working for me who took over the running of the Orsett Cock, while other staff looked after my other interests. This gave me time to return to New Zealand, where I had bought the house on the beach in Brighton. While I was there I also bought a restaurant and bar in the harbour at Dunedin. It was on top of a tower, where you could see all of the city. I called it Bruno's after New Zealand's most famous actor Bruno Lawrence[6]. I had exhausted the local chefs and had to bring a chef and head waiter from England. It was a 30 hour flight from London to Auckland, then you had to board another plane to Christchurch before the final leg of the journey to Dunedin. I had some business to attend to back in the UK, so I settled the pair in my house on the beach, arranged a car for them after a few days flew back to England. I phoned them a week later to see how things were. The head waiter answered the phone and said they were very busy. I asked to speak to the chef, and there was a deathly silence. I asked the head waiter again. "I'm afraid he's drunk," he told me. "Let me speak to him," I said. A rambling voice came on the phone – completely incoherent. I was shocked because I had given the chef a three month trial before flying him out to NZ. There was never a sign of him drinking. The next day I flew back to New Zealand with a return ticket for him.

I kept Bruno's for a while, but all the flying completely put me off New Zealand, which was not fair because, as anybody who has been there will know, it is one of the most mystical and exhilarating countries in the world.

---

[6] The late actor/musician Bruno Lawrence was born in Worthing in 1941, and migrated to New Zealand in 1946.

I was at a loose end when I sold Bruno's. I had moved the family and myself into a nice house in the country, 18 miles from London. There, I was approached by a couple of friends who asked me to join them in buying Scarborough Football Club. Jan was completely against the idea, for obvious reasons.

One of the friends was an accountant. He had looked at the books and said we could make it viable. He also said he would run the club as secretary, my other friend wanted to be chief executive, and were both going to take salaries. I invested my money and was made chairman. To my horror, the club was losing money hand over fist. I went to a chairmen's meeting in London and Barry Hearn of Leyton Orient came up to me and said I was mad to buy Scarborough – surely I had looked at the accounts?

The first day I was there, I had 10 people come into the office asking for money – in all, a total of just over £200,000.

My accountant friend had worn his heart on his sleeve and told me there must have been two sets of books, as he had not spotted any outstanding bills. Over the next three weeks, another £300,000 worth of bills popped out of the woodwork, and I decided enough was enough. I had started paying wages out of my own pocket. I told my two friends I was resigning. They kept things going for a little while, but could not make the club stand on its own two feet. Unfortunately the friend who had invested the same amount of money as me, and who had gone on a salary at Scarborough, decided I should give him his money back. Needless to say, we fell out over it, and that was my last encounter with the Football League.

About a month later, I bumped into a friend who told me he had just come back from Florida. He had a business colleague in a place called New Port Richey who had met someone who was trying to sell a soccer academy. I decided to fly over to find out more about it. The owner of the academy turned out to be Gordon Hill, the former England and Manchester United midfielder.

Gordon wanted to move to pastures new, but his business partner wanted to stay. I bought the academy, which turned out to be quite lucrative. It had four girls' teams and seven boys' teams. That year, soccer scholarships came into the academic criteria, which meant if the pupil was good enough they could be awarded a scholarship – which could save his or her parents up to $100,000 in fees. Suddenly it became big business: middle class families were investing $500 a term, on the hope of saving $100,000. Because of the demand, I returned to England with a shopping list of all the things required for the academy. During the summer months, I brought young professional footballers out to assist with the coaching. Parts of Florida are still very racist, and one of the young professionals who came over originated from Barbados. I had booked my coaching staff into a well-known hotel in the area, where I was also staying. We were sitting down for dinner, when I was approached by one of the waiters asking if I could please go to the manager's office. The manager explained to me that he could not allow blacks in the hotel. It was the holiday season, otherwise I would have pulled everyone out of the hotel.

After dinner, I explained to the young man that the hotel was overbooked, and that there were not enough rooms in the hotel for both of us. We collected our cases and I found a very nice hotel five miles away that had two spare rooms. We booked in and went to the bar. I thought I had smoothed the situation over without him realising anything was amiss. But the young man was more than aware of what had gone on. He told me: "You do not have to explain. There were no other coloured people in the hotel." I must confess I had not noticed. He understandably insisted on going home the next day, so I booked him a flight. I then took him to say goodbye to the other boys, who were so furious they were all ready to go home with him too. But, being the gentleman he was he insisted they stay and make the most of their chance to coach in the sun. If only the bigots shared his incredible tolerance, the world would be a much better place. I took him to the airport the next day, and made sure he was paid his coaching fees. I am glad to say that I still see him on a regular basis. Although he now has a career outside of football, he still coaches kids' teams.

When I returned to the training group, there were more than 500 kids and I could not spot any black children - apart from one Mexican and one Brazilian child. We finished the summer season, and after the young pros had returned to England, sadly, but perhaps predictably, I had a number of parents express to me their disapproval of bringing my young Barbadian friend over for even one day. The season had been quite successful, with our under-18 girls winning the Cocoa Beach Cup. It was strange: the girls would turn up for matches, driving their jeeps and open-top sports cars in bikinis, acting very lady-like. But once they put the football kit on, they turned from Jekyll into Hyde, spitting and swearing during furious displays of gamesmanship that would make some of the worst Sunday League games look like a picnic in the park. Four of the girls went on to play in the US FIFA Women's World Cup winning team.

While I was enjoying my time in Florida, the racist undercurrent coursing through the academy left me feeling that my days were numbered. So, the gypsy in me decided to call it a day and I set off for pastures new.

I had not moved the family while I was involved with the soccer academy. I had been commuting backwards and forwards from London to Florida. My air miles had certainly been clocking up.

When I returned to England for good, I re-opened a nightclub. We opened at the end of October, just in time for Christmas. There was no other such club locally, and within a week of our first night I had sold out of tickets for Christmas Eve, New Year's Eve, and a Faces Night on the Wednesday before Christmas. The club held 1,200 people, and at £20 a head it didn't take much working out that this was going to be very worthwhile financially. After Christmas, I became involved with a large market in Stevenage, which had more than 500 stalls, and a staff recruitment business. All three ventures were very successful.

By now, my eldest son had left butchery and had moved into pub and restaurant management - ably assisted by my eldest daughter, Fleur. With the Iraq war looming, I decided to sell two of my businesses and take the rest of my family on a world trip. I went to see their headmasters, who agreed to release them from their studies – travel broadening the mind, and all that. We went via Asia to Australia and New Zealand, then the Pacific Islands and on to South America. All in all, we were away from home for about five months. When we returned, I had to bottle up the nomad in me while Ames finished her Uni course, where she passed a BA in Equine Studies. She was then offered a job at Sheikh Mohammed's[7] Godolphin Stables, near Newmarket, where she taught the prince and princess to ride and looked after their ponies and horses. She had become involved with a young man and decided she wanted to leave the Sheikh's stables and run a pub instead. In our opinion this was total madness! Jan and I desperately tried to talk her out of this, but to no avail. Sheikh Mohammed had bred an Arab horse that had won the 800 mile Desert Endurance Race but was also very highly strung. Ames was the only person who could manage the horse. So when she left, Sheikh Mohammed and the family gave the horse to Ames as a farewell gift. Now there's not many folk who can say they were given a racehorse as a leaving gift. Sadly, neither the pub nor the boyfriend lasted long.

By now, Jake had finished at Palmer's College, Wish had finished taking her school exams, and Ryan was 13. The travelling bug had a hold of me again, and it seemed to have rubbed off on all of the family. The time was right, so I bought a small company to give us an opportunity to acquire visas in the US. It included a pet shop – Tortoise Farm – and a T-shirt printing factory. Again, it was in Florida. I bought a six bedroom house with a pool which

---

[7] Sheikh Mohammed bin Rashid Al Maktoum, ruler of Dubai and vice-president of the United Arab Emirates.

overlooked a lake. Property is not expensive in Florida – even less so since the financial crash.

Ryan still had to go to school, which he did without any fuss. The only difference in the States was the hours. He started at 07.30 and finished at 14.30, so we had to wake him up at 6am on school days. Wish and Jake worked in the pet shop, and sometimes at the T-shirt shop we had on International Drive. Then Wish decided she would like to work for Disney, and was offered a job at Disneyworld Florida.

We had been there about a year when I had a call from a friend in the Caribbean called Harry. Years earlier, Harry had been a very successful businessman until his wife ran off with his best friend. As a result of this, he had gone to pieces – losing his business and living out of a suitcase. I helped him out by financing the purchase of a railway arch in Windsor and converting it into a night club and bistro. He went on to buy another restaurant and I am glad to say it was all a great success. Harry had since met a lady, sold up and moved to St Vincent, a small island in the beautiful Caribbean. He phoned to tell me about a restaurant and bar on the beach which had closed. It was called Ocean Allegro. He asked me to take a look at it as he thought it would suit me.

Jan and I flew to Barbados and then took a small plane to fly us to St Vincent. The island was very colonial and, as you would expect, full of palm trees, hanging bunches of bananas and coconut palms. You were never away from wonderful views of the sea. In town, loin-clothed men rubbed shoulders with men in suits. On every corner people were selling fish, fruit and coconuts – the tops of which were cut off with a machete and passed to you to drink. It was so laid back, it almost put you in a trance.

Harry met us at the small airport, which was next door to the international cricket pitch. He took us to our hotel and said he would come back in the evening. I invited Harry and his lady for dinner, which he readily accepted.

We were in the bar waiting for them to arrive when Harry turned up alone. He told us his other half was busy. They had known we were coming for more than a week, we had been travelling all day, and she was busy? Something sounded as fishy as those corner stalls. It was the season for crayfish, which they called lobster. The crayfish were kept in what can only be described as small swimming pools. They could be very large, but they did not have the huge pincers like a real lobster. Nevertheless, they were quite delicious.

Unfortunately, the crayfish season didn't last very long and if you were caught with them out of season, you ended up with a hefty fine.

Harry picked us up the next morning and took us to this beautiful beach and there, nestling under the palm trees, was Ocean Allegro – a deep red wooden building with a corrugated roof and a gorgeous veranda looking out over the beach of golden sands. In front of that was Young Island, frequented by the rich and famous. Bill Gates was a regular visitor.

The place was closed and overgrown bushes had threatened to strangle it. Harry told Jan and I that the owners were a Canadian lady named Lisa and her husband, Godfrey, a local man. Sadly, Godfrey had a tendency to hit Lisa on a regular basis, so she had returned to stay with her parents back home. Godfrey still lived in St Vincent, and when I contacted him, he explained that the business was in both his and his wife's name – and Lisa would not speak to him. I wonder why? Apparently the last time he hit her, he broke her jaw.

Godfrey took Jan and me to look inside the restaurant. The place was just a shell. I found out later that apart from being a wife-beater, Godfrey also had a drug habit, and sold off all the fixtures and fittings to finance his addiction. This did not deter us. Godfrey said that I'd have to talk with Lisa, as they would both need to sign the contract for any sale. I was given a figure from him of how much he wanted for his half of the business. Jan and

I flew back to Florida, still not having seen Harry's girlfriend Edna. I think the name should have told me everything.

From Florida I phoned the number I had been given for Lisa. The phone was answered by a very protective father, not prepared to let me speak to his daughter. But he took my number, and one hour later the phone rang, it was Lisa. I explained the reason for my call. She told me she would never return to St Vincent. I could hear the fear in her voice. But she was prepared to sell her half. So, after travelling to Canada and back to St Vincent, I eventually snapped up Ocean Allegro.

My first job was to refit the property. At the same time, the whole place was repainted, with the veranda leading on to a brand new patio and bar. The job of refitting turned out to be much harder than I thought. The month before, the island had been hit by a huge storm that had devastated nearby Grenada, from where St Vincent received most of its business and household goods.

I decided to buy all I needed in Florida, and ended up going to lots of auctions where restaurants had recently gone bust, some after just three months of opening, so most of the fittings were practically brand new. I filled one 40-foot container, and half of a second one. I had noticed that you could not buy mattresses in St Vincent, and most of the locals slept on the floor. There was a company in Orlando that had the job of refitting all of the Disney hotels every couple of years, so there were plenty of mattresses going very cheap. I filled the remainder of the second container with them.

The containers took a week to reach St Vincent. I had flown back with the family and everybody, including some helpful locals, helped empty them when they arrived.

The kitchen equipment had to be converted for the local utility services. While Harry was organising the workers, I put up a sign asking for new staff, giving a time and date for the interviews.

When the day came, the queue was nearly half a mile long. I hadn't realised there was hardly any work on the island. I interviewed some very experienced and educated people, while others came in wearing loin cloths who could hardly speak. These people lived up in the hills, wore no shoes and looked as if they hadn't washed for a couple of weeks. I did pick one of them. He was huge and everybody seemed frightened of him. I made him my night watchman. He lived in a shed in the grounds, to keep an eye on everything. I was told that the Vincentians believed that if a person had more than one thing of a kind, you could take the extra item – as you only needed the one. The way he treated the shed, you would have thought it was a palace.

Strangely, he had no name, so we called him Goliath. His birthday was the same as mine and we liked to say we were twins. He had no shoes and I noticed he was always looking at mine. I wear size 12, and I gave him a pair which took pride of place in the shed and were only used for special occasions.

I ended up employing 16 locals: four bar staff; four waitresses; three kitchen staff; two cleaners; two gardeners/handy men; and one manager. I had heard of a chef who made the best chocolate cake in all of the islands. He was once Princess Margaret's personal chef when she stayed in Mustique. I was told he now lived in St Vincent. I managed to track him down, and it looked like he ate more than he made. He had recently suffered a bereavement in the family and was not working. I caught him just as he was ready to return. He was an excellent chef, as were the other three kitchen staff (all very large ladies) – one of whom made the best fresh bread and rolls I've ever eaten.

We opened Ocean Allegro at 11.00am on Good Friday, with all the front of house staff dressed immaculately in black and white. We had the only jetty on the island – about 50 yards long – where the small glass bottomed boats went back and forth to Young Island from. There were usually a couple of taxis waiting there to pick up or drop off people, so we seemed ideally situated. From the restaurant you could look over the veranda to the crystal clear blue and green shimmering water, with the odd yacht sailing by. On opening day, there was just a hint of a breeze which made the palm trees in the garden shimmer very gracefully. Inside, the ceiling fans were going about their business of keeping things cool. The gorgeous smell of the bread and local fish being cooked in traditional spices made the whole setting perfect.

But by 3.00pm, we had not had a single customer. The only people who had come through the doors were local fishermen who asked the chef to go down to their boats to look at the fresh fish they had caught.

At 4.00pm, the head waiter came over to me to advise it was taboo to open on Good Friday, and that no other businesses on the island were open.

I had all these locals working for me and helping me set up for the grand opening and not one of them mentioned this before. Perhaps they thought I knew something they didn't and I had organised a massive party or something with hundreds of friends.

I had not realised how religious the people of St Vincent were. I told the head waiter we would stay open until six and then close.

Around 5.30pm, a taxi pulled up and two young white males shouted out to me "Oi, mate – are you open?" "Of course," I replied. "Thank goodness," they said. They took out their mobile phones, and explained that there were 300 thirsty sailors looking for somewhere to have a drink. They were from HMS Liverpool, and had been at sea for two months.

Within half an hour the bar, restaurant and gardens – that had been virtually silent bar the gentle rustling of the palm trees – were packed full of naval personnel. I asked the head waiter to find a steel band. They were there within the hour. By nine that evening, I had to phone the owner of the local brewery to bring over a lorry full of booze. I told the band to keep playing. I think they only knew three numbers, but nobody seemed to care.

Around midnight, the officers from the ship arrived. They had been to a welcoming party thrown by the Prime Minister. After talking to the young Captain of 'The Crazy Red Chick' (as HMS Liverpool was nicknamed), I found out that he came from Billericay in Essex. I had owned a pub there, and it turned out that his father was one of my regulars.

The party just kept going. The staff were all laughing, probably with relief because earlier they thought they would be out of a job as no customers had set foot in the place, or were likely to. The last of the sozzled sailors left at 11 am the next morning. Before leaving, the captain invited Jan and me to lunch on HMS Liverpool. We were delighted to take up the offer, and were given a full tour of the ship - whose main role was to apprehend drug dealers.

On board they had four US sharp-shooters and a James Bond-style speedboat. "Take a look at this," said the captain, as he pressed a button and up on deck appeared a helicopter, which already had rifles on the seats. Apparently the drug dealers moved about the islands in very fast, powerful boats – some quicker than the Navy's, hence the need for a helicopter to give chase and shoot out their engines. Everywhere we went on the ship, we kept seeing customers from the night before looking a little worse for wear. We went into the mess and had a cup of tea with the boys and girls off duty.

HMS Liverpool stayed in St. Vincent for four days, with most of the crew coming back to see us when they were not working. It certainly helped our trade although customers started coming into the restaurant and a few of the ex-pats had now made it their watering hole.

As HMS Liverpool left the docks, the captain sailed her around past the front of Ocean Allegro, with ship horns blaring and the helicopter roaring overhead. Most of the crew were on deck waving. Our beach seemed to be full of local girls waving goodbye to the sailors, with a glint in most of their eyes.

Things calmed down for about a week. Trade was picking up and a few old ladies started coming in for afternoon tea and cake – chocolate cake made by the master; word soon got around that he was working at Ocean Allegro.

One afternoon, I was in the bar doing very little when some English and American men arrived. I had a chat with them, and incredibly one of them came from Stanford-le-Hope – three miles from the Orsett Cock. He told me he was in wardrobe in the film business and had worked on Ridley Scott's Gladiator. I asked him why he was in St Vincent. "We are making Pirates Of The Caribbean 2 & 3," he replied. I almost yelped with excitement. I managed to stifle it and not look like a star-struck teenager. "You're going to be very busy," John from wardrobe said.

Over the next two weeks, our bar was full of every type of person involved with the film industry. I had two burly men come to see me. They were American, and in charge of security for the film's stars. "They will want to eat and drink here some nights," said Tom, one of the security men. "Who are the stars?" I asked. "Johnny Depp, Orlando Bloom, Keira Knightley, and many more whose names I cannot remember," Tom said.

The actors were staying at Young Island and were to come over to our jetty to pick up boats that would take them to another part of the island where Pirates was being filmed. I and the staff were sworn to secrecy but, as you can imagine, that lasted all of three days and pretty soon our bar was full of photographers all hoping to get the shot that nobody else could. A couple of them offered to work in the bar for nothing. One kept saying he knew my face, and my name came to him after a couple of days.

Eventually the big day arrived, and all the stars converged on St Vincent. While waiting for the glass bottomed boats to return from Young Island, with temperatures in the 90s, everybody made a bee-line for our bar. If you have ever seen any of the Pirates films, you'll know there are a host of other stars involved –

including Geoffrey Rush, Jonathan Pryce, Mackenzie Crook, Bill Nighy, Chow Yun-fat and Rolling Stone Keith Richards. It was a real red carpet affair.

The next day, I was working at Ocean Allegro at 6am, and already most of the film crew had left the jetty and set off for work. In the afternoon, the two security men returned with four others. "Mr Depp, Mr Bloom and Miss Knightley will be dining here tonight," said Tom, "So we need to keep the media away."

At about 5.30, the boats started coming back to the jetty. A very expensive blue speed boat arrived with Keira and Orlando on board. They came straight into the bar. Keira Knightly and Orlando Bloom, in the same bar as me, and not only that, it was my bar. I had to pinch myself every now and again to see if it was all a dream. Half an hour later, a 40-foot yacht moored on the jetty, and out stepped a man wearing a bandana, peasant shirt and what I can only describe as a loose-fitting skirt, smoking a very large cigar. He came into the bar. It was Johnny Depp. He asked to see the wine list and picked a very nice red. He then joined Keira and Orlando. They had a local fish dish with salad, washed down with some more very nice wine. All the time they were there, I could see security turning photographers away at the entrance to the restaurant.

It became quite a regular event to have the stars, director and film crew eating and drinking in the bar at the same time.

At this time Wish was working for Disney in Florida and Ames was at her soon-to-be-forgotten boyfriend's bar in England. Ryan and Jake were with us on St Vincent and found themselves work as extras in the film. They wore red coats and had to learn to row in unison.

Wish booked herself time off from work and flew out to join us in the hope she'd meet Johnny Depp. Ames was discovering that her boyfriend was not really cut out for a pub, and he had started to become very aggressive toward her. There was a parting of the ways, and before I knew it she was in St Vincent too.

While all this was going on, I was told about a medical school which was closed for the holidays. It was for American kids who had failed their final exams to become doctors. They mostly came from wealthy families, who paid for them to try again in St Vincent. The students returned from holiday while filming was still in progress, and the girls soon found out that Johnny was in town. Unfortunately, this forced him to keep a low profile, and he mostly stayed on his yacht until after filming had finished.

Ames and Wish were helping out in the restaurant now, but had arrived too late to see Johnny eating and drinking there. Wish had her photo taken with an obliging Orlando Bloom and Keira Knightley but, much to her disappointment, not Johnny Depp.

Wish returned to Florida, but Ames stayed on and became friends with the film's makeup department head, Ve Neill. She had worked with Johnny (and also film director Tim Burton) for many years, including Edward Scissorhands and Ed Wood. Ames explained about missing him and Ve said "Why don't you come with me to see them filming on Saturday? They're doing a sword-fight scene on the beach."

So Ames went with Ve on Saturday and watched the filming. When it was done, Ve called to Johnny who said "I have not forgotten." He went to his trailer, and returned a minute later with a signed photo 'To Wish' and other memorabilia. "I thought you had forgotten," said Ve. "How could I?" asked Johnny, opening his hand to reveal Wish's name written on his palm. When we returned to England later, Ve came and stayed with us when Johnny was filming Sweeney Todd: The Demon Barber Of Fleet Street in London.

While all this was going on, I had a few run-ins with Harry's girlfriend, Edna – a woman with hair dyed bright red, who continually talked about her conquests with married men. I know now how the word 'slapper' came about. Harry had a nice pool at his home, which Edna always maintained was her home. I would sometimes take the kids for a swim there, and Edna always seemed to make a point of hanging out her smalls by the side of the pool and would sit on the steps talking to me and the boys – without any underwear on. Poor Harry.

Edna came swanning into the restaurant on opening night looking like Cruella de Vil. She immediately started to tell the staff what to do. Eventually, I had to ban her from Ocean Allegro because she managed to upset so many people. Harry's life must have been hell. He told me she would not get out of bed until he had taken her a cup of tea and a plate of biscuits – her own personal butler. Rumour had it that Harry came home early from work one day to find Edna in bed with three locals. Great.

Ocean Allegro became very busy with people from the many yachts sailing and anchoring out front. They would get in the dinghies and tie up at the jetty. Some came to use the hot shower we provided, as there is not always a lot of room to shower when sailing and most on board would use salt-water. We also sold provisions, including fresh bottles of water. Most came just for a meal. There were two companies on St Vincent from who you could charter yachts and sail around the islands. People came from all over the world to do this. So business was good.

Ryan had a private tutor on the island, but he was now of an age where he needed to finish schooling and sit his exams. I personally found the island a little claustrophobic. Pirates moved on to Dominica, and Ames joined them. She had been offered a job with the production company, and spent the next three months helping to finish the two films.

In all, we spent just over a year on St Vincent. During that time, the beer company Red Stripe was sponsoring the international cricket match between Pakistan and the West Indies. They had the end of match dinner at Ocean Allegro. We also saw many well-known actors and pop stars coming over from Young Island during our stint there. But we decided it was time to move on, and Harry took over the running of the place. With 'help' from Edna, that lasted six months.

Epilogue

It's fair to say I've led an eventful life and my children's mouths never fail to drop when I relate some of my many stories from way back when. Football has been the central theme and has given me many highs. I'll never forget the day Rotherham played at Carlisle a few games before the end of the season. I had not been thinking about promotion but we achieved it that day and I shall always remember the roar in our dressing room. Football also gave me my low point, which was being arrested, although in a strange sort of way I am actually glad to have experienced that, it gave me an insight into just how badly things can go wrong, and how quickly it made me appreciate the horrific feeling many people have suffered by coming close to, or even being, jailed for something they did not do.

As for the game today, there is no loyalty anymore and the way it has gone in recent times saddens me. But I must say that I saw it coming. Some years ago I gave an interview to the News of the World predicting the greed that exists in the game today and the fact that the players would become highly paid celebrities like pop stars. Football was always a working class game, which is why it was played on a Saturday afternoon and why the grounds were always near to stations. Nowadays it is out of the reach of working class men and clubs are owned by companies, rather than families and individuals, who write off the money to taxation.

Having said all that, I would be interested in owning a football club again because I am still ambitious and I believe I still have a lot to offer. I have had approaches and recently came close to buying Falkirk, but the offer would have to be right for me. So watch this space.

This book has taken me nearly three years to finalise. As I was writing it, memories came flooding back to me as if the events mentioned happened yesterday. The last few pages were penned while sitting by my pool in Florida. My life (so far!) has certainly been eventful, but I would not have changed it for the world.

For the last few years, Jan and I have been assisting and watching our brood grow up:

Chi is now busy with his restaurants and butchers' shops with his partner Nicki. They have a great son and daughter, Kalen and Amelie.

Fleur has two beautiful girls – Fenn and Lani – with partner Lee. She still works for Chi.

Ames is now a police officer, with partner Rob and they have a beautiful son, Tide.

Jake is running a golf club and playing the field.

Wish is in Florida, working for Universal at The Wizarding World of Harry Potter at the Islands of Adventure in Orlando.

Ryan is now a hair stylist to the stars in London's West End.

Anton's purchases:

Rotherham - £67,500, sold for £250,000

Bournemouth - £150,000, sold for same amount

Southend - £300,000, shares valued at £1.5m when the club was taken over

Lightning Source UK Ltd.
Milton Keynes UK
UKOW05f0915021213

222213UK00001B/35/P